BACK TO WILD

BOOK FIVE OF THE ALASKA OFF GRID SURVIVAL SERIES

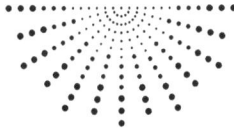

MILES MARTIN

ALASKADREAMS
PUBLISHING

Back To Wild
By Miles Martin

Book Five of The Alaska Off Grid Survival Series
©2021 Miles Martin
Artwork, Photos, Original Poetry ©2021 by Miles Martin - All rights reserved

Published by:
Alaska Dreams Publishing
www.alaskadp.com
1st ADP Edition August 2021
PRINT PAPERBACK ISBN: 978-1-956303-06-3
PRINT HARDCOVER ISBN: 978-1-956303-07-0
This book was previously published by Miles of Alaska

Visit www.milesofalaska.com to find a bio of Miles, additional photos, stories, how-to videos, handmade artwork, and raw materials for sale.

In front of my Nenana home.

Mt. Denali viewed from one of my remote cabins.

NOTE FROM THE AUTHOR

This is book five in an Alaska adventure biography series. It is not necessary you read the previous books, but it is good to know what has gone on as an introduction. You can find a summary for all the books in the back if it has been a while since you read the other books, or forgot.

CONTENTS

CHAPTER ONE

ART TRAIN, CLEANING SKULLS, TRAPLINE AND HOMESTEAD TRIP

"No crock pot or oven on the homestead, Miles?" We both laugh. I have kind of a convection oven, not a real cooking source a woman would call an oven. I have a single hot plate to cook on I am happy with. I eat out of the pot, cook one pot meals. I'm used to it.

"Been doing it for how many years now?" Will understands, he eats the same way. When we want to eat differently, we go out to dinner someplace. *Spend $10 and splurge!* Another State Fair is over. Now I'm in a hurry to get the garden harvested, and hope the first frost is late. Sometimes it arrives in August during the fair. But this global warming stuff has moved the freeze date ahead! No disasters here. The garden is harvested. I have enough for the winter. The boat is put away. The snow machine is out, looked over, parts ordered from Dennis Kirk, or Snow Machine Salvage. My winter moose is shot.

"$10? What happened to the Oriental place on College Road, buy meals for $4.50 if you buy a twenty meal coupon?"

"Yes Will, I still go there, but only in Fairbanks. Here in Nenana, we have higher prices. But now and then free food. The church groups put on feeds." It seems like at least once a month there is a feed someplace! We both agree it is a good life. We guess. Sort of.

Will adds, "Be nice to have a woman around though." I have known Will a lot of years now. His arms are still as big around as my body, and he can lift an engine out of a car. He has not lost his Iowa farm accent and slow personality. We are like Mutt and Jeff! I am a tad over five feet tall—a bit like a hobbit.

One room in the shop stays an even fifty degrees this time of year, perfect for hanging the fresh moose meat. It hangs for fifteen days with plastic on the floor below it for drips. I make 200 pounds of sausage, wrap 300 pounds of steaks, and have enough soup bones to last a year. I eat the heart, tongue, and ribs first. The ribs dry out fast and seem not to be worth wrapping.

I tell Will, "I figured out if I slow cook them in a crock pot I do not have, then put them in the oven I do not have, they come out tender and moist! Yum!" We both laugh. Moose tastes good any way we fix it. "Yes, a woman would know how to fix moose proper!"

"Yea, well, women say the same! How nice it would be to have a guy around to fix the car when it breaks, and the sewing machine, and the water pipes, and the roof, and the drain…and pay all the bills and…"

"Yea, Will, if she's grateful for it, that is OK. " I look at Will, wondering if he will ever get married.

Will takes ten seconds to process what I say, nods, and begins to reply. "It's the woman who thinks it is us who should be grateful." He has a point. Each has to appreciate what the other offers I suppose.

Yes, it's all about 'love' and what is love? It is that which makes one forget reason. I think this but do not speak out loud. It's just my thoughts.

Do I wish to voluntarily lose my ability to reason? *I answer myself in my head, "I am not sure it is correct to assume all women want to hypnotize men!" Love is nothing but a sword through the heart.*

I never say that to anyone because I know the reply would be, "It is better to have loved and lost." My mind wanders about 'stuff' I do not need to share with Will. The blade of grass shifts in my mouth, moving with my thoughts. My mountain-man leather floppy hat hangs over my eyes.

There was that one local gal who was taken by me. I did not know her. She invited me to her place for dinner and a movie. She expected me to spend the night. The date got strange. She ended up chasing me down the road naked, screaming for me to come back. I felt so bad for her, cars are going by honking. She didn't care. I still have this image in my head as I turned around, watermelons flapping in the wind.

I hardly hear what Will says, and change the subject, "You ready for winter, Will?" He's got some firewood cut up and thinks he has work running a snowplow on the local military base a hundred miles away. Sounds like he has it together, and will make it through another winter. He used to want to live like me back when we met in '74, when we were both still kids. Will does not want to change the subject.

"Miles, you still hear from Vicki?"

Ah yes. Her. "The one who came to be with me during my time of tribulation—as a murder suspect." I forgot I tried to get her and Will together, got a date for him.

She had said, "Well, Will started to preach religion to me." She paused and left it at that. Like there was more, but that was all I needed to know.

I reply to Will. "I heard from her off and on—sort of. But no, we lost touch. I guess." I'm deliberately vague. Most women who are attracted to me call me 'cute.' I'm not especially pleased. Cute is not what I want to be. However the whole Vicki deal was very strange. Will still thinks of her. Hmmm. Yes, she is beautiful. Willowy build, long blond hair, maybe Dutch, hard to place her nationality. I change the subject again, "By the way, Will. I have the snow machine on my mind. You understand engines well. I have a cylinder that does not catch till the engine is warm. I thought it might be the carb, but now wonder if it is electrical, but it's not the plug. In old style machines, I'd guess a coil going out, but these new machines with brain boxes do not seem to have coils, so what should I check?"

"Could be the brain box—but no way to test without a special computer. New brain box is $200."

"I have to buy a new one to find out?"

"That's about it, Miles. It'll cost $200 just to bring it to the shop to find out what is wrong anyhow."

"You mean 'break out another thousand' like what 'boat' stands for?" We both laugh, and miss the days it was easier to work on our own stuff. That is part of the wilderness subsistence life of independence disappearing fast. So, I will have to buy a $200 part I may or may not need. To save money.

"Yea, one more straw on the camel's back. Fits in with my rabbit cycle theory of civilization."

"You mean the stuff that causes people to scream, pick up a gun and go out and blast a bunch of people? Road rage, stuff like that? Banks being a Ponzi scheme, civilization being lemmings marching off the cliff. Events since 911."[1]

"Yea, like that." We both laugh again. *What else can we do? We are not going to change anything. Just make more money!*

"Nothing money can't solve, huh, Miles?" I sigh because I kept all such thoughts in check when I was out in the wild. Civilization is amazingly depressing. "Watch yer top knot, Miles!"

"Yea, stay below the horizon, Will." He is off to his life. We still exchange the old mountain man lingo that separated us from ordinary people when we shared a longing for the free trapper days.

⁂

I NEED CHEERING UP, good positive news! Art Train is here! I have been working on the project many months, with a good several hundred hours volunteered into this event. I am the first one here early in the morning as the train pulls in and stops. *It is so cool! So amazing! A traveling museum*! "Here in remote Nenana!" It all comes together well. I meet the artists. I had been informed this is American Indian art, with respected, well known artists coming to talk to us. As expected, very gifted; well dressed; educated. Inspired to show their work, and pass on the good word to the community. My hope is, the young local natives here who are artistically gifted will be inspired, know they can make a living with art, and be respected.

I know from my volunteer work with the children at the living center some of the kids hope to return back to their village some day. One big issue is lack of work and opportunity. The beauty of being an artist is this trade can happen anyplace, even, and especially, back in the village.

Many villages are small enough not to have a high school. So Indian children come to our village and stay in a dorm to attend our school for a formal education.

One female Southeast Native artist comes off the train, and I hear she actually spins her own gold thread to use in her southeast Indian blankets! *How cool is that!* I think to myself.

The train cars are galleries with walls of hanging art, tables have art laid out on display. Much like a high end gallery in a big city. Not like anything in Alaska that villagers could expect to ever see. I was raised in the city somewhat upper-class. I was exposed to museums, opera music, and such things referred to as 'class.'

I take the head guy out fishing as promised, before the big work begins. We get out in an early fog, with an awesome view of Denali. The sun is just coming up over the river. I take a nice picture of him. He is about as happy as a person can get, catching his lifelong dream fish. The picture tells it all. An experience that would cost $10,000 if he made a special trip for it.

I did not have to say, "And this is our culture, welcome!"

The train car is unhooked from the engine. City power is hooked up. Stairs are set up to get in, art is set up on the walls. All the details are worked out. I line up a couple of our local Native artists to be guest artists for part of the show. The news media shows up from the big city, visiting Nenana, population, 350 people. I am in the background, no, not even mentioned. The mayor is interviewed. The Chamber of Commerce as an organization is given credit. I was in fact a one man operation making this happen. The train would not be here if I had not talked them into it and done ninety percent of the work. More important than credit is that the train is here!

School buses arrive with children to view the museum first, in groups with their teachers. Everyone who volunteered shows up, and does their part. Locals are needed to direct people, dispense juice, clean up after. The train is along the river with a great view of the railroad bridge and Nenana Hill. The bright new train is an amazing contrast to everything around it.

Dinner and potluck follow at George Hall—the Native Center. The locals put this on to honor the visitors. All you can eat king salmon, with all the fixings for anyone who cares to show up. We serve 200 people. This is half our entire population. The Natives put on a great dance, all dressed in Athabascan Native clothes of leather, feathers and such. Art Train is impressed. I was told, "Treated better in Nenana than Fairbanks, even Anchorage." Better than communities with 70,000 people, with a much bigger budget. I accomplished what I wanted, showed our visitors what culture is to us. Feeding visitors, making them feel welcome.[2] I did not personally pull off the entire event! It was a community effort that I spearheaded. I'm proud of my community.

The Art Train has a small gift shop associated with the exhibit. Much as our Culture Center in Nenana has a gift shop that helps support its museum.

"Miles, some of this exhibit is permanent, and travels with us everywhere we go. Your own work is so nice! You have been such a great part of our success here in Alaska. We'd love to carry your work among our gifts." The guy I took out fishing OKs this—thinks it is a great idea. I like and get along with the gal who runs the shop. We had emailed off and on as part of the preparation. I'd had no thought of any personal gain.

"Sure, I am open to suggestions and opportunity. I'd feel honored to have a place in the shop, with my work and books, thanks!" I write up a receipt and leave $700 worth of art with the shop when they leave.

I tell Josh, "See how things can work out when you volunteer! Wow! This could be a major outlet for my work!" Josh was a bit miffed his son's work is not included. Josh's son is Athabascan, and doing some nice Native style art. Partly, I think the reason is, he is not around to promote his work, and partly I think he charges too much. He has not had a lot of success so far. I let that conversation drop. I was not trying to show off to Josh, only share my excitement with a good friend. *I've learned there is a lot of good art in the world going unsold. Much concerning the selling is not about the quality of the art, but in marketing it!* Art Train is in Nenana for three days. Several thousand visitors are recorded passing through. The village Indians are impressed, and inspired.

"I didn't know art could bring so much respect!" This begins a conversation about my own choice in life and my art, how it is possible to choose this as an occupation.

One village Native thirteen year old comes up to me. "My friend said you have been to Ruby, who you know there?" The question is asked as an interrogation, in Native slang. I am used to this, and understand. When I first began volunteering to teach art to the Indian children at the living center in the evenings, I was asked a series of questions. Who do I know? Why was I in their village?

In the white man world, we name drop. We ask for, or offer up 'references' when we engage in business, or require respect. Most professionals put up degrees, permits, awards, on the wall for visitors to inspect. Natives have another way.

The thinking I understand is, "Why should I listen to you? Are you honest, running a scam, have an ulterior motive? Who will speak for you if there is a problem?" The children do not understand the White world, may not trust it. They may not care how many degrees I have, or do not have, or what school I went to. 'Who you know' has to do with respected elders in the village they know. A respected person by way of a reference, or who can be counted on to be responsible for me if there is a problem of any kind.

Since I understand the question and why it is asked, I respectfully reply, "I was living on my houseboat and stopped in Ruby for gas. I became friends with Emit Peters, the dog racer." Big smile and less tension.

"Emit? He's my uncle! He should have won that last race he was in!"

I reply, "Yes, but he does not have Nugget, that good lead dog anymore, so it is harder now!" Proving I walk the walk I am talking. Now, what I have to say will be remembered. I'm not just some educated idiot teacher with a degree from another planet, getting paid to pretend I care and understand. I do understand, and see that many of the teachers are incredibly rude, insulting, naïve, ignorant about other cultures. I just heard this morning, a teacher telling a student the food they were eating is disgusting, and will not be allowed in the building. Parents had sent some special, native processed fish, white people are generally not fond of—that would not even be legal to serve to white people. The Art Train visitation fits in with my time spent with the children. What I am trying to teach is frowned on by many of the teachers, maybe the school system and its mission.

I am not especially respected by most of the teachers. I think partly because I volunteer. This is sometimes perceived as taking away work from a union employee. At least this subject has been passed on to me through rumor. "Someone said."

I have no degree, or formal education, so in some minds makes a mockery out of the education process. *How can anyone know anything without a degree?* I believe the school has an agenda, not totally up front. This agenda is to integrate the Natives into the dominant white man's world. Partly to help Natives get white man jobs they need, or at least into the assembly line. I see many Natives buy into this thinking. I see the entire villages smile and nod. Parents decide to send their children to the white man village and school to give them a chance to survive, because they see their own dying culture. The government shows up with free food, fuel to heat instead of wood, boats made of aluminum, outboard motors and other cool stuff.

"White man ways is the way to go!"

Perhaps. Sometimes it is a good choice, I agree. The choice depends what you want out of life. Is 'all this talk' about what the Indian needs? Or is it the white man's need?

I do understand this is best for many of the children. There may be fewer job opportunities in the smaller villages they come from. Many wish to leave village life. They have dreams white children have. I notice the military presence in the school. We have a military base not far away. Recruiters show up in the school. They show free movies that glorify war, give speeches, discuss the many wonderful opportunities the military has to offer impressionable minds. Again, this may be a good choice for some!

I think they need to understand these recruiters pay the school to come talk. They have a financial interest in doing so, as the government has a reason to want young, impressionable minds to train for war. I agree, you give something, you get something. You go kill the government's enemy, and the government offers you the GI bill, interest free loans, the VA to take care of you. I know, *been—there—done —that*. I am politically savvy enough not to discuss such issues out loud.

I think what I have to say is also worth considering by some. That is, it is possible to live in the village and survive, be happy, make an honest living, if you like the wilderness and subsistence lifestyle connected to the land, as your ancestors were. 'Art' is one of those answers. One native girl about fourteen looked depressed while I was doing my voluntary art class in the evening. I engage her in conversation. "What village are you from? What do you do there?" She brightens up a little. I could tell no teacher or dorm parent asked this and did not care.

You are taught, you are here to forget those savage ways!

She says, "I am from Fort Yukon." Said very proudly, in loud defiance.

I reply. "Ah yes, the Black River, one of the best trapping rivers in the entire state!" I pause. "Is that little house still there in the center of the village, with the satellite dish on the roof bigger than the house? I always wanted to take a picture of that!" I have thus proven I know her village, and have been there. She laughs and opens up. I can tell she is homesick.

"That little house is Auntie Sue. She loves her satellite TV. I'm not really into that."

"Why not, what is more interesting?"

"Oh, my family owns a lodge up the Porcupine. We have half a dozen cabins, a fleet of boats, a plane, and I want to run the business, teach others about the subsistence life." I see nothing wrong with this goal. I think it's realistic, very workable. I can tell it is her passion. I'm guessing by her depression, she is not impressed with the white man schooling. It is not what she and her family expected. She is not interested in becoming a white woman.

I say, "Well, maybe you can learn about business, advertising, computer stuff, that might help you run a business. The school is required, so you may as well make the best of it, get out of it what you can." Art Train, and what it was all about has a lot to do with this type of conversation.

I recall a single school incident when I was about her age. A guest speaker came to my art class. A professional, who made his living with art. This artist knew little of our curriculum, or what was on our next test. He pointed out some facts of life, if you wish to be an artist. Life experiences from someone who does it. All my art teachers made their living teaching, not being artists. The goal of the teachers did not seem to be to teach us to make a living with art. Maybe the goal was to have culture and appreciate art. Or do art for fun. Or even to baby sit us so our parents had free time to work. This artist impressed me, because he brought business, advertising, costs, credit, interest rates, loans, gross compared to profits, history, into the art world. I never forgot. This as well has a lot to do with Art Train as I see it. A single event that turns the lights on.

The school methods did not seem like reality to me. A bell rings, "Ding!" Now we will be interested in this subject for exactly forty-five minutes. Not a second more, nor less. "Ding!" now we will shift gears and be interested in that subject for forty-five minutes, and then at an exact time to the nearest second, it will be lunch time.

In the real world I find myself in, I have something broke that needs fixing. There is no bell to tell me when or for how long. I work at it till it is fixed. I might be doing math for a week straight. There is a planning stage, a doing stage, a follow up stage; that is very rewarding. I did something.

School is nothing at all like this. In the Native way of teaching this student was raised in, grandpa takes you out to fish camp to teach you all you need to know to catch, hang, and prepare fish, and feed yourself. Along the way might get some history, how to run a boat, something about ethics, and maybe some math.

"How many fish do we eat? What about the dog team? How much might get lost to the Ravens?" This education is about life through the eyes of those living off the land.

I raised two girls on the homestead in similar fashion. How to grade fur ends up being a math problem. How much gas to bring for a 200 miles trip with a six mile an hour current, ends up being algebra. I hated bells telling me when to be interested in a subject. Since I have seen another way, lived it, taught it, I can understand this particular student.

There is nothing wrong with wanting to take over a resort the family owns in the remote wilderness as a life goal occupation. She is already a pilot, flying the family plane at fourteen. I feel badly that school would teach this child she has nothing going for her, except some drone job being a worker bee in a white dominated world. I'm convinced this has a lot to do with many teachers and those running the school, being antagonistic towards me. I'm not suggesting this girl or any others be rebellious, or beat the system. School can be a test in learning how to do things you do not want to do. Life will be full of that.

Some of these village children look up to me because I live their lifestyle, have been to their village, know their parents, relatives. In their eyes, I am successful by measurements that matter in the village. I feel inspired to be a good example. Is it this that bothers the teachers, when they wish for the students to feel this way about them, as a role model, while the village idiot is not to be admired! That will not do! I'm lower class, and need to act my place properly. One does not say, "Yes, dumpster diving is so cool and lucrative, go for it!"

Perhaps there is another whole issue here. Children are getting stressed and committing suicide over bad grades. The world does not have to begin and end with grades. Not for everyone anyhow. It's not worth dying over. My parents cried over me, over the embarrassment I was, over what would happen to me if I could not pass the classes. *Oh well.*

After the big Art Train event, I have business to catch up on.

Internet saved file, Thursday, October 31, 2002 Art Prices

"Miles, how come this necklace cost so much—isn't this a rip off? $45? Come on—the materials were free—you found them—and it didn't take you more than half an hour to make this. $10 would be a lot—$45 is a scam—a rip off!"

How do I give a quick reply that will be understood? I think it over. This is an attitude that is becoming a common thing. Worth giving a lot of thought to, since I want to run a good business and do not want people to feel scammed. Partly, I think our society is not taught 'culture' anymore, like it was once. The value of things like art, is lost. The basic appreciation, the time it takes, is not taught. Even 'products in general,' where they come from, what is involved, and the costs. I think, "Big money is made within the system producing copies of desired famous originals." *Why buy an original painting to help your neighbors' kid? When you can be cool and buy a Van Gogh print from us? Cheaper, from China! Not even Van Gogh made money off his own work!*

I have a reply saved to cut and paste when needed.

"Yes I do understand how you feel and just wish people understood better where the price comes from. No, I'm not getting rich—but it would take a while to explain. OK, I found the ivory used in this necklace. Do you know what it cost me to be in a situation to find the ivory? I need a boat motor, camp gear, the cost of the time to go look—like a week's time. Even though I would own the boat anyway and be camping anyway—still, the money to support a $10,000 boat motor has to come from some place. Anyone who gets this ivory is going to have these costs to cover. Those who just happen to stumble on a piece and make a necklace as a hobby may not charge as much, this is true! But, consider this factor in the equation. What brought you and me together here on the internet, creating a situation where you get to see this product? You and I do not travel in the same circles. All this infrastructure needs to be supported that has us meet.

Yes, there is imported art that looks similar to what I sell for the $10 you speak of.

To get the price this low, thousands of the same item have to get sold. Usually the quality is not the same. Usually it is not hand done, or if so, done by slaves. Much depends on what you want. I do have places on my website to go view that explain what I offer and do not offer to help customers decide, in my effort to have honesty and understanding between us. People who are happy with my work want unusual one of a-kind, hand done, quality. Possibly wanting to support 'made in the U.S.' and or 'Alaska made' or support a lifestyle they believe in that is also part of the story behind the art. I'd rather you not buy it, then to get it and feel like you got ripped off. I'd be happy to refer you to sources that sell something similar for $10

I am thinking this might be overly 'wordy,' *But better to offer too much than to little?* "At least if the customer does not understand now, it is not because I did not try to explain." I can feel I did my part, the rest is up to them.

My saved reply to a letter.

Hello Gary and Sally!

Yes, I am fine. Still surveying though. I am supposed to take off tomorrow for Galena for a week. This will be the last survey job of the season. I have had days off at a time, and looked over Chapter 10. It looks good, but wanted to use a split screen and bring up the 'original' and compare changes with how it was. Had trouble getting my original to come up—crashed the computer—the entire book is too large a document, have to put chapter ten in its own document, I think. Just have not done it yet. I also have trouble—unsure how to explain, but trouble 'unwinding.'

I can't get my mind out of work summer mode. I need to be scan-disk and defragged. (Smile) It often takes a week, then I can get back into my art, book writing and 'other things.' It is like shifting gears or programs or something. It is harder to 'shift' as I get older!

I explain a thought that has been on my mind a lot over the years when it comes to finding a partner. I write it out in my email. One of the greatest romance images is of a knight and a damsel in distress.

I think of the story I tell often, as I convey it to my friends.

So we have this knight who is used to eating wild game and sleeping on the forest floor by a campfire. His life is about killing dragons. A rather bloody affair requiring skills involving weapons, treachery, tracking, and physical strength. He is used to being with other like-minded people, storytelling around the fire. He is used to the rain, mud, cold. That is his world, and he loves it.

The damsel lives in a castle. Spends a lot of time in one room. She is used to brushing her hair endlessly, getting dressed, and undressed in clean finery. She eats at a dinner table. Meals are cooked and served by others. Conversation is polite and reserved. She spends her days dreaming, staring out the window at the world beyond. She has 'an opinion' of what life out there must be like, based on her limited experience viewed out the window, and reading romance books. Looking, longing to be rescued. Someone who will solve all her problems, sweep her off her feet. Treat her the way a lady should be treated, at the same time offering adventure she longs for. She's sure Sir Knight knows exactly how to treat her. Just as certainly, he is sure she knows what he wants and how to please him.

She sees Sir Knight off in the distance and hollers her 'female in distress' mating call, shows her gorgeous hair. He's impressed. He storms the castle, and there they are. Together. In each other's arms. Leaving us all in happy tears.

The story ends here, romance stops somewhere in here.

There are many versions of the basic story. The question I struggle with is, "Now what?" Is he gonna live in the castle with her? Doing what? He's a trained killer. He is used to physical activity outdoors. He likes the rain. What will his trade be? How will the bills get paid? He's going to enjoy helping her pick out clothes and brushing her hair, reading her poetry, taking up some new trade within the castle. Starting with washing the dishes, since this is all he is qualified for in the castle. He will be going from 'respected, front of the line in the pecking order,' to minimum wages, last in line in the pecking order. It is hard to imagine him being happy like this forever. At some point, the infatuation over her beauty will wear off. His chemicals will mellow out and he'll look around. I'd guess he would miss the good old days in the woods.(?) Yes? No?

Will she join him in the wilderness killing dragons, sleeping in the mud, eating half skinned critters cooked on a stick with leaves, ashes, and sand as condiments? It is hard to picture her enjoying such a life. I want to know why the story is never finished! Because reality is, they look at each other's life and say, "No!" Each goes back to the life they love and know.

Interesting and puzzling is—why would the damsel be interested in the knight out the window in the first place? Why isn't she looking among those who live like her in the castle? And why would he be looking in castle windows for a partner? Why isn't he looking at the village girls—or those living in the forest? When he sees her there in the castle window, why doesn't he just smile, wave, and keep on riding? When she looks out the window and sees him, why doesn't she pull her head back in and stop messing with the heads of heathens?

Does nature favor the cross breeding of those with nothing in common? I sell, and even live a romantic way of life. Rock stars, dog racers, sports hero, and Mountain Man. I'm resentful of the myth. I'm seeking reality. While not knowing how to get there. Coming to terms with what that means, is a big part of who I am.

Survival, is how to get what I want, contribute something, and be happy. Doesn't that require 'reality?' Is reality about engaging in the myth?

I shake my head to clear it and get back to my letter.

> Thanksgiving? Sounds like a plan. I can pay for the trip if you can put me up. I have not been to Anchorage in a while. Maybe I can bring some art and look around for an outlet, and take in some sights. I'm thinking of getting a laptop computer with my Alaska dividend.
> **Sunshine Miles**

Valerie covers her nose as I visit at Senior Center lunch. The smell of me is 'nothing' compared to in my house. I'm asked to leave. Back home, a phone call interrupts. I have to explain, "I have maggots trying to escape out of the bathtub. Please call another time, as I'm rather busy at the moment. I have to wash them down the drain before they get out. No, I do not have time to explain. Just call back." The smell sometimes gets so bad from cleaning the rotten skulls, I worry the fumes will ignite and blow up the house. Once again, "Why do I do this?"

Well the analogy I often give is, "Like a mother who willingly cleans baby diapers. Something about love? As a woman loves her baby and does not mind the work or the smell, so this skull cleaning is to me."

"Out of respect for the animal." Somehow it just doesn't bother me all that much. The animal died. Probably suffered. Fought the trap. What the animal went through to 'get here,' is so much more than what I put up with. Ya, it stinks, but 'so what.' Partly, too, is the finished product. A cool skull people appreciate. Similar to how cleaning baby diapers eventually leads to a young man that does not resemble baby poop. I'm glad to be part of that process. Someone has to do it. God created me with the ability to happily step up to that plate!

"Cool, huh! God's pretty amazing, right?"

A dog barks in the street. My view on loose dogs and barking dogs seems to be very different, so needs explaining yet again! Tired of the subject! I'm puzzled more people do not feel the same. An aggressive barking dog—even in someone's yard is like this situation; A guy steps out his door as I walk by and starts yelling and screaming at me, telling me to go someplace else! How he's going to rip my head off if I don't.

"Get off my sidewalk!"

His wife comes out and says to me, "Don't mind him, he's harmless—no need to be afraid of him," as he waves a gun around. I wonder then, if he is harmless, why is the guy foaming at the mouth, swearing, and insulting me, and waving a weapon? Yet the wife is not embarrassed, or asking him to leave me alone.

Afraid? Well, it may not be so much about 'being afraid.' *Why is this about fear?* I can blast this guy to hell, about as easy as he can blast me, and do so first. But why? I do not even know this guy. I'm not mad at him. If he wants to die, it is his own business, but seems a waste of all our time. If I have to blast him, I am more upset about all the paperwork that follows, and potential risk that society will not appreciate I put a man out of his misery, and defended myself.

"He started it!" Might not be a legal defense. I'd be seen as no better nor different than him. But I resent having to walk away steaming. My whole day is affected, and I'm in a bad mood.

Put another way, if this guy said these words to the Federal government or a police officer, he'd be shot, or in prison as a homeland security risk. You can't say you have a bomb and are going to blow the school up, for example. So? How is it a dog has more rights than a person? I'm puzzled. Because that is exactly what the dog is saying.

Often the owner of the dog says, " Just walk up to him, talking nice, scratch him behind the ears and he'll calm down. He's nervous—he's OK. Let him sniff you. Don't be afraid". I'm shocked! *Afraid? Lady, my only fear is what will happen when you are covered in your dogs gore after I slice his throat with my knife.* Why is this situation about making the dog feel better? Making sure the dog is OK and feeling safe? That is not my job. This is not my dog. Again, if some psycho guy screams threats waving a weapon of some kind, is the answer, ' calm him down, give him what he wants. Make him feel good. Talk nice, bow down, and be non-threatening, so he is happy.' Why?

A cop would put a gun on him and holler, "Drop the gun, get on your knees, now!" or be shot.

Why is a dog any different? When the dog barks, no one tells it to shut up. When I bark back, and tell the dog what it can do with this attitude, someone is sure to open the door and scream at me to stop teasing their dog!

I know this. If a dog of mine ever—under any condition growled at, barked, acted aggressive toward a human being I would be extremely embarrassed, apologize, and reprimand the dog immediately. If a dog of mine ever bit anyone, I'd kill the dog. If anyone was constantly made afraid by a dog of mine, I'd shoot it, and I have done so, not just talking.

A barking dog interrupts my tranquil walk. A barking dog causes lights to come on in the neighborhood, curtains to part all up and down the block. I'm trying to be unobtrusive, not stand out, not have attention drawn to me. I do not feel 'safe' when people are scowling at me out the window, wanting to know who I am, what I'm doing there, where I'm going. I do not wish to explain my presence, defend myself. I feel like a stranger—an intruder- someone who is not welcome. If no one is telling the dog to shut up or apologize, now or later, for their dog's behavior, then I feel the dog's behavior is found to be acceptable. The dog reflects how people feel.

"A stranger comes, beware, wake up, pay attention! Attack the stranger if you can!" How do people find peace—call this a friendly neighborhood? Now and then, joggers get bit. Now and then, a child gets knocked off a bike. Now and then, the dogs pack up and harass game. In my opinion, one day a pack will seriously hurt or kill a child or elder. *Oh well! I'm done saying anything.*

"Smile and nod." I will not attend the funeral. I assume this is what people want. "What you dish out, thus will blow back in your face when the wind blows." *Did God say that, or is that Peter Paul and Mary—the singers?*

I explain to Josh, "There seems less of an issue now. I think only because I am not dealing with quite as much animal products as I once did. I used to smell like moose or bear, with blood odors on me."

"I guess, Miles, most civilized people would sympathize with the dogs more than you, understand the dog better, and consider you a dangerous person."

I agree, but, "Josh this is a wilderness Native community, sort of like rural farm land. This is not civilization. I have a legal occupation I am proud of, normal for this kind of community. *If you do not like the smell of cows, why are you in cow country? If forced to be, you have no right to stop your neighbor from farming.* That's what I'm thinking. "My view—dogs need to accept and understand my rights, and it should not be me who has to understand any dog's rights." I'm more hurt and depressed then I am mad or afraid. I'm wanting to feel part of the community, not being beneath a dog.

Josh understands. "Well, you know how I was raised, Miles. Competing with the dogs of the village for rotten food in the street and on the river banks. No one cared." He shrugs his shoulders. As a child, Josh even slept in dog houses in winter to keep warm. His parents were neglectful drunks. I guess this has to do with why Josh has such an uncanny ability to understand dogs and their language. He was one of them.

"The good news, Josh! Is that there seems to be fewer issues. Perhaps the dogs all know me by now. Or I have shot all the ones who feel I am not welcome."

Josh confesses he too has popped a few loose dogs. "Not that I'd say anything to anyone. You got to keep quiet about that, Miles!"

"Ok Josh, I think I understand your instructions on switching burners in my furnace, that's why I came over. Before I forget, I better get that job done!"

Switching burners in the furnace, Josh tells me, should only take half an hour. After all, it is only three bolts and one fitting. *But we both know it is going to take all day, right? Should we explain? You want to?* "We might have to duct tape the listener's mouth shut though. You know as well as I do the listener will either interrupt with advice—or burst out laughing. So I'll just talk to you and you pretend you are the listener, OK?" My unconscious: *OK and I'll try really hard not to interrupt or burst out laughing till you are all done talking.*

The job is to take the burner out of the greenhouse furnace and put it in the shop furnace—which I do every season. A few years ago, someone stole the burner out of the greenhouse furnace. Probably the neighbors, because their furnace went out. So rather than get a new furnace, I got the bright idea of just switching burners with the furnace in the shop. The burner only has three bolts, an electric plug, a fuel line, and two screws holding the thermostat wire. No problem. Done this a dozen times.

I forget what tools I need—but probably a crescent wrench will handle the three nuts—a screwdriver for the thermostat, and some vise grips to help hold the fuel line nut while I turn the plug fitting. The shop fuel line has a plug in it. I recall that. I go out back and shut off the main fuel valve so I can disconnect the fuel line. I go in the shop and take out the fuel line plug. The plug has a small leak, so I have a cup under the fitting to catch the slow drip. While taking the plug out, I tipped the cup over.

"Rats! I can't find a rag." I go into the art shop next door and find some news-paper to put down in the puddle, then to the greenhouse across the yard with a few tools I think I need to get the burner out of that furnace. Right off I see the crescent wrench will not fit two of the nuts. No room. I have to go back to the shop to get a socket. I do not know what size socket, so I bring the whole set. The size I need is not in the tray and think I left it with the tools in the house. I walk to the house and look. I find one. On the way back to the greenhouse, I see the handyman Jack I took part way to the shop while heading that way, pick it up and get it as far as the greenhouse.

Back at the greenhouse, I find out the socket is quarter inch drive and I have three quarter inch drive ratchet. I think the adaptor is in the shop and go there to get it. While looking for the adaptor I find a box of turquoise I forgot to take all the way to the art shop. I know if I do not do it now, I will never remember where I set it. This is hundreds of dollars worth of turquoise. *I better stop to put this turquoise in the art shop.* "Even though I promised myself no more interruptions!" This reminds me that my friend Helm asked for a chain saw bar, so I stop and grab the spare. Rather than make a special trip to the house just to put the saw bar in my 'going to town' box, I take it partway, and set it down in the boat. Hopefully, I will not someday next year be hundreds of miles in the wilderness on the river and wonder why I have a chain saw bar in the boat. Or, spend three hours looking for the saw bar I promised Helm, and know I have it someplace, never dreaming it is in the boat which is on the way to the greenhouse.

I still can't find an adaptor, but think I can make the crescent wrench work if I work at it slowly. Back at the greenhouse, the crescent will not work no matter what. If I cannot find the adaptor, I need to find a three quarter inch drive, half inch socket and return to the shop where I find one. However, back in the greenhouse, I realize even this socket will not reach the nut. I need an open box wrench, so I go back to the shop and can't find a half inch, open end wrench. I think I have one in the snow machine tool box, so go out and take the tarp off the snow machine and look in the toolbox.

In the greenhouse again, I get all three nuts off. The fuel line is off. Everything is done. I take the burner to the shop where I discover the replacement burner studs and furnace nuts are a different size. The furnaces are not the same model or even same brand. I had to do some adapting in the past I forgot about. Now I need a larger socket or wrench and think it is in the house. Not in the house. I think I can make vise grips work. Back in the shop, I decide vise grips might strip the nut. *In the boat tool box*, "Yes, in the boat, I think I have the right size wrench." It's not in the boat tool box, or snow machine tool box, or the house. I think after all, I can make the crescent wrench work.

After the burner is mounted, I inspect it and realize the fuel connection in the greenhouse requires an elbow, while the one in the shop goes straight in. I have an adaptor on the furnace shelf to make the switch. I take the elbow fitting off, then the bell housing, and see the nipple in the furnace is the wrong size. To get it off would require ruining it. I have to use the bell housing. Nothing fits it but the elbow. I look in my furnace pipe fitting box in the house for anything that fits the elbow. Not finding one requires a trip to the store to buy a straight fitting that fits the bell housing on one end and the fuel line on the other end. On the way to the hardware store, I run into someone who needs to talk to me at the café, so I have coffee. After coffee, I run into someone else who wants to buy a wolf skull. I need to bring it over, but explain I am busy. They saw me come out of the café and tell me I do not look very busy. I explain I'm trying to fix my furnace. All I get is a knowing smile. I find what I want at Coghill's store, and ride the three wheeler back to the cabin. I forgot Teflon tape, so go back to Coghill's. I still have to clean up the fuel spill, as I am kneeling in it. I go back to the house and get a rag.

Now it's time for lunch...and while having lunch I recall how so many friends have asked, "But Miles, why don't you just have a set of tools and whatever job you need to do, you simply bring the complete box of tools! Wouldn't that be simpler?" The question implies I am stupid and never thought of that. I have done that many times—bought a set of new tools. What happens is— I'm in the boat 100 miles out in the wilderness and need a crescent wrench. It's in the toolbox in the shop. So I leave the crescent wrench in the boat, and that is where it is if I ever need it. Except I'm 200 miles out on the trail on my snow machine and need a crescent wrench. I buy an extra crescent wrench. In fact I have seven crescent wrenches. One in the boat, one on the snow machine, one in the house, one in the shop, and one just to change the oxygen tank when doing torch work. I cannot afford seven complete sets of wrenches. I go to buy just one wrench so I have the main tool I need to take the rewind off the snow machine on the trial, and am told a single wrench will be $20—

but for $30, I can buy a complete set. I tell the guy what he can do with his wrench. I look for wrenches and sets at garage sales. I buy whole sets for a few dollars. But you know what? Murphy's Law is that the most common wrenches are missing from the set. I can buy ten wrench sets, and none of them have a half or 9/16 inch. I end up with fifty wrenches I have never needed in my life.

Ideally, I would like it set up so there is a box labeled 'snow machine' and everything in that box is what I need to do the basics. Another box says 'Chain saw' and another says 'Boat' and 'furnace' and all I have to do is grab that box. But it never seems to work; because I never have seven sets of what I need.

I would like about five boxes by the front door of the house, the shop, the greenhouse. Every box has a label: 'headed for the shop,' 'headed for the greenhouse,' etc. Then—whenever I am in the house headed for the greenhouse I simply grab the box that says 'everything in here goes to the greenhouse.' This way, I do not make a special trip out the door across the yard and waste my time going to the greenhouse just to put a pot away. Nor make a special trip to the shop, unlock it and turn on all the lights just to hang a crescent wrench up. I don't have room by the front door for five boxes. When I have one box, the box ends up not getting returned, and when I am working on a job it is easier to leave all the right tools I need to complete the job right on the spot so I do not forget what tools I need and waste time making trips for each tool again.

But sometimes I do not get back to the same job and…well, never mind. Each tool indeed has a place it is supposed to be. I am very organized. Eventually tools end up where they belong—just not all the tools at any given point in time. It would take a day to go around and put all the tools where they belong. That might have to get done once a week. It doesn't seem very efficient to spend one entire day a week putting all the tools back. Anyhow. My unconscious only grins. *What a great story!*

I spend time keeping my thoughts in the computer in a diary-like form. The computer is a nice tool for such storage. I imagine what kind of space it would take up in a hard copy, like a file cabinet. It is so easy to find things, change things, and move the written word around, using a computer.

I get my winter moose—again this is a big event, and relief that food is not going to be a problem for another year. As with other subjects, I tend to not give out a lot of details, but keep my activities more low profile. Laws are getting so complicated it is hard to be 100% certain I understand everything correctly.

A conversation with a friend in the café sums it up. "Miles, my father and I saw a bull moose while we were out hunting but did not shoot it."

"Why not, was it too far away?"

"No. We spent a long time discussing if it was legal or not. We got out the map that shows all the management areas. It's a book as big as the phone book. We were pretty sure we were in unit 20-A. The bull sure looked like it had a legal fifty-four inch rack. But how do you really know for sure till after you kill it and measure it?" I nod that I understand. "We were near a road, so had to look the rules up on that, but it looked to be far enough away from the road. By the time we spent the half hour looking it all up and deciding, the bull wandered off."

I add, "And if you shot it while you could, then looked up all the rules to verify the legality, what if you were wrong?"

"Yea, front page headlines in the paper, confiscation of our guns, truck, thousands in fines, lawyers and maybe jail time."

I explain something that happened to me, "Once upon a time, I got my legal moose. The papers required that I send in information about the moose and where I shot it—a green card where you write down what drainage, what day, and size of the antlers." The hunters I am addressing know this card. "I forgot to measure the antlers in the field because I was not trophy hunting. I separated them so I could carry them out to the boat. The set was too big and awkward for me to carry through the dense brush." I tell how filling out the paperwork seemed less important than taking care of the meat. I can fill out the papers later when the job is done. I explain, "Later, at home, I cannot be accurate as to the exact antler size, since I cut them in half. I do the best I can, and basically make up a number, just to get the paperwork in. That seems easier than writing a letter explaining I screwed up. I assume the legal antler size is the same as it has always been in the area I am used to hunting in, so fill in the guesstimated size, and press on with the rest of the form." The hunters nod they understand this situation. "I later read the antler size needs to be an inch bigger than in the past. Probably my moose met the new requirement, but I had just made up a number, since I had cut the rack. The number I wrote down was an inch under legal!" So here my friends are going to go without food, for no other reason than it is too hard to figure out what the rules are. No, you can't always know ahead of time what the situation you will run into will be. Sometimes decisions must be made in split seconds when a moose jumps up and runs.

"Yea, well, Miles, subsistence is different." But not really. It used to be so. There are management areas and boundaries, arbitrarily marked on a map, but not in the field. A GPS is required but does not always work. In the Far North, satellites are not always lined up. Batteries get cold, and it takes time to lock in and get a reading as the moose runs. There are specific days to hunt. Not quite as bad as for sport hunters, but still, sometimes unrealistic.

I do notice there are fewer people talking about their hunts, sharing meat, celebrating. People are a lot quieter now, more secretive. Too many stories of hunters talking, and getting busted when they thought they were legal. Someone else thinks not, and turns them in. A whole lifestyle is becoming a secret. The joy and the thrill are not made visible. No more good hunting stories. I do not say I got my moose, and do not offer to share my meat with someone who did not get theirs. I let them go hungry. It is not worth the risk I did it wrong.

Anyhow, "no big deal" I tell myself. Anyone who signs up for the road kill list gets meat from moose killed along the highway. The train kills an average of 800 moose a winter. That fact is not made public. The railroad does not want to spend the money to save moose. If the meat is salvageable it goes to the needy, through a government program, if you are eligible. So the answer for the needy and dependent on the land is, "Just get on the road kill list and we will make sure you have meat—problem solved!" *If you do not sign up, the assumption is—you are too lazy*. This offer figures you have a phone, are near it, and have a truck to do down the road to fetch the meat. Meaning you are, in fact, plugged in and not off the grid. I see a dependance created. For now, it sounds good, "free just sign up!" *In the future you may need to meet requirements to qualify, pay a fee, fill out a lot of questions.*

In Fairbanks.

Crafty tells me he believes I pulled the fire in that burned my cabin down, because of my bad life and energy. "You need to change your ways, for your life to get better, Miles!" He wants me to follow his Scientology philosophy, so I can be more successful—like him.

I am reminded of a story from the North Country. A pastor has been gone from the village for a visit to the lower states. When he returns, he is greeted at the Fairbanks airport by someone who will give him a ride to his village. There is news!

"Pastor Pastor! Someone got robbed, his home broken into while you were gone!"

The pastor shakes his head, replying, "Oh yes, the ways of the wicked shall be weighed and measured and a price paid. We must pray this one comes to the church more often."

"But Pastor ! There is more! The house and shop burned, too!"

The Pastor interrupts, "Oh yes, my child, this is sorrowful, we must bring this one to the Lord, whose house was it?"

"Pastor! It was your house!"

"The ways of the Lord are mysterious, beyond our understanding..." Remembering how my buddy Crafty sang a different tune when it was his shop that got broken into, vandalized, and wiped out. I'm a little hurt Crafty would blame me for a forest fire. But amused. We all tend to make what we do look correct, and wish others saw the light of truth as we see it. It is easy to believe in the rightness of what we do, and the wickedness of others.

My buddy Crafty. I have known him many years now. A top Scientologist.

Money is still his God, and I still respect him for moving a million dollars a year in craft inventory as a one man show. He once looked like Grizzly Adams, but has white hair and a hunched back these days. I trade Crafty some of my art for supplies.

"I am here in town to pick up snow machine parts, Crafty."

"I thought you would always be a sled dog man, Miles, gave that up after all these years and knowledge?" He knows telling sled dog stories sells more art then telling the tourists about machines. This is in fact a sore subject. I miss my sled dogs. However the road to happiness is not in regrets. I will find the rewards that can be had in machines.

THE PARTS ARRIVE for the snow machine and get put in. Nothing major—new plugs, new drive belt, a special spark plug wrench, spare headlight bulb, and new gas line filter. I always cut the gas line and install a separate good, big, filter in all my engines. There are other things to do. I adjust the track tension, grease it, look at gear case oil, and inspect the windshield and make sure the skis have enough skag to make it through the winter. I add a little de-icer to the gas and test drive it. No, there is not much snow, but I like to be the first one out with a snow machine. I make sure I go by the school so the kids on lunch break get to see a snow machine go by. I do a drive-by at the city office, the post office and the store.

I admit to Josh, "Yup. I just did about $100 worth of wear and tear on the machine going out early. That's fine. It's worth it." My big splurge for the winter. I'll be the first across the river. I have to go down and see what it looks like. Still running ice flows and black water as expected.

Two days later, during the night of our first fifteen below zero spell, the ice jams. The morning after, I am there at the edge inspecting it. I have been the first one across for over twenty years now. My main concern is actual open water. In theory, one can jump open water with a snow machine, but I am not willing to take such a chance, unless I have an emergency. The ice pans are a good foot thick; black ice between them is newly formed ice holding the pans together. This new ice is half an inch thick and is only the glue holding the pans together. I do not need to get the entire machine on half an inch of ice. At any given time there will be a foot of ice supporting half the machine. Safe.

"Miles, you said all this before."

"The years blend together." We both smile at so many memories. "I never get over the thrill of being the first across the river, Josh. It must be in my blood." Josh understands, he has to be the man out front, when it comes to sled dogs and racing.

Josh is among the top ten in the world at what he does, running long distance sled dogs.

I see the safe route I can take across the river. A route with no ice pushups or new ice to span more than two feet long. So at about fifteen miles an hour I take off across ice with no snow on it. Not even a hint of an issue. No sag. No cracks. I have to stop at the bank on the other side because I cannot get up the bank without making a snow ramp first. There is a spot out front I know is a sandbar, with no water under it, where I can stop to build the ramp. There is no snow on the new ice, but snow on the river bank from a week ago. A snow shovel for the snow, a machete for the brush I will lay down first. In about an hour I have a nice ramp.

It is nice to be making the first tracks in the snow. I do not think about trying to prove anything. It means a lot to me to see the fresh snow, the new tracks of animals in the snow. No one has seen this in eight months. This makes it my private world for a while, maybe a week before others decide to venture out on my trail across the river. There is only two inches of snow. Tan sedge grass, as tall as the snow machine hisses against the sides with the sound of a snake crawling in the grass, except for the loud engine noise as the background. A raven watches from a scrub spruce. Perhaps there will be some food of some kind stirred up in the disturbance. *This scene I view has looked the same since the last ice age.* This thought gives me hope for the planet and is the source of my joy in life.

There is nothing especially exciting to look at this trip. Lots of moose tracks, some otter tracks in the swamp. I did not haul the sled with me this first trip out, so cannot head home with any firewood, but see where there is some wood I can come back for tomorrow. Eight Mile Hill is reached. I go to the top, look around, and head back home. This is my trapline trail. I have been here many hundred times.

Josh is usually the next one across the river after me. He is training his sled dogs for the Iditarod race.

"Miles, I see you crossed the Nenana. Did you get to the two sloughs?" He does not want to take the dogs out until the two sloughs have been crossed, and a trail made. His dogs are too hot in that first two miles to control. He may not be able to get them to stop.

"Yes, Josh, the first slough is as usual. Go slightly to the right because of the hotspot that is open a little bit. The second slough you have to take my trail to the left, not go diving straight off! We need more snow, but I think you can make it." Once out in the flats, he is fine with the dogs, they slow up a little, and everything is reasonably safe.

Back home at the computer, I bring up a checklist and review it. This is the major list for long trips fully outfitted which I can tone down for shorter trips. Some items are with me all the time. It is not difficult to keep all this in a backpack, and toss the pack in the sled. I have the room to spare. Even when out cutting firewood, I can break down if I have to spend a night. Or get injured falling through the ice, anything like that. [3]

Food

A way to cook it—pan, cup, handle, fork, spoon, Thermos, muffler cooker, snacks, rice, matches, gun, and spare ammunition.

Fire

Matches, candles, bow saw, machete, chain saw.

Shelter

Tarp, machete, knife and stone, rope, twine.

Clothes

Spare boot liners, hat, mitts, socks, chains saw, and wrench, bow saw, sew kit, flashlight and batteries, reading book.

Communication

Pencil, paper, tacks, trail tape, map, GPS.

Transportation

Machine stuff—plugs, spare bulb, crescent, screwdriver, rope, spare drive and fan belt, plug wrench, electric tape, bail wire, spare 2 stroke oil, winch.

Sled hitch pin spare, rope tie downs, tarp.

Snowshoes.

First Aid

Band-Aids, antiseptic, needle, dental floss, brush, pills, aspirin, Tums, toilet paper, ear plugs, matches, Vick's, sun glasses.

I mount a machete sheath on the hood of the snow machine so it is within reach while sitting on the machine. It is common to need to cut overhanging branches over the trail, or clear the trail. A rifle scabbard is mounted on the other side within reach, so I do not need to get off to shoot. Animals are less frightened by the sight of the machine, then the sight of a living thing. I have many times seen moose stare, trying to figure out what they are looking at. As soon as I step aside, the moose recognizes a living thing, and runs. Even a rabbit or grouse tends to take flight more often if I move off the snow machine. Sight seems to mean more then sound. I can hide my motions behind the machine. While sitting, I can draw a gun without being visible.

It means a lot to me to get out of the house for exercise, get firewood, and while getting wood, look around for a fresh edible game. Hare, grouse, ptarmigan are normal. The feathers of the birds are saved for my craft use. Left overs can also make good trapping bait. It may not pay economically to hunt. At least I have had the discussion many times, and had to back down, from claiming it saves money. There is simply pleasure in taking care of myself, living with the land, having the land and nature provide for me. There is reward and pleasure, even in the process of cleaning and preparing, as it brings many memories of good times, fine meals had in the past.

While hunting is on my mind, I need to call Seymour, my survey boss. I wonder if he got his moose? He loves moose season. I want to know how those last two village survey jobs we did shaped up after the data was analyzed in the computer and turned in.

"Hey Seymour!"

"Miles! I was just thinking of you and going to call! I was reaching for the phone and it rang!" This happens so often I pay no mind.

"Did you get your moose?"

"Had a good hunt, all right. Was able to use my plane and went in with my son, had a good time in camp. Took a couple of trips to get all the meat and gear back out!" He tells me the jobs worked out well. "Lime village came out within a tenth!" That's a tenth of a foot in several miles of line we surveyed. About 100 times more accurate than required. But all our jobs are like that, so it is what I expected to hear. Seymour is very much a numbers man, and very meticulous. Everything he does, he does first rate. He's more intelligent than I am. A real pleasure to work with. In my defense, Seymour is not as artistic or innovative as I am, so he could not do what I do, as I cannot do what he does. Seymour and I have been working together a lot of years now and he still looks and acts much like John Lennon.

"Seymour, how is your son? Is he still taking water and ice readings for the weather people?" His son is fifteen and has been taking water depth readings in the Manley Slough on the way to school each day. He gets paid $5 a day to call in the depth. That is fine for someone his age. I think it is great, teaching him how to be responsible, and gives him pride and responsibility.

"Actually, no. He was told he is too young, and the job is not safe enough. He had already been doing it for three years!"

"Geez!" Seymour explains how it has been determined to be unsafe. He might fall off the bridge and drown in the slough while lowering the weighted string into the water. So he lost his job. But he is graduating soon, and thinks he has a job with one of the local airlines as cargo handler, after he turns sixteen, in a month.

"He likes planes and might be interested in being a pilot." That would sure be great, since Seymour flies and owns two planes. A nice father—son thing.

"So how is your son, Miles?"

"I guess he is OK. We email back and forth and keep in touch." Seymour knows my son and I are not so close. My son seems to not be interested in the work I do, or being part of my business, or hearing about Alaska and the wilds. He is into malls, is raised in the city by his mother. I need to respect that. It would be nice to have some good father-son stories. But—oh well. I wonder if my son misses a father as

31

much as I miss a son? I kind of doubt it. He's never had me around, a father in his life, and does not seem to have any longing for that. Certainly no sense he wished his mother and I were together as a family. Meaning then, he is glad I am gone. I thought it best to leave it that way.

There was a chance at one time to go to court and fight about joint custody— being able to help raise my son. His mom took full custody, with me getting super- vised visitation. Meaning she controls the visits and the relationship. I had to raise my son how she felt I should. If I got off track, she'd reel us both in. I thought it was better not to fight. The lawyers get rich; it seems to hardly ever be best for a child. Better he has one good parent without fighting. Getting yanked between ways of life, schools, far off places, would probably not be good for him. Especially when he has not expressed any interest. He is very protective of his mother. The head male in that household. I am competition, not a valued member of the family. But anyhow, nothing to get into with Seymour. *Love is nothing but a sword through the heart.*

So glad Seymour got his moose. Seymour does not enjoy civilization, but he does well as far as the rules go. He knows where he can get a moose, how, when, and under what conditions. He does not need to study for it much, nor does he find it confusing or stressful. He is lucky in that way.

"Miles, did I tell you about the bear?"

"What bear, Seymour? When?"

And Seymour tells me, "When I went out by myself to do some last details at Lime Village. I had to fly in by helicopter." He got dropped off in the tundra some- place. A bear started to follow him around. "This happens sometimes. I tried to just run him off." I know, because we have this happen to us sometimes, usually no big deal. We simply run the bear off. "First, he gets into my lunch while I am someplace else setting up the instrument. Then he followed closely and I can't scare him off. Pretty soon he is getting bolder, moving in on me through the thick brush." Sure, that would make anyone nervous. "I'm thinking, the heck with this, and decide when he shows himself, I am going to shoot him."

I can picture the situation. Seymour is a more nervous guy than I am in the woods. He doesn't like unknowns, nor does he get any thrill out of danger. He is not nervous like stuttering or freezing up. One time, a moose attacked him and the dog team on the winter trail, and he does not recall, but his empty gun is in his hands and the dead moose is behind him. He recalls one shot and a moose flying over him as he ducks down. He simply doesn't enjoy it as much as I do.

He is saying, "I have my pack on, so can't move fast, have a job to focus on, with a helicopter waiting for me at $700 an hour." His lunch is gone, so he will have to do without. His pack is ripped. The bear already got a snack. Now the bear thinks Seymour might be an easy meal. In the past, we have had bears knock down and damage the survey equipment. In this case, it would take all his profits on this job to cover the loss. Seymour always carries a .44 Magnum.

"Was it that the new Taurus your wife got you?" He had shown it to me. We had both tried it out. Nice titanium, light weight, heavy duty gun, on sale for $600. Easy to carry, compared to his old Smith and Wesson.

"Yup. So out comes the Taurus. No fooling around anymore with this bear. No more hide and seek and tag, you're it." The bear shows itself. Seymour blasts it. "Went down like a ton of bricks, all right. This .44 is very effective." I smile because he knows I prefer my .357 Magnum. Half the power of his 44. I know my .357 still leaves a hole in flesh you could drop a bowling ball in. How much bigger a hole does it take? Seymour goes on. "I finish the job, and when the helicopter comes to pick me up, I tell him all about it. "

The pilot was very nervous. Wanted to fill out a self defense report. If it is not reported, it is not legal to kill a bear the same day you fly. The pilot could lose his license and helicopter. Better to be safe and just make a report!

"So we go to Fish and Game and make a report, Miles." Seymour pauses and goes on, "You would not believe the problems that followed!" Oh, I can believe it all right. It is Seymour getting his first taste of that branch of the government. I smile, because till now, Seymour has told me Fish and Game is fair, honest, and I am creating my own problems.

"Miles, they wanted me to prove it was self defense! They wanted me to prove I did not take a trophy hide out." In my own mind, I would consider it a plus if some of the bear could get salvaged. I consider it a crime to kill an animal and waste it, even in self defense. I do not recall ever wasting any game, not for any reason. "And take them to the spot." Seymour pauses. "They want me to take them to where I killed the bear! On whose dime, and whose day's wages?" So Seymour is facing fines, a criminal record, and the pilot is risking the loss of his license and helicopter. Seymour has some comments I can't record. I only grin. Now he knows what it is like dealing with 'Them.'

I assume it is possible to have good experiences with government agencies. I only assume, because public opinion appears to be how great government is, and how helpful. How important it is to vote, how great our system is, how grateful we should all be, and how much worse it is elsewhere and on and on.

"Isn't it great, how the government has rules, cares, keeps us all in line, protects us." and such talk. How important it is to follow all the rules. How rules are there for a reason.

Heck, Seymour himself has argued this with me countless times! "Otherwise, what would we have, Miles?" Indeed. Anyhow, Seymour was not locked up, but it cost him a lot of time, paperwork, being under suspicion, and he is probably now on the 'person of interest' list.

"Well, it is the last time I voluntarily go in to see Fish and Game, that's for sure, Miles!" He does not have to tell me about it! He's telling a mouse the cat cannot be trusted.

The subject turns to hunting, getting meat in general, and having moose meat for winter in particular. I feel good Seymour has his freezer full of moose meat, and will have a good year of eating ahead. Living remote makes it hard to get anything fresh, so it is not even a matter of how much money he has. The village store does not have fresh meat at any price. What it does have is limited and old. Maybe freezer burned. It's OK, but no comparison to good moose!

"Yea, Miles, my wife has health issues, and is on a special diet. The meat from the land is really good for both of us. I think the city meat with steroids and preservatives and such has an effect on our health." Seymour had some sausage made by a friend of his. "He raises turkey. So we trade some meat with him for his home raised turkey!" I chuckle as it is good to share, because 500 pounds or more of edible meat off a moose could use some variety in the diet, if someone else has a surplus of 'whatever.' Trade seems to be part of Alaska—certainly village life.

We talk about health and food for a while…

"Got to go, Miles, time to feed the sled dogs!" I can hear them outside the house. Seymour has about twenty-five sled dogs he races and leases out. He enjoys this as a way of life. He is not like Josh, as Josh prefers slower long distance races. Seymour like the hot sprint races.

I recalled over twenty years ago Seymour gave up a high paying job as head of a big company during the pipeline days in Fairbanks. He was not happy, over stressed, even though 'rich.' He realized what he liked best was being out in the field, one on one, with small crews he knew and trusted. Seymour and wife moved to a small village to live a simpler life. The only regret is the wife's family disowned them, cut her out of the will, barely on speaking terms for turning down such good money, respect, prestige.

"I'll give a call towards spring, see what kind of work is possible for the summer!" I'm glad to be off the phone. I still do not like phones much, and use them as little as possible. Time to get away for a while. Away from people, rules, permission, depression, madness of civilization. I think of this many times. *Getting back to how man lived for 100,000 years. Man has only gotten modern in the past 200 years.* I tell myself I do not mind the snow machine, even like it. I tell myself I do not miss the sled dogs. Because, what good would it do to wish for what can't be? It makes sense that happiness is on the road of accepting what is. Seymour having sled dogs is different. His team is recreational, and he feeds them town bought dog food in bags at $200 a month.

I HAVE a list of things to replace at the homestead, lost in the fire. Also, someone showed up on the trapline last winter, and left traps on the slough where the homestead is. A guy named Kevin contacted me, and is interested in buying my trapline, or being partners, or working out a deal of some kind. He lives 300 miles away. This seems a long ways to drive, then snow machine to get there! He is a carpenter by trade, and in construction of all kinds: cement work, land speculation, heavy equipment and such. He tells me it is not hard, nor time consuming, to replace my burned cabin with a small frame place. Maybe two to three days work.

I do not see how this is possible, but hear this from construction workers who know how to build a cabin fast. I need about five days just to get the basics up. But anyhow, this Kevin wants to set up a small cabin for me if I buy the material, by way of being nice and getting a deal on a place to trap in the area where he might get left alone.

I'm open to the idea, because I know I will never be able to re-cut all those trails that burned, that took me twenty years to put in the first time. If some younger dreamer thinks he can open it all up in a few years, who am I to say he cannot? One of the trips in summer was to meet this guy on the river, haul in supplies and get the cabin framed in.

As he said, "It only takes a day."

We built the walls on the ground, and lifted them into place. I did not know how to do this. We got something small up, eight x twelve feet, but good enough for shelter and storing a few basics needed to be out for a week or two. I haul in insulation and shelving.

The second trip out is routine. There is a foot of snow, temperature is plus ten degrees. About perfect. I haul the fiberglass insulation, and a few basics I want. There are a few logs in the way, trees that fell over the past summer. I am the first one out this way, as usual, and as usual, there is brush hanging over the trail I need to stop and cut with the machete. This has been an ongoing issue, getting worse each year. I cannot keep up by myself with trimming fifty miles of trail. After twenty-two years, the original bulldozed trail has brush that is more like trees— thirty feet tall on the edges. In fact, if it had not been cut by me each year, the trail would be impassable.

Thirty foot alder and willow, when laden with snow, arch over the trail because they are already leaning in to get light. Normally they arch up fifteen feet or more over my head. For years I could just run over the smaller trees and knock them down, or hit them when cold and break them. This creates fallen trees in the trail on the return trip, but I ran them over till they were chips.

Now the trees do not break, the snow machine does. I can no longer smash them down by running over them. I do not know how many more years the trail will be passable. One advantage to having someone like Kevin in the picture is, he might open the trail better. But in return, I may have to give it up as my trapline. Or offer him a deal of some kind. We are still talking about what might work. He has two buddies who want to come out and hang together. I can see the future. I cannot do this anymore. My back after surgery is fine, but is not a young back anymore. Cutting, twisting, tossing brush all day long in the cold is not going to happen. Running rough trails, jumping logs, yanking my machine back on the trail when I run off it, fixing the snow machine in the dark and cold is not going to work well either.

One trip at a time. For now, I am trimming enough to get through one more trip. It is still exciting, and a thrill to be the first one out. I love the way the light dapples through snow covered branches overhead. There are wonderful memories at all the spots along the way where I have set traps over the years and got fur. Images fill my head of the various marten, fox, otter and lynx. I have an uneventful trip home.

Josh and I have talked about the subject of sled dogs or snow machines for reliable transportation over the past twenty-five years. He loves the old way with dogs. He refuses to change, and move to snow machines, and never will. One thing we both notice is the increase in 'idiots' out here in the remote wilds. Idiots who in the old days, could not get to the wilds. In earlier days, travel took skill. There was, in the past, a certain amount of respect meeting anyone else 100 miles in the wilds. They had to make camp, and know how to spend a night.

"Josh, now in an hour, someone can get to my remote cabin!" I point out there is now a machine race between Fairbanks and Nenana. Fairbanks is seventy miles on the river. Winners make that in twenty minutes! I laugh, "Gee, Josh. In twenty minutes I might still be adjusting my hat and gloves, and not left yet!" We both know as well, that to be safe you should never go further than you can walk. "If the machine breaks down, then what, Josh?" Josh and I both have short legs, stout bodies. Good for strength, not as good for long distance.

I get nervous going way out beyond my cabin without a safety net, so to speak. If I break a new trail, the soft snow would not be easy to walk back on. The trails I used to make in the woods were 'forever.' All winter long they were constantly being packed like a highway. I could walk them through the woods out of the wind where there are trees for shelter and fire. When I lived out here, and this was my only home, there might be only two trips to Nenana all winter. The sled dogs cost a lot less. Certainly when I was fishing for them and building my own dog sleds, making my own harnesses and such. I did not need much money. It was a whole lifestyle that trapping was only part of. I do love what I am doing, and enjoy all this very much! Nothing is free! *How do I support this lifestyle?*

The average person who comes to the wilds for recreation covers costs with a high paying job of some kind. Another main group that is successful is the retired elderly with outside money coming in. Those who are poor tend to have unreliable equipment, and tend not to get out far from the village. A few Indians can make it work. Because? I go over the reasons in my mind. One huge factor is the white man gives Indians money they did not work for. It's supposed to be settlement money for occupying the Indian's land.

I get told by civilization, "We did take their land. We owe them, Miles!"

I often give a puzzled reply, "Many races throughout history had their land taken, what makes the Indian so different and deserving?" *Even Indian tribes took over land, stole, robbed, enslaved other tribes. This was before white man ever showed up.* Beyond all that, heck, I have been on the Indian's side as best I can. I always wanted to be an Indian. As a kid playing cowboys and Indians, I was always the Indian getting laughed at. I read all the 'how-to' Indian books. I practically worshiped the Indian way. I do not hate Indians, nor ridicule the Indian life. At any rate—a few Indians can afford the $10,000 snow machines, gas and gear due to having more money than I without working for it because their ancestors were persecuted. This has not been competition for me, there has been enough room. But it does affect how people perceive my lifestyle.

"Oh, the Indians still live like this right? So why can't you? Are they smarter? More knowledgeable? " No. The government gives each of them thousands of dollars a year. Free medical, free housing, free land, preference when hiring, and restrictive racially biased laws that favor Indians. I'd about sell my soul to be an Indian, but oh well! Sometimes I feel like the inferior race, being punished. That thought leads no place, so I push it out of my mind and focus on the good stuff. Some Indians can still make this life work on their own, and do get my respect.

A few remote people are outlaws, up to something that fetches extra money. Growing pot, and illegal guiding are two big ways that come to mind. Tom and Lana are a rare neighbor couple who both work in Denali Park all summer, and make pretty good money. Enough they can take the winter off and run dogs, race, fool around, make a little money, but if not, no great loss. Maybe collect unemployment all winter. I run into Lana on the trail on the way home to Nenana with the snow machine. I have not seen her in a long time, maybe two years. She is still running sled dogs.

"Good to see you, Miles! I come across your snow machine trail sometimes, but our paths do not cross as much these days!" She and her husband have changed lifestyle a little, like I have. They invested money in house rentals, and have four to five places they rent out, manage, and earn income from. The sled dogs are more for fun now. There is no freight hauling with the dogs for mountain climbers as they once did. "I always envied you, Miles, and the life you have. You spent all those years out here, full time. We never could. I wished! But we worked all summer to support the winter time." I suspect it was more her husband's plans. She would be happier living as I do. But life is filled with compromises.

"I see you still have sled dogs Lana, can you fish for them?"

"Fishing? I guess. We try to get a fish wheel out in the fall when we can. The laws are better now, finally." Better? I suppose, with lots more control and regulations, paperwork, permits, times, dates and fees. We need to apply, and be approved with a chance of denial if certain criteria are not met. A way to turn the screws down on us. But, yes, it has little effect on Lana. They have money, get to town a lot, have a phone, one of these new cell phones, a home in town, and plugged in, connected, able to easily comply. The laws are set up for people like Tom and Lana. Hard working taxpayers who are plugged in. They are among the protected. I'm not sure they understand or care how it is for others. But for sure, I like Lana and have no hard feelings. But still, I am a little evasive. I do not say much about what I am up to or my plans. We do not talk about the forest fire. She may not even know I have a small place built to stay in.

There is a possibility her husband, Tom, had something to do with the loss of my home. It seems strange a sprinkler system was set up but never turned on. Tom was the boat operator for firefighters.

"Too much smoke, Miles!" But not too much smoke to set it up, and he did not sound sorry. No sympathy expressed for my loss. *Couldn't get to the home?* "Maybe did not care to try."

Lana's dogs are laying down in the snow resting. One rolls on his back to scratch it and smiles at me when I look over. I recall these close relationships with my transportation. Not far behind us on the trial is a brush tunnel covered in snow. Lana has not changed a lot, still thin, full of energy, intense blue eyes, now in her fifties.

I am reminded of the Kramers. They are recreational new people in the area, who hired Tom to built a log cabin from a kit on a lake out behind my place. They are only around a few days a year. I surveyed their place. I gave them a picture I painted for the new cabin. They love my art, and seemed nice. We get along as sort of friends. But by the grace of God, their place might have burned. Their cabin was spared. Only half a mile, maybe a mile from me. They are kind of Yuppies. Ok, just a different lifestyle then mine. Environmentalists who do not hunt or trap, more likely to take pictures. Lots of money. Live in Anchorage, 500 miles away. Come here for two days to "Ooh" and "Ahh" over the beauty of nature. I smile. I know a lot of people like this. Better friends, more in common with Lana than me, which is why it is on my mind.

I like them. So when my cabin burned I wrote, and asked if I could use their cabin for a week, while I built a new place. After all, it could be the other way around. Them with a lost home and no place to stay. If I was not there I would say, "Sure! Of course!" But they told me no. They preferred no one use their cabin while they are gone. I suspect that Tom would say the same thing. Polite friends without being close. Without as much in common as I once thought. A sorry conclusion to come to after twenty-five years of being neighbors.

"The dogs have a nice broken trail to follow from here to the fork, I'm glad for that, Miles !" Yes, the dogs will enjoy being able to run in my trail for fifteen miles before Lana's trail forks away from mine. The tripod that once marked the fork is falling down. We used to leave notes for each other at the tripod. I'd pick up mail they left at the tripod, and bring it to town for them. I wish her a good trip. She takes off before I do, so my snow machine will not scare the dogs. Many years ago, we had worked together to cut a trail by hand all the way from here to Nenana. It used to take three days sleeping on the trail with sled dogs to get to town. Now it takes me two hours. Something lost, something gained.

If I did not have my Nenana home, no electricity, no computer, and I lived full time on the homestead, *how would my life look?* "I'd be breathtakingly dirt poor." As my survey boss described pure subsistence.

"Yes, if you like working fifteen hour days, and all you got to show for it at the end of the day is a pot of beans." If you get sick, you die. I'd be dead already. Without back surgery? Where would I be? Without blood pressure pills? If the fire wiped out the only home I had in the world?

Now I have my art, the web site, and more money, more tools, more nice things. But it means I cannot be gone for more than a few days at a time or my web site falls apart. People are waiting for orders they paid for. I'm still in hopes I can catch enough fur or somehow at least break even trapping.

It is very nice to get back to Nenana in two easy hours, warm, not tired. I could easily make a round trip in a day without a lot of effort.

I am expecting a reply from Art Train that came and stopped in Nenana. I have been anxiously waiting to hear if any of my art left in their traveling gift shop sold! *Maybe this will be an ongoing permanent outlet for selling!* "Wow! I have been honored and accepted." I left a lot of my art with them on consignment. So far all I have heard is, "I think we still have your art, someplace. I am not sure. There are now new people in charge. We have a high turnover." Even so, *doesn't someone do book work and keep track of inventory you do not own? Are you treating everyone like this?*

Crab pot with Roger—Nome trip.

My art. Opal ivory turquoise.

CHAPTER TWO

INTERNET ART SALES, SEATTLE GIFT SHOW

I glance over my emails

I decided on the first claw, and we asked about changing dollars to pounds, and it turns out that it would cost almost as much to convert the money as it would to buy the claw...so I can't, really...let me know if you can think of a solution to the problem...

Thanks Richard

I reply

Hello Richard! Well, I just closed a deal with a guy in France and we had the same problem. He told me he was a member of this thing called 'Pay Pal'—a method of paying on the internet.

PayPal might become a solution for international money issues and the only way it can work easily so business can be done between countries.

I write one of my customers:

Hello Jean! I have been in Fairbanks—among other things to do—trying to get a credit card, a merchant account, debit card, and get all plugged in so I can better do business on the internet.

This will be the first time in my life I have a debit card, just about required to run a business these days.

Dear sir,

We are a Taiwan Art Company to sell high quality artworks. We are interesting in your artworks—sculptures. please send your catalog, price list or more information to us. thank you very much.

GU

I reply

Hello GU Thank you for your interest in my work. My art is one of a kind and no two are alike. bla bla bla…

I know of no one else anywhere but I who carves precious stone and combines it with other materials from the land. Wings and ivory are a tight fit and pinned with gold wire so it is strong.

The birds are 'Ptarmigan' the Alaska state bird. This bird loves the snow and cold. It flies low to the ground and flies in a special way in groups. This sculpture is how this bird looks when the flock flies.

The crystals are how the ice looks on the river when the river freezes with chunks pushed in the air by the river current. The wind will blow the snow off the ice and it sometimes looks exactly like this crystal. I freeze this moment from the life I live and offer it as a dream.

The art belongs to someone who understands this moment frozen in time. The retail value of this item is $1,000 selling wholesale for $500. If interested, bla bla bla…

Wow! An inquiry all the way from Taiwan! *Amazing!* "Isn't the internet amazing?" Still, *I wonder how come Taiwan would be interested in Alaska product to re-sell?* Well, maybe there are rich people over there who collect stuff, even if it is a high price, if they want it. Some aspects of selling on the internet are confusing, with varied opinions. No one I know has been scammed or spammed, the terms are not even in the English language yet. I am discussing how to edit pictures, what format to use, and how Ebay works with a customer. This Randy guy runs a web store, and sells for others on consignment. This works well for people having trouble figuring out how to do it themselves. Ebay is sort of new and has some bugs to be worked out. Not everyone can figure out how it works, or how to offer things for sale. I have an Ebay presence, but my gut feeling is, I will be happier with my own web site, set up how I want.

I reply to my next email:

Hello Randy! I use jpg on my pictures as much as I can. Some older pictures may have been done in gif. I now try to do with about 200 dpi (I call them 'dips') and try to keep them under about 50k, many are under twenty. Probably my lifestyle pictures are the oldest and have the most energy, and done in the gif format.

But yes, I need to keep a better eye on that—maybe relook this over and get the pictures down in energy. But jpg is fine? Not tiff or gif or any other format? Why then do the other formats even exist? Is there better quality with the other formats?

So I'll pick a few things out and send them to you. I have a brochure—pictures and basic write up about me and can do some info on each item and you can decide how to use this info—either have it go to the buyer, or have it go on the ad in Ebay.

Before sending my email off, I review what he first wrote me, that I have stored in a computer file.

Monday, I go to Fairbanks with the guy who wants to buy my trapline and remote homestead land. We go to the land office to check on the status of the land and set up some kind of deal. I get back to review where I am with the Randy consignment.

Subject: Beauty! Your handiwork is amazing
Hello again, Miles

I didn't know you had a website. It is very professional—and your handiwork really is amazing—and I have seen, bought, and sold thousands of pieces of Alaska over the years.

After the Native Land Settlement Act, the gang from the North coast had the money to come to Fairbanks every summer for the carving competition at the State Fair, then they would come to us to sell it all so they could hang out on two street for a couple days before they went home. Quite a few of them, like Ed Penatak decided to stay in town and carve, and handle carvings from the craftsmen who went home. We helped Ed start making cribbage boards out of his tusk carvings, and he got to give one to President Nixon when he stopped in Anchorage on his way to China.

If you are not home on a regular basis to ship sold items out, then I agree with your basic thought on sending me groups of items to sell. Dealing with me as a wholesaler with a thirty day pay would seem to be workable…

So one idea to run my business, and still be gone a lot, is to work with someone else, like this Randy guy. It's a new concept to be business partners with someone far away, staying in touch by instant emails on a regular basis. Instead of working in the same building with people one on one.

So I'd send this guy my art, he'd sell it for me and keep half. I'd lose half, but my time is free to live the lifestyle I love out in the wilds. Money is not as important to me as being happy.

I see another email having to do with resources, and getting help finding customers. It is a time to try this and try that. It all costs. It all takes time to sort out. It's a learning process.

> **We at World Wide Arts Resources** would like to let you know that we have processed your arts related resource submission. Below you can find out more about your specific submission—i.e. what category you were included in, your page title and much more. If you subscribed to www.absolutearts.com Arts News Service you will be receiving your first Arts News within the next couple of days. We would also like to invite you back to http://wwar.com to use our search engine, arts chat room or bulletin board on a regular basis.

I cruise to another web site…

Polygon—Website services
 http://polygon.net/products/docs/webservices_mfg.html
 Offers web managing, promotion, domain etc.
 Retail Jewelers Jewelry Manufacturers/Suppliers
 Diamond Dealers Estate Jewelry Dealers
 Colored Stone Dealers

I pause. Here is an interesting one. Because. Well because I am finding as I deal with other cultures and just 'people,' from all over the world, that we define things differently. This can cause misunderstanding and lost deals. So here is some sort of standard for terms like 'hand -made' and exactly what that means from a legal standpoint.

Guides for the Jewelry Industry
 http://www.ftc.gov/bcp/guides/jewel-gd.htm
 Friday, January 28, 2000
 A useful list of info only, not a selling place, but guidelines and info:
 § 23.0 Scope and application. § 23.1 Deception (general). § 23.2 Misleading illustrations. § 23.3 Misuse of the terms "hand-made," "hand-polished," etc. § 23.4 Misrepresentation as to gold content. § 23.5 Misuse of the word "vermeil." § 23.6 Misrepresentation as to silver content. § 23.7 Misuse of words "platinum," "iridium," "palladium, "ruthenium," "rhodium," and "osmium." § 23.8 Misrepresentation as to content of pewter. § 23.9 Additional guidance for the use of quality marks.

And about fifty more like this.

Some of what I see, I never thought about much, since I am not 'in the box' with no formal education. Like the fact I am melting down metals of unknown origin and content, remixing, then adding other metals, and making jewelry. It never occurred to me I might need to know what to call it, or not to call it, or must by law call it! In my view, I am selling my art, not the metal. In my mind, who cares what metal it is? You look at it, you like it, you like my art, you like the price. If it has copper in it and looks yellow, is not expensive and is not gold, I call it brass or bronze. *Who knows? Who cares?* "But others might?"

So I need to increase my knowledge about what is legal, accepted, done, and not done, and what is it people expect. In truth, brass and bronze have specific percentages of exact ingredients and guidelines. Outside those guidelines would stretch the definition into the realm of a kind of metal with no name.

How then would I reply to a simple question, "This is nice, what metal is this?"

Should I, or even could I, make up a name for my metals that fit no category? In the stone business it is common to refer to a stone you do not know the name of, as 'Leaverite.' (The customer smiles and nods.) It means leave—her—right—there. Or 'who knows!'

Someone got rich in Alaska off a product they called 'Borealis Stone.' It's not a stone at all. It is some kind of powder mixed with epoxy resin and put together with colors—like baking a marble cake. Light green and blue. It's pretty enough. Many think it is a natural stone. It looks a little like azurite and malachite. Copper based stones. Since this 'borealis stone' is a liquid mix, it is cheap to cast and mass produce as it does not need to be carved like real stone. No one called the inventor a con artist. Is it misleading? Is it ethical? Is it legal? Every Alaska gift shop has it, and a ton of money is made.

'The Man of Magic,' who can wink and supply you with that which you so desire? Could I be arrested? Has anyone been harmed? Has the environment been hurt? I already know if I use the term 'imitation,' well, we simply cannot use this word—extremely few do. 'Replica' is a little better, 'enhanced,' 'stabilized,' are all more pleasant sounding words than—"I altered it" Or "fake."

Meanwhile, I have sent Randy some of my art to market, and have not heard back …

Hello Randy! How is the internet business going? I wonder if anything of mine has sold, and what is going on. I sent an email a couple months ago inquiring. You might have been busy, but do let me know what is going on and if you want different items (do an exchange) or if we should keep trying, or what to do here. Talk to ya' later!
Miles

A reply to file…I only glance at it and press on…I'm having trouble figuring out how to keep a file of all my emails in some kind of order so I can find them again.

Geez! I have a hundred or more emails in a random file. But this Randy is the one who has my work on consignment.

He replies,

Miles, Hello! Hope your holidays were wonderful!!! Sorry about the slow responses, we have been going slightly crazy around here. I've been looking at your web site from time to time—it's evolving quite nicely. Keep up the good work! I have a page up on our site with information about you and your work with links at the bottom to all of your art and your web site. Let me know what you think…**bla bla**

One of my pieces described on Randy's site I look over.

Box-prehistoric horn Swallow Not just art—but a way of thinking ID# B-ph-BS Retail price—$250

Hand done, one—of—a—kind. This is about three inches in diameter and three inches tall. The box is made from 40,000 year old bison horn found by the artist along the banks of the Yukon River, 300 miles in the wilderness. This animal lived at the time of the mastodons.

I pause here to think. *It seems easier with all the work involved, for me to offer high end items in the $150 to $350 and up range.* "But is this the market people will spend in on the internet?" This conversation with myself reminds me, *Hey, we have not heard from Art Train. Seems odd, even if nothing has sold, not to get a reply to our inquiry.*

Hello Stephanie at Art Train!

I hope the museum train has been a success, and wonder where you are at now! Hope you still think of Alaska and your visit here.Bla bla moving along…I know you are busy, but if anything sold, it would be nice to be paid. If not, I wonder why, and ask if we should consider I take it back so I can have it someplace it might sell. I had been so hopeful when we parted in Alaska!

I have not heard from Art Train in quite a while. Hmmm. Oh well?[1]
So much for the rich bringing culture to the savages.

The business is at least similar to 'trapping.' Getting customers to buy, is much like putting bait out for predators. The term 'shark frenzy' is appropriate. No customer wishes to be viewed as 'being trapped,' nor the product they seek as 'bait.' Yet one secret of trapping is to not have the item of interest seen as bait! If the wolf thinks 'bait,' he will not step in the trap! The goal is to get the wolf to see what you offer as desirable, natural food, necessary, worked for and earned, and as a reward. The wolf is suspicions of a free gift, just as a customer is. The customer seeks a deal they cleverly spotted ahead of everyone else. Discovered because they are smarter than the average bear. A good seller says,

"Why yes, step right this way, sir, you are indeed clever." *Wait! Back up, start again, you must put your right foot forward first; see the guide sticks, very good, the trap pan is right there, thank you! With fur you catch the foot, with dear customers you catch the wallet.*

I tell my customers.
And post on the web site,

I want everyone in the food chain to be happy. I want to treat those I buy from well. I want to be treated well, and I want you, the buyer, to be treated well, with no one being ripped off. How can I accomplish this? Decent prices that are not a steal, but fair. Honesty, reliability, a certain amount of personal service, a story with the item, a connection of some kind all the way from the source to the end user.

The issue I am beginning to have with my outlook, is running into so many people I simply disagree with. People who feel as strongly as I do, that are morally good people filled with the correct intentions. There is so often no known, for-sure villain.

I explain it to Josh, because he is a good example. He is Native American and I am white. We have cultural differences to overcome to be friends. He was truly shocked I put a burglar alarm in my shop, that went off when he, my best friend, went in the shop to borrow my lawn mower.

'Treat others as you would have them treat you,' does not work here. Because what Josh did, I would never do! If I went to someone's shop when the owner was not home, with the intention of taking anything without permission, I would expect to get shot if I was caught. I believe a man's home is his castle. Nor do I think much of stealing. There are countries where they cut your hand off for stealing a piece of bread. Some cultures are more communistic, believing every-thing belongs to everyone, and is shared by all. There was a time I thought a man had a right to make a gun set. If anyone broke in they should expect to get shot. My friend, Josh, would be dead now. Is he a thief? He is as shocked by my behavior as I am of his. Imagine a situation between people who do not know each other and are not friends! Black and white is not so clear anymore, as it once was.

The situation between seller and buyer is similar ground. What is fair?

I talk with Josh "I'd prefer to say, 'Porcupine claws that look like hawk,' and do so as often as I can, when I can. But people are not often looking for truth and real-ity. Many cannot handle that. They are for the most part buying dreams. A dream home, a dream car, a dream job, dream clothes that do not make them look fat, accented with dream jewelry that sparkles and looks like diamonds and gold, but is not. Because they can't afford real gold. Yet they wish to falsely impress others."

Josh only says, "Miles, the man with the golden pen" implying I can make anything sound like the truth. I could sell snow to Eskimos. Convince you red was really blue. Win any side of a debate. Does it make my arguments right?

I did not make up the rules. I do not even like the rules. I wish very much we could all be honest and see the truth. I struggle with how to run a successful business and what's going to work. If selling is like trapping, it is also like fishing. When we fish, the one who catches the most may not be the one who invested in the most expensive quality lure, or has the best product. Catching the fish has a lot to do with the jiggle. The fish in general responds to anything shiny moving in the right way at the right time. Under specific conditions. But companies invest in research studying, and making marketing a science. There is a formula. To some extent almost any product can be plugged in. That bums me out. Speaking as an artist with skills that took years to develop. Skills and a quality product do not count for as much as I once believed. No. A good product does not sell itself.

I myself was sold a bill of goods when I headed out into the wilds trying to be a Mountain Man! The life of the free trapper! Davey Crocket. Indiana Jones! The truth did not set me free. Not one book or movie told it like it really is. It's all hogwash. My only chance to survive was to smile, understand, and accept. Not to be angry. To smarten up. Get wise. It's part of growing up.

We are not going to find a real diamond ring in a bubble gum machine, even though it says 'diamond ring' on the plastic bag. 'Genuine turquoise" for $9.95 is reconstituted rock dust with resin, dyed, baked, and smells like plastic if you heat it. This is the world I find myself living in. I am not pleased. But given the rules, I plan on surviving. As honest as it is possible to be. *Let's see how it goes.*

So, how can I offer a $250 item for $50? Instead of hand making every single part, one at a time, one of a kind, as I have been doing for thirty years, I have been learning to cast. I make one item by hand, make a mold, and can then spread the time over ten or twenty items. I have, so far, never made even 100 castings from the same mold. My molds are cheap and fall apart after fifty casts. But before that, I get bored and make more molds.[2]

I'm trying to offer 'story pieces'—another idea that I want to be a connection between the customer, myself, and the land the materials came from. In the days of cheap mass production, do people miss a connection and a personal story? I believe they do. I am reminded of what I learned at the Seattle wholesale gift show.

Past Flash[3]

Years ago. The Seattle Wholesale Gift Show is designed to get suppliers and vendors together in one place. The market is the gift shop industry for the entire

Northwest. Tourism companies as well as mom and pop operated shops come here to hand pick items for their shops. There is a $10 fee just to come in and look, so only serious customers show up. The show is a few days before the big Tucson show, so I combine it with the same trip. I'll do the wholesale show for two days, repack, and press on to Tucson. I have done the Seattle show three times already. I know the routine. I have the same table, and know most of the vendors. I'm trying to understand the gift shop business, and see how my products can fit in.

I have a conversation with a guy much like myself a few booths down. "Good to see you, Miles, hope you had a good season! It's going slow for me. I hope I can make up for it here." I look at his work, and admire it. I have looked at his work before, and pondered what is going on. He does one-of-a-kind handmade, really nice stuff. Very much like my work, with a similar story. That is rare, so I am paying attention. His prices seem to me, to be way too high. "Sure! High, Miles, quality costs, you know that!" Yes, I do. I know he is not making profit. "I take pride in my work. Each piece designed and never repeated."

Yes. I know quite well. I have used the same exact line for many years. He begins one item and finishes creating it, then begins another item. Extremely time consuming. His average price is in the $150 range, with nothing less than $100. His work is worth the price. He makes $15 an hour at these prices. He is not selling well. He does not agree with me. I told him my opinion several times.

"I do work much like yours. I think we need to come up with items in the $50 and under range, if we can, what the average customer can afford. It's hard to do! I think I have figured out how." And explain about casting to duplicate parts I can use again. I can buy rough stones and other materials, then cut them myself. Come up with a unique cut, and different look. I can get free metals to cast as scrap. I can keep the same high quality and still create four to five or more pieces at a time in an assembly line. I have the tools out for each step, and finish a dozen items at one time which enables me to offer more quantity for the same inventory value. I have seventy-five items, or 100 items, for $40 each. That's a total of $4,000, spending the same time and money as forty pieces selling at $100 each.

My fellow vendor says, "Fine, but I am not lowering my quality and sacrificing my artistic talents to mass produce!" *Will people care, and will he do well?* I'm interested in seeing. The answer is no. He's practically in tears. He does not even sell one item.

I do not rub it in, but point out, "I made $2,000. I honestly think your work is every bit as good, even better than mine." I leave it at that, and hope he figures it out. Or finds a market someplace that buys what he offers at his prices. If so, I'd be curious. I have not found such a market. So far, neither has he. I know a few who have made it big time. In my opinion, it is not about their product as much as marketing. *I learned much of this from my buddy Crafty!*
Past flash ends

ONE COMMENT I hear over and over is, "Many customers can find your web site, but, so what, who the heck are you?" *There's a lot of scams and bull crap operations going on.* Because of this, it might be helpful to offer up some references, phone numbers of happy customers, artists who buy materials from me. People I have done business with, my local Chamber of Commerce, anything to show I am who I say I am. I begin posting pictures of products customers made using my raw materials. This makes me, and my products, more real, homey, hopefully gets people thinking, they also could create this from my materials.

I'm seeing an increased interest in my surplus raw materials as part of my business. Other artists need wolf claws I can easily get locally. I set my web site up to encourage trades.

I'M HAVING a little more trouble keeping track of deals and customers. Now and then I space it out! I have no understanding of spreadsheets or information retrieval. I use word documents with bookmarks to find customers, but no way to cross reference, put in reminders that I am happy with. I try using the email calendar, but then change email accounts. I try using a tax program with the capability of remembering customers, but this has issues, mostly it takes too long to open the program and get to the right spot every time I want to review something. I try an 'I owe' document and 'owes me' document, but forget to keep it updated. Some deals are ongoing back and forth for a year or more. Some information needs cross-referencing capability.

Seeking a moose molar. Can you help?

I reply

(jdkenaf---'who'?) Don't recognize who you are—emails don't even let one know what state or country the message is from. (DO I know you?) Moose molar eh? Well ya—I got a whole moose lower jaw. I could sell half a jaw for $15 with all its teeth—or pull one for $5. If I pull one I have to pull them all and sell the teeth individually—lower jaw value would be gone. So give me a hint...Is this my neighbor? Someone who found me on the net?

His reply

Greetings Miles,

Not a close neighbor by any account. I am in New Market, Maryland. I found you on the internet in a quest for a moose tooth (aka mooth tooth).

So, if possible, I would like to purchase a tooth. If you could let me know the actual cost of said tooth with postage, I could mail you a money order for that amount.

Thank you so much for your response and I envy you not living amongst the madding crowd.

Have a great day! **John DeNoma**

I recall a free gift after reading another email [4]

HEY MILES I sent you out a fossil whale tooth as a gift, Will get you a fossil GATOR as soon as I come across one! Just wanted to say THANKS FOR BEING SUCH A NICE PERSON! **JEFF RIEGEL** (HOPE YOU REMEMBER ME)!

There is a term I hear more of, called, 'paying it forward.' I agree with the concept. We help people when we can, and it is repaid by someone else as a Karma type idea. I often give something away to the needy, for those who will appreciate something, or items I can have and gift, but cannot legally sell. I do not often give, when asked for something free. I simply decide on my own, to give something to someone who I think is a good person, who I wish to reward for being who they are. One reason is because of others who have done the same for me. I have not always been able to repay them, or even get in touch again. I try to remember, and pay it to someone else. I'm aware the one I help may not have a way of paying me back, maybe not ever. Now and then I get scammed, but the reward is greater than the loss I sometimes have. [5]

I had an elderly Indian woman come past my table at a local bazaar one time. *I retell this story often. Here we go again!* She was old, frail, bent over, could hardly see. Looked poor, uneducated. She kept looking at one lynx claw necklace. But kept leaving without saying anything. I assumed she could not afford it. Finally, she got my attention, pointed the claw out, and told me she had no money. With a big smile she asked if she could trade—make me a pair of slippers! You know, the traditional, smoke-tanned, beaded with fur trim, so popular. I did not believe her. She looked too old and frail to sew. She could pass for a local drunk. I sighed and went along anyhow.

"OK, that sounds fine." She went through the motions—found a piece of cardboard and drew the outline of my foot. Told me it would take at least a month to make. She was old. *Uh-huh.* I handed her the necklace. She thanked me. I assumed I would never see her again. I just donated a $35 necklace to a worthy cause. *Oh well. I hope she likes it.* I forgot all about her and the deal. A day later I would have had trouble remembering! In truth, this sort of thing is a common occurrence with me. As much as half of everything I create simply disappears. I can't explain where it went. "Someone out there in the world has it. It was created, my job is done." Actually, selling it is secondary. Because of this outlook, I will probably never be rich with money. *Oh well.* My friends sigh and forgive me for being such a sucker, and so absent minded.

An old lady came up to me, maybe a year later. I did not know who she was. She smiled. I still did not know who she was. She handed me a paper bag, I opened it. Inside is a pair of beaded, smoke tan slippers I could not afford to buy. Easily worth $300.[6]

What about the rock guy! My unconscious reminds me. Yes, the rock guy. A very long time ago when I had no electricity, and worked by kerosene light. I was at the Tanana State Fair. Even before the days I could afford a booth. He must have been a tourist. Some old man standing there, letting me tell him Alaska adventure stories! How I do all my art by hand without electricity. He only smiled and nodded. Just one of a gazillion. I still happily talked to him even though it did not look like he would buy anything. I share my love of the wilds with whoever will listen.

"Do you ever use rocks?" he asked out of the blue.

"I never thought about it. I have no way to work rocks."

"Rocks would look nice with your metal work." *Uh- huh, yes, well how interesting, next!* The old man took my card and that was that. An hour later, I could not recall him. Weeks and months went by. I got a box in the mail. A huge box of sliced rocks. Some big enough to be clock faces, pre drilled for the clock mechanism. Fifty pounds of polished petrified wood, jasper, agate. Easily $1,000 worth. Just a note in the box.

"You might like to try this." Not even a return address. That is how I was introduced to the wonderful world of rocks in my art work. *One act of kindness can make up for a thousand scams.* I remember this when it is me who has something I can give. That old man never knew if I tossed the rocks out, gave them away, appreciated them or not. Just as I rarely know when I give.

Hey Miles!

I have no idea how to put this dream together, that is why I was going to have you put it together if we could keep the cost under $75...

Yes, the subject of dreams again. Special orders can be rewarding. However, few customers understand that if the item in stock is $75, to have one special made for you is twice that much. It cost me twice as much to make. I do not have time to explain, it's 'complicated' Maybe later.

Time to say "hi" to my son,

Dear Mitch

So how is life with you? Yes, my life is changing. Getting plugged in. There are exciting challenges I enjoy. I'm certainly not bored. Ha. Running the art business is fun. Trying to overcome business issues. All the various kinds of customers to deal with. Are you still delivering pizza? The GPS in the car sounds interesting. It has a map and everything, huh? No, I have never seen such a thing. I suppose I focus in the new technology on what will help me in my work.

There is more going on than I can keep up with, for sure. You seem happier in your life these days than when younger. I guessed that when the time came you could drive and get out some, you'd enjoy more freedoms. Now you are making your own money, you can be in control of…

Yes, I have city water and sewer now. I didn't tell you? I actually preferred my own well and leach field, but Oh well. I did get lucky! It did not cost me anything for the hook up. I bought all the fittings to hook up myself and had them ready when the equipment was here digging the ditch and laying new pipes. They dig a ditch, and before they back filled it over, I jumped in and cut the plastic pipe, made the connection, and was ready for them to fill it back in. I still have the well and pump and the leach field if the city source fails.

I review his last letter to me, before sending mine.

Hey dad. Yeah, maybe during the fall before school starts. Maybe around Christmas would be good time to see each other. and i did not leave Alaska hating it. i did not want to leave i wanted to stay. but mom wanted to leave. i didn't care about the food or the water. i just wanted to see you. well i am older and a bit more mature. and there is always ketchup. yeah. well talk to you later. **Love Mitch**.

Christmas comes and goes. It is rarely a good uplifting time for me. I do hand painted water colors and send out seventy to friends, relatives, people I know, customers etc. This has been a tradition most of my life. Since I was a kid, I made my own gifts. I sent out handmade block printed cards. It's the darkest, coldest time of winter. The sun creeps pink above the horizon about 11:00 am. About 1:00 pm the same pink sun creepy—crawls down again. Temperatures are often forty below zero. I'm amazed even God is on time, gets it together enough to load the sun in His chariot and haul it across the sky. I'm told light deficiency affects one's mood. No one talked about this till recently. Now there has been a study and it's the talk of the dark climates.

I keep one room in the big shop heated. This year, a new oil stove goes in. I keep it warm all the time so I can go in and work anytime. I work each day to justify the oil cost. This room is a steel Conex container, ten feet x twenty feet, with holes cut for a door, access to the other rooms, and one window. One thing to like, it is hard to break into, being steel. There are bars across the windows. I have valuables I am concerned about—opals, gold, ivory, and such. It is time to gear up for the big Tucson show again. See my aging mother, get in some warmth and sun. Buy material to sell the rest of the year on the internet.

Many of the best worldwide dealers in things I use and sell are among the elderly. The elderly are not up to speed with this new fangled internet stuff. They do not know how to offer their items on this net. So, if I can buy wholesale, and offer on the net, my retail price can look like a wholesale, for someone who has no other source. It's almost a monopoly on some items.

I can buy cut gem stones almost by the pound. As low as five cents each. The dealer from India has totes full of sorted stones in various price categories. I have trouble selling gem stones, though. *Oh well.* But there is one guy who is a world supplier of fossil cave bear fangs, I go see, and high- grade him as my first stop each year. If I buy enough, I can get big fossil fangs for $20 that can retail on the internet for $100. Sure, it takes all year to unload what I buy, and I have to spend $1,000 to get the price, but still, it beats working for a living. I'm out of these fangs, so Nord is on my list of people to see when I get there.

I invest my entire savings in product, slowly recoup, break even, then get ahead as the season progresses. Last year, it only took two months to break even after the show. That is exciting. A new win, a new thrill, to replace the old thrills of the wilds. Not everyone needs thrills and goals to meet, or a higher purpose. But I am one who does. I ponder that whatever goes up, comes down. So, OK, this is the down time, I understand this is the springboard I will bounce from when I get to Tucson. I will schedule my high in a controlled flight. I smile. I am at a bottom. I miss my sled dogs, miss a lifestyle I once had, that I feel is gone and I will never get back. *If I must ying and yang, go up and down, why not see, believe, and be in control of the rise and fall? One issue I see often is people wanting to be up all the time, like it is necessary! Hate and fight the down, even take drugs to stop it. Ha! How can we fool God? How can we beat nature? Why try? There are times I can afford to be down. My only goal is to survive. Tough it out. Like any storm.*

It is more like hibernation I will awake from. I sleep more in winter for sure. I made a few trips back and forth to the trapline. I take a break during the coldest, darkest time. After Tucson, I know the light comes back. I go back out again to trap, and catch the end of the season. What furs I have I can bring to Tucson to sell for more money. I have them tanned locally.

When I come in off the trapline, Josh is at his dog yard by the Nenana River, He looks confused, which is unusual for him.

"You look lost Josh, you ok?"

"Wolves just killed two sled dogs, I feel bad, just now sorting it out." Only now do I look around. I take in the fact there is blood all around in the snow, then my eyes follow up a trail taking off in the woods. Fur tuffs and bone pieces strew the trail, mixed in with the normal dog yard trash.

I'm puzzled, "Well why, Josh? Why would wolves come in for your dogs?" Usually wolves are wilderness animals, but do come down our streets at night. I see tracks in town, but usually pay no attention, nothing going on. I had wolf trouble once long ago though. Similar to Josh now, an attack on sled dogs chained up.

"There is a wolf kill moose not far away, so no reason to eat the dogs, Miles, but who knows the ways of wild animals. They may not need a reason!" Josh has a little shed where he cooks dog feed and can hang out in. "I think I will stay here a few days to protect the dogs, Miles."

"Want me to set a trap or two, make sure your dogs do not get lose, maybe catch one of these wolves?" He only nods yes. I add, "If we catch one I bet the rest will not come around anymore." No answer. I have traps with me so set one for a wolf. *Hopefully I do not catch any lose dogs, but these sled dogs in the yard look traumatized by what they saw, and for sure Josh cannot lose all his dogs to wolves!*

Me encountering a young Great Grey owl on a survey job.

CHAPTER THREE

SELL TRAPLINE ADVENTURE, BUYING NATIVE ART, AUTHENTICITY

Friday, February 28, 2003

I answer the knock on the door. Trooper Dan Hickman shows me a badge.

"I'm here to ask you a few questions. May I come in?" I hesitate. *Plain clothes, elderly investigator, disarming, relaxed, but serious approach.* He seems friendly enough. Assume he has no warrant, or he'd be telling me he is coming in, not asking.

"What's this about?" Trooper Dan has questions concerning the long ago Gene Graham murder. *There is no statute of limitations on murder.*

"I'd like a DNA sample and fingerprints from you, Miles." He is assigned to cold cases. Trooper Dan tells me there has been funding to investigate some unsolved murders. He is assigned to review all the evidence, present a new perspective from a new person. I was the main suspect. At one point, the only suspect. That's understandable. Gene did burn my house down, then five days later disappeared, with his body found in the river a month later, with a bullet in him. I can understand being a suspect. There was evidence of a struggle, and probably a crime scene. This happened only 100 feet from my houseboat, where I lived at the time. I talked without giving a lot of information. *Know nothing, see nothing.* "It was a long time ago."

We go down to the local cop shop, and get me fingers printed (again) and a mouth swab done for DNA. There is a hint there is old evidence that can be reviewed in the light of new technology. I assume some piece of evidence that has a DNA sample on it, connected to the murder. I see little use in being uncooperative. We can do this the easy way, or the hard way, so it may as well be the easiest way. I am wondering if anyone else is being visited.

Pat had scratch marks on his neck, he covered up on the day Gene disappeared, Pat told troopers he was not on the river that day. "But I saw him on the river. So why did he lie? How did he get the scratches? Why is he hiding them?" None of my concern. Or more like, at first I was open and honest about what I knew. Till I saw there was zero interest. No notes taken concerning anything I had to say about anyone else.[1]

I'm also aware that whoever killed Gene saved my life. Gene tried to kill me, and said he would try again. To quote one of the cops at the time, a week before Gene turned up missing, "I don't really care. One of you will be dead, and the other will go to jail for murder."

Life goes on. Much of this goes through my head as I am being fingerprinted and swabbed, wondering what evidence they have that they might reexamine for a connection between me and the victim. Gene and I had once gotten along. I had touched many of his things. My prints could be on almost anything. Is this a case of shaking the tree to see what falls out? Is there anything I need to be concerned about? Could I be set up, and framed, if I act like I know too much?

"Yes, Miles, I was involved in that case with Silka. I was in the helicopter when the officer got shot." I told the trooper I had almost been one of the victims in that shootout that ended in ten local people getting shot when I lived on the houseboat in Manley Hot Springs. Dan and I had been reminiscing about past crimes and local murders and such. I stare at his back deep in thought as this trooper heads away to his car.

NATE—A trapper guide stops by:

"I like your art Miles, because you bring two worlds together so well. You show the rustic and rough, mix it with the modern advanced and delicate."

"Yes, Nate, I try to do that, maybe in my writing too, but like this piece—with a rough tooth direct from the land, that's pretty raw." We ramble about life in general. Few people in civilization would wish to look at, or even touch a raw tooth as nature presents it, much less wear it. It smells, is stained, bloody, and probably will crack if left natural. I know how to clean it, stop the fang from smelling, dry it slow, take the nerve out of the center so it dries evenly, and does not crack. When I am done, I think of it as a finished product, not raw anymore. Yet the rest of the world calls this product 'in the raw.' If so, what do they call still smelly and bloody? I combine a cleaned stabilized fang with an opal, add delicate silver work, paying attention to fine finish work so it is not 'rustic' looking. Yet the basic centerpiece is rustic in itself. *I can then spoon feed reality to civilization in a very watered down palatable version.*

"Miles, I know we sell dreams, both you and I, but it is nice to put at least a little reality into that dream we sell. Trapping, too, is a dream many have and few can make it pay. Yet trapping attracts so many! We fight so hard to keep what little we have. I think it is about dreams."

I interrupt Nate with the question, "You have six wolf skulls for me, huh? $25 each? Yes, I will boil them up, clean them, and make them acceptable to others, to where they will be interesting and worth something. I enjoy that." Nate knows most trappers will throw the skull out in the woods, or dump them in the river with the rest of the carcass. $25 is hardly worth messing with, or worth the time spent getting them to me. But this is all the raw skulls are worth. Nate spends $150 flying from Minchumina to Nenana in his own plane to look me up, and spends an hour of his time.

"Miles, as for your trapline, and us having to look over the map? I see the map here on the table, so guess you want us to look it over. Well the area you show me does not affect me. I know that from flying over the country when guiding in the fall. Ketslers and Terry are going into Mucha Lake here." Nate points to the lake on the inch to the mile scale topography map. "And going around and over Bearpaw Mountain now. It's been a few years since you were there. Rollick is out there on the other side of Bearpaw more these days, but not hitting it hard. In ten years he has not cut more than ten miles of trail. He has the advantage of being a pilot and flying in. George put a cat in from Wien Lake over to the Dead Fish Lake. But that misses your old area."

"Yes, I was on the trapline, when George went through with the bulldozer. He flies for most of us out here, so hate to say much. He seems reasonable enough."

Nate only nods a reply and continues, "A few Twin Lakes homesteaders come down your way, but not serious. Spears claims the whole county, but everyone knows he lands his plane on lakes and does little cutting – so trails you have are not a problem. These new guys you speak of, who do they affect?" I had mentioned in the past, some new trappers, new trails being cut, and I am not sure who they are. I thought Nate might know. Part of the issue is, some trappers think of controlling a trail, the trail they cut usually. While others think more of a trapline area, by the square mile, like a block of land. This can create conflict if trappers like Spears, who cuts no trails but claims a vast area, runs into someone like me who has cut 200 miles of trail and expects to be respected a mile either side of my trails.

I reply, "Well, Dim for sure is affected. New trappers went as far as Black Bear Lake. I do not know if this is the guy named Don who traps out by Geskemina Lake. Someone crossed Dim's trail two years ago. I think they will not be back in a serious way, though. They told me when I ran into them on the trail in spring they had covered 3,000 miles and got twenty lynx. They said they can't make that pay—not that trapping is about making it pay, but he has a wife, kids, bills and am told his main concern is money." He also has pissed off enough people, I told him he'll be lucky if he does not disappear in the river. He wanted to take over Tom and Lana's area. I told him that couple has been there twenty—two years, even though they do not trap, they cut trail and run sled dogs. I told him if he tried to go on those trails trapping there would be a feud over it, and he'd lose. "The guy told me his name but I couldn't understand, he was talking through his fur parka ruff."

"It sounds like a lot of people and a lot of activity!" I remind myself we are talking about a dozen people in an area the size of Montana, over a ten year time period. Still, relative to twenty years ago, it's a lot of people. There was a time, if I saw a blaze on a tree someone made fifty years ago, I'd call the country crowded. When much of this land I cover was last visited by people in the Stone Age.

"I'm not sure I have any trapping country to claim anymore. I gave it twenty years of my life, and what's to show for it but memories?"

"Miles, I think if you yourself showed up in your old stomping grounds, people would accept you back. The Carvers never did go out much beyond five miles of their cabin. They are just talking. Many of those others screaming 'invasion,' are lazy trappers, claiming areas they never went. I wouldn't worry about it." I'm not so sure Nate is right about Carvers, as I ran into one brother more than once, way out in the wilds. We have so far managed to respect each other's area. "An uncivilized area, not off the grid, off the map. Whole mountain ranges not named, unsurveyed and not mapped on the ground."

I reply out loud, "Well Nate, I will not likely ever go back at it hard like I did, but it would be nice to sell it and pass it on, have the old cabins I built used again and such. I told this guy if he buys it, he may still have trouble. He buys only whatever rights I had to the area."

"Miles, I think no one would respect this guy, only yourself. But just be sure to tell him what he is in for. I'm not sure I want to fly him around to show him the area. I may not like the guy—but if you want to go up yourself with me and look over what burned, I'd be glad to fly you, just give me a call—got a new plane, be nice to go up with you." No rules, ways to behave, or rights are universally agreed to or in writing. We all have to talk to each other, figure out how an individual thinks, and try to respect this. Different agreements with different people. *This is not much like how civilization operates.*

Diary Tuesday, February 27, 2003 **Trapline for sale**

Kevin and Vern have been trapping my line. Vern puts up sign 'This is my trapline.' I am shocked to see such a sign up on 'my trapline' that I cut and have run for over twenty years. I run into this Vern guy and he is happy to see me, thinks everything is fine.

Vern comes to my homestead to meet with me. "Hi Miles! Remember me? I met you when I was about twelve! My parents homesteaded land five miles downriver from you. I always remembered meeting you, and dreamed of living this lifestyle! Now I have taken over the parents' homestead, and plan to live here full time, just like you!" I'm speechless. I muster up as much politeness as I can. People get shot out here for doing what he is doing. What I see before me is the pup wolf running around on his own for the first time peeing on everything to practice marking territory.

I clear my throat, "And what makes you think you can trap out here, anyplace you want?"

"I talked to someone at the Fairbanks Trappers Association about a trapline. They suggested I set traps out and see if anyone says anything. They no longer have maps with trappers lines marked because it has got confusing with people claiming areas they do not trap. There are conflicting overlaps." Maybe so, but it seems like not such a great idea to move in on a trail you did not cut that obviously someone else cut. I also think the Association's response is inaccurate, and would refer to how to handle situations around the immediate Fairbanks area, where there are few professionals.

I say, "Well, can't you go cut your own trails like I did if you want to live like me?"

"I can't find your trails! It's not your trails I follow! I follow the creeks. Trails I find look really old and not used. Looks to me like there is plenty of room, and guessed you would not mind!" Big smile. Young kid. Full of energy. Hard to just shoot him. And what can I say? I had been concerned for a while, not getting out here anymore as often. Lots of the country burned up. A young kid can cut, build, as I once did. If I do nothing, he will take it all over. I lose everything here.

"I might be interested in selling my trapline. Are you interested?" He'd rather buy it then take it over. A guy named Don I sort of knew, and sort of get along with, and sort of consider a friend, has a cabin on a far off lake. Geskemina Lake, the place and situation the pilot, Nate, had referred to seeing from the air. Don has to run part of my trail to get to his area. We have had an understanding, he can use the trail and not trap it. Mind his own business. I find out this Don bought the old Bettes Cabin near me, the old Native Indian claim that was on the map as off limits for home-steading, because it is a previous Indian claim. Many years ago I had to cut way around this area to accommodate someone who never came out, who said it was his trapline. Just like the Association told Vern, how folks claim all kinds of stuff they have no right to claim. Vern ran into this Don on the trail and relates the conversation.

"Don bought the Bettes Cabin and plans to trap out of it connecting to his other area. He told me you don't trap anymore, and have no claim anymore. The Trappers

Association says if you give it up for three years, it is open to anyone else." I and others feel the ownership transfer of a trapline is not that clear or open and shut. This 'rule' works OK around town where the trails were already in, and no one person cut them. Out here in the wilds, if you spent twenty years cutting, it seems you would deserve more than three years off. I feel if an area has been trapped hard for over ten years, it might need more than a three year rest to let the fur population build back up as part of proper game management. I'm not just talking and changing the rules to favor what I want.

I recognize Dim's area as a trapline that has been in the family more than a generation. He is Athabascan Indian, one of the Natives I have a lot of respect for. He does drink a lot, in my mind, a bummer, but I accept this. He works hard, has a lot of outdoor skills, a good attitude, a fine trapper, so I stand up for him and his rights.

Dim has not been on parts of his trails in over fifteen years. I still respect it as his. This respect cost me time and money, because I have had to run eight miles of his trail to get to my trapline for over ten years. Yet we all have our own ideas of what to respect and why. My beliefs follow 'the old way,' I feel have been in place for the past 100 years. The village, Native rules. I'm miffed the Association seems to be about the white weekend warriors, not the professional trappers out in the wilds, making a living trapping. Oh well. Maybe it is the weekend warriors who show up at the meetings, I'm not sure, since I can't make it into the meetings. A lot of us are too busy and poor to get to meetings. I'm a lifetime member, write for the magazine, do what I can, but yes, maybe the organization is run by armchair trappers.

It is also true when I first began trapping when I got to Alaska in the early '70's, I had no concept of space, and I, like this kid, thought the country vast and empty, with lots of room. I had all my supplies stolen, was left to die over a misunderstanding about land use rights. A lot like this kid before me faces.

Vern asked and is only following what he is told by those he feels are the authority on the subject. The writing is on the wall, I will soon have nothing. The Trappers Association is not going to back me up. Nor will the law, nor will locals. We settle in the old way, with money or guns. There are no cases argued in court over traplines. Legally it is all public land we are 'borrowing.' Society who owns it, has been kind enough to let trappers use it. Others can use the land, and our line cabins as well.

Vern is full of the energy of youth. I had seen where he dug a hole in the ice. I assume to make a beaver set, without realizing there was no water under the ice where he chose to dig. I could tell at a glance. He has a lot to learn. I saw another place where he fell through the ice in a place he should never have been. I was that young once, doing the same things. Having the same problems. The country looked big and empty with lots of room when I first arrived. All trails looked ancient. The cabins all looked unoccupied for 100 years. I had no comprehension anyone could claim the vast wilds I saw, when I was introduced to this new planet. I'm sure I too had a big happy smile as I moved in. Now I am at the receiving end.

"So Vern, thinking about $15,000. You can have any cabins the fire did not get, any traps you find, and 200 miles of trail. I will give you the maps. I want the fifty mile trail from Nenana to the cabin, and a few miles around my cabin. I hope to come out and fool around—do some small time trapping."

One hope is this enthusiastic kid will cut the trail open to the homestead better than it is now. I can no longer keep up with the brush cutting that needs doing. If he wishes to get where he is going, he has to run the same trail I do, so it has to be able to be traveled. Vern seems agreeable. He gives me $500 down. I figure $15,000 is more money than I would make trapping the rest of my life. An industrious young trapper could theoretically earn this in two years. *I once made $8,000 in one season.*

"What about your buddy, Kevin? How does he fit in, Vern?" Kevin does not seem as honest as Vern. They appear to be friends working together though. Kevin had set a wolf trap right in front of my home. How could he not know this home is occupied? It seemed at the time, like a challenge or a slap in the face. He may have done that to see what I'd do, if anything. The equivalent of parking in the boss's parking space as a newcomer, to see if he could, or see if the boss would do anything about it. To show who the new kid on the block is. Not very bright, in my mind. It seems pointless to me, if you are serious about trapping, to travel 100 miles to put a trap in front of someone else's house. Curious if this Kevin and Vern get along. Figuring if Kevin plays tough with me, he'll do it to his partner, too. If Kevin disappears out here, I would not shed any tears or be surprised and I would know nothing. He's older then Vern, so should understand the rules. Or does, and thinks it will be me who gets put through a hole in the ice. *We'll see.*

"Well, Kevin and I are sort of together, but not really. Kevin wants to find his own trapline." We are talking down at the boat landing looking out over the Nenana River we have to cross to get to the trapline. Josh comes down the dusty road in his pick-up. He is here to feed his sled dogs. Vern gets in his truck and leaves.

Josh wants to talk to me. I have not seen him in a while, "Miles, we protected the dog team from the wolf pack but there is a problem now." I am puzzled and wonder what he is talking about. "The wolf trap you set to protect the sled dogs caught a moose by the foot." Not great, but I know in most cases this is not a big deal for the moose. The moose can get his foot out of the trap. "The moose did not get out of the trap, Miles."

I let this sink in and wonder what happened. "So what is the issue Josh, did I lose my trap?"

"I never saw your trap, you got worse problems." I focus on this 'you,' stuff, instead of 'we.' I can guess something bad follows. "The moose pulled the tree up the trap was chained to. The tree got tangled like a drag. The ruckus must have attracted the wolves passing by. The pack showed up and killed the moose. Big mess right by the dog yard. Blood, guts..." He trails off. I can imagine what it looks like. I see what he means. It's my fault. Trouble.

"Did you report the mess, Josh? I hope not."

"I'd never report such a thing." A look of relief.

"Good." We both know what would happen if news of this reached the civilized world. Headlines in the news, jail time for both of us. Serious jail time, as in five years. A somewhat normal event in the wilds. I'd be in trouble for setting a trap out of season, reckless endangerment. I can hear it now, 'What if a child got caught in this trap?' Josh fed some of the moose meat to the sled dogs. That is illegal. But waste of a resource is also illegal so a catch twenty—two situation.

We know the answer we would hear is,"You should have reported this incident, and Fish and Game would have salvaged any meat!" None would have been given to Josh, and arrests could have been made. For sure, no good would come of it.

"Well Josh, you know the wolves will be back around, so better watch the sled dogs." Winter is coming; wolf fur should be prime soon.

"Miles, I know trappers who might want the wolves for the fur, maybe Dim can come stay here overnight with a rifle."

"Good idea, make sure it is a Native, a white man could get in trouble."

"Yea, I already mentioned this to Dim." Just nod. I briefly update Josh on the trapline events with the kid. It is still fall, so Josh only shrugs in understanding—it will be winter before there will be issues.

I let that thought go, and will wait to see what develops. Kevin begins guiding hunters all around me in the fall during moose hunting season. Later he looks me up in Nenana and offers to buy my Bearpaw homestead. This is further up the river then the area Vern acquired for trapping. Again, I could fight the guy and make him back off. He is illegally guiding without a license. Locals do not like this, because they depend on the moose meat for survival, where most hunters who can afford to hire a guide, are out of state sport hunters. The laws reflect this, so assign designated areas for guides. We locals prefer to be tolerant and easy going. Often reputable guides will donate the meat to the locals in the area, while their client happily takes the trophy antlers. Kevin is not doing this. There is a possibility he is leaving the meat behind to spoil. Most of us locals will tolerate poaching, or not following the civilized rules exactly, but waste is something we feel strongly about, in our own local sense of law and order.

Meanwhile, this other trapper, Don, has bought the Bettes Cabin. He was, in the past, claiming the trapping area just out in back of me. A Native named Bettes owned it previously, and told me he trapped here, asked me to cut around his area and not cross through. It took me several years to cut around someone who never showed up. Me being nice cost me dear. Several years of wasted work, Bettes never showed up and died of old age. Now the area is being moved in on by an outsider.

Don has talked to Kevin and Vern, but not me, and not stood up for me. Told them I have no claim. If this old timer Don is believing in the old ways as he once told me, he would recognize I am next in line if the old Bettes area is open now. I have been here a lot of years, and could use this area to cross over to my other lines.

I hear from Vern, who moved here to Nenana, "Miles, Don says you should be trapping more wolves at the bluffs." It is against local etiquette to discuss what you see going on in someone else's area, especially if you are passing through as a guest. In civilization, this would be the equivalent of having permission to pass through your fenced in property to get to theirs and then discussing with the community how you feed your dog—that you do not agree with. *It's not cool! This is a good way to say you are not friends. It's a good way to get told to stay off property.* I, in fact, decided the wolf population in my area has been hit hard by rival trappers around me, and I prefer to create my own buffer zone sanctuary for the wolves until their population gets healthier. I am not going to go public with this, and don't tell anyone at all. This information in the wrong hands could mean rival trappers showing up to trap these wolves. I should be able to run my trapline in the way I choose.

In fact, Tom and Lanna long ago told me they do not trap, do not believe in trapping. It is me who suggested they claim all the trails they cover as 'their area,' and tell trappers to stay off.

"Call it your trapline, manage it however you wish. There is no law concerning how much fur you must catch. You could have a trapline and catch nothing. Believe in building up the animal population for a healthy environment." I add, "I will honor this and think most local trappers will as well. Most important is you run the trails and maintain it as your territory." I have no problem with maintaining a sanctuary. So, for a rival trapper telling another trapper how I manage or do not manage my area is out of line. Especially implying this is reason to say I have no right to claim the area.

The 'bluff' referred to is 'Chicago,' as named on my trapline map the past twenty-five years. Yes, lots of wolves congregate here to hunt for moose down below. It looks like a lot of wolves, however this is simply an ideal hunting spot all wolves for a hundred miles around come to exploit. I wish to call it off limits to trapping wolves, they need his area. *It's my trapline, I'll make the rules. You will respect them. I will in fact defend the wolves if this comes to a battle. Trapping is about a sustainable resource. It's my area. I understand more than anyone else, so most qualified to manage it.*

Don is also not honest with me about where his cabin is, nor told me that he is trapping part of my trapline, using trails I cut, and not offered to buy, compensate, or discuss. This looks to me like he has been playing me for a sucker, and not been my friend. *Maybe he wants to start a feud between Vern, Kevin and I, so he can grab the spoils.* In civilization, this is about business take over. Who to partner up with, who to ace out, how to go about it. In civilization the choice of weapon is lawyers, judges, rulings, laws. In the wilderness it's guns. I do not see a lot of difference. Someone could die either way. *Occupation taken away, in jail or dead, is there a lot of difference?*

With Don and I both being old timers, I'd think he'd side with me, fighting off the next generation of punks. His move appears to be, to use the punks to get rid of me, and assume the punks will give up and leave, as often happens with the energy of youth. Then Don will claim it all. I do not see it like that. I think he is too old to pull it off, and does not have the energy to outlast the next generation. I believe Don will be sorry for his decision not to side with me. *His choice.* "Lock and load."

There had been a similar issue further up the Kantishna in earlier years with a guy who bought a remote cabin. That cabin I'd had permission to use from the owner. The cabin sold, and new owner tossed my things out in the snow, put a lock on the door, and took over the trapping. I arrived expecting my supplies to be there, in emergency mode after a week on the trail with sled dogs. Only to find nothing there for me. I had to accept he bought the cabin. But why did he think a trapline came with that? Similar deal as now.

"**Boom, boom, boom!**" I yell, as geese fly over—followed by "Yum, yum, dinner!" My tourist customer laughs. This is a common comment when I see geese, cranes, or ducks fly over. Usually I get a chuckle, or this leads to a hunting story or conversation. This time I hear a friendly question.

"Miles, how come you like to kill stuff?"

Well, it is not so much the killing of stuff. I have to stop and think. To me the question could be the same as asking a farmer how come he loves pulling healthy plants out of the dirt and watching them die. *Because that's where food comes from.* Does a cattle rancher acquire his ranch for the love of watching cattle die?

"It's about getting food, good food. I suppose hunting fills me with good memories." I had not thought much about it before, but those who have lived in the city may not associate guns and 'boom, boom' with good thoughts! It may conjure up memories of news reels of violence. Memories of the sounds of sirens following a robbery, gang activity, and such. I have no such memories or association. I spent my life in the wilds, where 'guns' mean good thoughts of success, positive self defense, dinner on the table, great hunting trips. It brings memories of the smell of fall sedge grass, blue skies, fall colors, good health. My thoughts go to freedom, not needing to know what time it is, lack of stress, the geese flying and the blast of getting food becomes a symbol in my mind of a whole lifestyle. It is hard to imagine anyone thinking differently, with the opposite reaction. Spring is a wonderful time of year.

I recall a memory I relate, "Once it was spring and I was holed up at the homestead. Hungry, hadn't seen anyone in months. Longing for something fresh to eat. I hear the first geese fly over." I drool. *I know a good place to go wait for the geese to land on a sandbar on the river.* "It is one of the first places they land each year." I go there to wait for them to land. While waiting quietly, and patiently, I look around and enjoy the smells, the sounds, the feel of spring. I spot a wolf across the river! I watch. He is crawling on his belly through the willows to the edge of the sandbar where geese can be expected to land. He lays and waits, as I am doing. He too, knows this is a good place for early geese. He too, is waiting for a first fresh spring meal. Instead of hunting, the wolf is just watching, as the geese come in low and land. I watch the wolf get a goose. "It's a memory, I suppose, not like memories most people have."

It is therefore hard to sing from the same sheet of music, share the same experiences, or share the same feelings, with word association. It's a lonely feeling to have such times, then have no way to share them with people I wish to communicate with. Worse, have them misunderstood, and creating hostility. So this person and who else, thinks it is all about liking to kill stuff. My fond memories bring 'Belongs in jail!' thoughts in others. Sigh.

One of my emails:

Miles, do you sell any bear claw necklaces? Your website states that it's not legal to sell grizzly bear claws, but are there other bear claws that are legal to sell? What I'm looking for is a single claw with a plain cap that can be put on a simple leather cord or rope to wear around my neck. If there are no bear claws available, how much is it to buy a single lynx claw w/a plain cap to allow a leather cord to go through it? And, is a lynx claw available in a black or dark brown color? **Thanks**.

I reply:

Hello- thanks for your inquiry. All bear claws are illegal to sell in Alaska—sorry![2] I can put work on a claw someone has is why I even mention them. Lynx I have and some already capped. I have to go see how many and the price range—depends on size of claw and amount of work done on it but from $20 to $40. I can send a picture of some when I get them together if you are interested. I might have some that are darker than others, but in general Lynx will have clear—softer lighter colors. I'll look for the darkest I have...

And that email ends
It's a big issue that so many customers do not know much about the items they

are ordering. It sometimes makes it hard to please them. There is an image in their head of what this animal product looks like. Many do not know the difference between a tooth and a claw, nor care, yet they want me to supply what they have as an image in their head. I work on a 'how to' and 'identification' and 'answers to basic questions' section of the web site to improve the website and educate people. Many customers do not understand they are inquiring about a $5 item. The knowledge they want in return occupies an hour of my time. *I would never in a million years go to a grocery store and pick out $5 worth of food and occupy the clerk for an hour asking how oranges are grown, where they come from and what the laws on pesticide use are. etc.*

I reply to yet another email discussing how to use PayPal.

Hello Colin! Yes, I have used Pay Pal and have used my account for only a few times and forget if you need any info from me to use it. I didn't know I could put their icon on my web as a way to encourage people to use it—will go to the site again and see how to do that. I especially like it when dealing with another country, especially when we don't know the money exchange rate—and also when the customer does not want to give a credit card # over the net on a line that isn't secure. Yes, I have a moose leg bone, and also the 'buttons' we call that burl—depending on size about $10 each— they are about four inches across. I only have three to four but have a source for more I think…

and I ramble on about other stuff.

A lot of emails come in, as many as thirty a day. Some involve interesting lessons to learn, are informative, educational. Others are more routine. Some I do not deal with. It's like an endless river of humanity that is overwhelming. Now it is time to order greenhouse garden seeds. Playing in the dirt tends to get the mind out of 'stuck in fast forward.' Some seeds get started as early as March, to go in the greenhouse by early April.

I think I will get a better wood stove in the greenhouse this season. A new rack of fluorescent grow lights are set up on abandoned shelving so I can start about twenty-five flats of seeds. Almost half are flowers for hanging baskets all along the property line. The garden interest keeps me physically active as a balance to the computer time. So does going out to cut firewood! The long trips on the snow machine seem to not be as healthy a form of exercise. Such trips have too many incidents requiring extra effort beyond what is healthy. Not everyone agrees.

There are a few village elders still out, living active lives in the wilds, with snow machines, trapping, cabin building and such. We each have our own path we are on.

My buddy Crafty comments, "Not so wild anymore, huh?" I pause at the bait. Staring at his T shirt with "For you, a special deal' written on it. I suspect he does not like me referring to him as 'Crafty' like a first name. There are now four to five people I know who Crafty has disowned and he will not talk to, whose names will not cross his lips. People he has told cannot come around anymore, they do not exist. Sure, I know what happened. The same thing that would happen if I rose to the bait. Reeled in and made a fillet of, like a fish. I do think Crafty is getting more extreme as he gets older.

"Life is ever changing, Crafty. Look at the changes you have made in forty years! Did you ever think you'd be here?" The focus is now on him and away from me. He brightens up.

"Yes Miles, I gross near a million dollars a year now!" He does not look like it. Rumor has it he gives 90% of it to his Church of Scientology. But I understand why, and that's fine. If it makes Crafty happy, what's it to me what he does with his money? Others talk like he is a nut case. When I met Crafty, he could not read and write well enough to make a receipt, so he was dead in the water, would not likely get ahead. He told me at the time, that he had been pushed through school. Graduated from high school, yet can hardly write his name correctly. He was one level up from a dumpster diver. Kind of a used stuff, flea market business, living out of his truck kind of guy. He had a wore out trunk he set on the sidewalk and sold used stuff out of. I'd get rusty wrenches, used oil, wore out military sleeping bags, and such things from him when we met.

The Church of Scientology got hold of him. In his mind 'cared.' Cared enough to teach him how to read, out of the goodness of their hearts. He owes them everything, and is forever grateful, and they can do no wrong. I can understand how that feeling could come about. If some such group had taken me in, I might have reacted the same way. We were both street people in those days. It was so long ago it is even hard to really remember what that was like with any kind of reality.

"So, Crafty...I myself have been earning in a day, what I used to live on for a year. That's a big change! But change is not free! It comes with a price. We gain something, while at the same time, it cost us something, right?" There are in fact some aspects of the old life Crafty says he misses. Crafty's days are now filled with obligations, appointments, deals he has to make, in order to pay bills. He longs for escape, to get away sometimes, but can't. Is he really in a position to call the kettle black? To make fun of the fact I am not as wild as I once was? Where is Crafty's heart? But that too, I understand. He was abused and neglected—father an alcoholic —poor. Never been married. Money is his God. It all comes with a price. I do not feel sorry for him, nor dislike him.

If I fell on hard times, Crafty would be among the first to give me a place to stay, and a job. He did in the early days. I see others take advantage of this trait of his, move into the building he owns and not leave. Live off him for weeks, months, even years. He asks for nothing more than thanks. Often, not even getting that. Life can be very strange. We make our bed, and then have to sleep in it. My buddy, Crafty.

"Miles, you need to change. Being a murder suspect, your homestead lost to a forest fire. Doesn't that tell you anything? Everything happens for a reason." Because he brings in a million a year he feels he is a God among us mortals. Well. Good for him. I'm glad he is not negative, and can feel so good about himself. I smile. God loves him. Crafty is willing to give me advice, get me on the right track, because he cares about me so much. I too am a God among mortals. I live what Crafty can only dream of. Time to hunt, fish, enjoy the great outdoors. I live most people's vacations. *Yes. It's awfully hard to be humble isn't' it, Crafty? When you're perfect in every way?* I smile, words taken from a country song we like and have stuck in our head. *"Oh Lord, it's hard to be humble…"*

"Thanks for the advice, Crafty! I'll be sure to change!"

"You find that amusing, Miles?"

"I do!" *Have I no shame?* But Crafty likes me, and as a Christian coming by to read Scripture, is in hopes I will one day be saved. As I hope he will one day be saved. Yes, I find that hilarious. Define 'saved' and saved from what, and saved for what purpose? One person's heaven is another's hell. It allows for a lot of diversity. Maybe for every sort of thing needing to be done to support a society, there will be someone who is dedicated to that as the only thing meaningful in life. Crafty is not a deep thinker, and simply does his part. I'm glad. God is very clever and amusing.

Crafty changes the subject. "Are you still the buyer for the Nenana Cultural Center Gift Shop? Can I sell you anything? What's been selling there the most?"

"Mostly Indian art sells best, Crafty. It's an ongoing discussion with the city who owns the building and runs things. It's a Culture Center. There is more than just Indian culture. We have a railroad history, a homesteader's and trapper's culture, and one of the first radio stations in the Interior" I pause. "But anyhow, a lot of grant money, and funding is in the direction of the Noble Savage." I pause because I do not know how to take this conversation from here without sounding prejudice. I review one of the concepts Crafty and I have talked about again and again over many years. The concept of wholesale prices when selling to a shop. "Crafty. I even tried to get the Chamber of Commerce to give a class on buying, selling, and pricing, geared to the local craft people who do not understand." *Meaning mostly Natives.*

Crafty and I have reviewed this lots of times. As a buyer of art for a shop, it is hard to deal with the Natives. The typical village Indian doesn't understand 'wholesale,' and is offended if I explain, it means the shop gets 50%. I myself lose 50% when I sell to a shop, and everyone I know does. Sometimes it's a 60% loss, up to 75% these days in the finest galleries. It's hard for me to go to the Indian with a different set of rules. Extremely few I talk to have a business license, business card, pay for advertising, a brochure, displays, a written biography, pay taxes, or have the sort of 'overhead' white artists have. That is their choice, and fine. I started out the same way! There are rewards to this choice! *No mess, no fuss, no stress, total freedom.* "But they should not then expect the rewards to be the same as for those who have invested."

Crafty runs into the same situation, saying, "The Indian basically wants to sell his art retail to shops. They holler 'discrimination' if I offer the standard policy. Picking on them because they are an Indian. Thinking a ten percent mark up is outrageous and ripping them off. How do we deal with that, Miles?" Crafty is more disgusted than anything else, "The heck with them, they need to straighten out and plug into reality!" *It is easy for me to understand and agree! However the difference is, I have lived like the Indian, with the Indians, and understand the culture a little better as a result.* Crafty interrupts my thoughts, "Some Natives understand business, like Richard Strand!" We also agree the Eskimo and Indian have been shrewdly trading and negotiating for thousands of years. Therefore, we wonder what is going on. *Is it us being conned?*

"Oh yes, I buy from Richard, too! He does the handmade miniature fish wheels and caches, great job! He understands wholesale and is shrewd all right. But still"… I go on. "In fact, they get a pretty sweet deal compared to white artists. It is hard for me to go to white artists and tell them I can't give the same deal I give Natives. Yet, as the buyer for a cultural center, I am trying to promote the Indian art." I pause because I am trying something new. "I am trying to figure out how to offer it on the internet, come up with ways to pass the Native ways on and keep it going. Grant money and funding is available to pay Native artists to do art, but not white artists. It's an awkward situation as a white buyer. I sigh.

"I may not choose to be the buyer this year, Crafty." I explain why, "I feel if the main or only culture considered is 'Indian,' and Indian art is where it is at, then it should be an Indian in charge as the buyer." Crafty is upset because he isn't going to be able to hand me his box of goods from 'Indian Traders' Company, made in China. He wants, and expects me, to put this 'fake' stuff up in the store and sell it as an authentic Native craft. *Because we are such good buddies. Because it will make all of us money, including the city of Nenana.* I am the one who set policy for the Cultural Center. "Honestly 'local made,' even if it cost a little more, is a good direction. If we get a reputation for that, and even though we are off the beaten path, I think, given time, those who seek out true local crafts will arrive and buy. Independent travelers, as well as the tour busses will stop. The Nenana Cultural Center will be a unique shop for doing this. I even would like to see 'Interior Alaska' art, not Eskimo. Crafty, so much on the market is Eskimo art. Yet in history, if we study 'culture,' the Eskimo and Indian hated each other, and were at war. At best, willing to tentatively trade. It would be an insult to the Interior Indian to mix the cultures as if they were all one and the same, in the same shop. Since, the Alaska tourist market is already saturated with Eskimo pieces, a good niche market might be Interior art, Athabascan, and then other races of crafts using the materials of the Interior." [3]

"Miles, it might be asking and expecting too much, to have a niche market. Tourist want 'cheap.' They do not care who made it." Yes. Maybe. Somewhat discouraging, since Crafty is the expert. This is another reason to back off as the shop buyer, and focus on my own art more. I had been filled with such 'Ra ra lets do this!' when it came to helping Interior Natives and homesteaders. This other view is Crafty's way of selling, that works well for him. He dominates the Interior at what he does. But there is room for only one Crafty. I envision a niche market. One Crafty does not specialize in. Though our ideas spring from the same well. *Or swell from the same spring.*

He once told me, "I had the concept of a Craft Market, Miles. I envisioned a lot of artists working together as a co-op—maybe even me providing the space and tools for them to work and marketing our work." Yes, but this also describes a sweat shop. I've seen Crafty make offers and accept workers. They work in his dingy basement with no window, filled with dust, a dirt floor, noise, and Crafty overworks them, saying, "I'll give you a place to sleep and some food for payment!" People like Wess the Mess find that attractive. Not the 'together, successful and smart.' I myself started out this way working for Crafty! Crafty makes his million, and what do his workers make? Room and board. Money talks. Customers seek out made overseas 'garbage' with fake stickers saying it's authentic hand made in Alaska at the sweat shop prices. Crafty hauls in his million. I am not sure if the customers have been brainwashed, the shops push what makes them the most profit. Maybe the customer really wants what I'm talking about. *Or yes they do, at the slave labor prices.*

Crafty can show me some items that fit the bill. Art his local Athabaskan Indians create. I will buy some local soapstone carvings, and moose antler work.

I think about Tucson. I seek out the gem supplier from India with genuine stones hand cut for ten cents each. Because some poor worker in India hand cut that stone for less than a penny. *But that poor guy can find food to eat for less than a penny.* "Somehow that worker is alive." *I do not know how. Should I care more?*

I know as a worker, I do not want to compete and make ten cents an hour. When I buy that cheap stone I put it in low end art. I mark it up to make a profit. But I do not call it a $100 stone, nor hand crafted in Alaska. I call it the 'You get what you pay for' tray. In my opinion that is the difference between Crafty and I. He buys it for ten cents, puts 'hand made in Alaska' on it and asks the hand made in Alaska prices. That screws the local artists who compete with that product. I forgive Crafty, money is his God. I would not trade places with him. The smart local craft people see what is going on, and do not think much of Crafty for that. How can Crafty truly care and be their friend? Again, I feel respect is everything. *Respect can bring money, but money does not necessarily bring respect.*[4]

I get another email from a female I have an interest in.

Am curious...after listening to your tape. How many personal ads have you placed? And one more thing...I'm not sure why you wanted to live the life you did. It seems you almost abused yourself...why with freezing and being hungry and all...I can understand wanting to get away from the city and people and live in the wild and remote but to jeopardize your life?...when it was not necessary...difficult to understand...talk some more to me about the **WHY.**

My response

Hello Bobbie!

I'm on the computer answering as I watch TV. So you ask 'Why'? You didn't read my poem "twelve answers to what for?"

I write several pages explaining this and that. And my reply ends. Unsure if I should even send it. A very lengthy reply. Better to make a one sentence joke and let her go?

"Next!" But it is always next. I have probably met hundreds of women over the years. I'm no longer optimistic. This is off my mind as I have an art show coming up in Fairbanks fifty miles away.

I do about as well as anyone else. The Arctic Travelers Gift Shop is having a show. I gross $400 in three hours. Sounds good? The show took half for their part right off the top, so I have $200 in my pocket. I spent $50 to get there.

The few artists I know, who are trying to make a living, tend not to do these shows. They run shops. They have other answers for making money. Others can make it work by doing an event every weekend. They have a routine and regular customers. They gross about as much as I do, but have less overhead. I've talked about it with vendors for many years, and review the various options. Doing shows every weekend is not what I want to do.

TUCSON SHOW

I have piles of money from the Tucson show I am trying to keep track of. Thousands of dollars of cash a day pass through my hands. I do not set up next to Eaa anymore. He has decided to stay in the same place doing the same thing in the same way, with his one table. But he looks me up for his year's supply of Alaska jade.

"Had a good year, Miles? Looks like you are doing well!"

"Yes, Eaa, hope your year has been good as well. You look like you have not changed. De—ja—vu. Same happy smile, same Jesus robe, and same bare feet!"

He smiles back,"Been time traveling." I only nod. We have joked about this over the years, speculating where all this amazing stuff we see around us comes from, and how unbelievable people's individual stories are.

"Including your stories, Miles!" We laugh.

"Speaking of stories and time travel Eaa," I pause and look to the right and left to see who might be listening in. It's part of the sales pitch. "Eaa I found some black jade for you." His eyes light up. He claims to be pure Mayan, and his entire village carves stone in the way it was done since before Christ. Stone masks. They of course sell at very high prices. All done with primitive tools. I supply the jade. "For you, a special deal" *I need that T-shirt my buddy Crafty has with these words printed on it.* I get out my ten pounds of jade, worth over $1,000. Eaa gets this amount for one inch of this carved into a Mayan God mask.

Eaa takes one sample thin piece and holds it up to the light, looking for flaws, inclusions, imperfections. "Perfect, flawless. Are you sure this came from earth?"

"Maybe not present time, but yes, earth." I keep a straight face. Being Mayan he could believe in a variety of things. Some things true, and some things part of his own story and sales pitch. I toss that out like a fly on a calm Alaska glacier eddy to see if grayling bite. Magic material sells for more money. Even a story you got told, passed on to your dear customer—one reputable dealer to another, is worth more money.

I picture Eaa saying, *"Got this exclusive source in Arctic Alaska, claims to be a time traveler, comes up with this black jade no one has ever seen before."* I like to think we are both smart enough to see the legal advantages to the story we are sticking to. Unscrupulous dealers might try to find the source and get there first to make the money we do, thieves. Legal beagles may want to know if the source is legit, and we have all the proper permits, paid off all the officials along the way. No permit is needed for time travel. Because it is not possible. We are obviously kooks. Nothing traceable up our sleeves.

Eaa shows me intricately carved ancient looking masks of jade he makes from material he previously acquired from me. I'm an artist. This work is impossible to do. He tells me it is done without electricity. If he told me he went back in time 3,000 years ago, it would be no less believable. So what is his truth?

He must wonder as well, where pure clear black jade comes from that the civilized world knows nothing about, in Arctic Alaska. *I have my sources, and I know enough to keep my mouth shut.*

Magic. Setting the groundwork for a silly grin if interrogated.

"Sweet, Miles, you came through for me again." He pays me in gold. It's $1,500 worth of gold. I have a customer who stops by who will pay $2,000 cash for this. *Beats working for a living.* My buddy Eaa drifts off into the dust of the dirt parking lot, Jesus robe blowing in the wind, right out of a Clint Eastwood spaghetti western. *Headed for where?* 'The Twilight Zone."

Art materials. I have nine sheds looking much like this- tons of material.

CHAPTER FOUR

PASSPORT, FINDING MAMMOTH TUSKS, HOMESTEAD CHANGES

Diary Tuesday, February 25, 2005 Homestead trips—cost of trips. I made a round trip to the Kantishna on my Yamaha Viking snow machine and it has me thinking how things have changed over the years. When I get to the homestead I want to make repairs on May's cabin so it can be used. The repairs are only to raise the roof three feet so there can be standing room.

She made the cabin when she was ten years old and three feet was tall enough. I think of her mother, Karen, who I lived with for years helping her raise the two girls in the wilds. May's cabin is still bear proof. I note May used pegs to pin the logs together that still hold. It's been twenty years. She had one sled dog to haul logs with, and her toy plastic saw. The forest fire did not burn her cabin.

I jack the roof up on one side. This might have been good enough, but only allows head room on one side. I decided I have to raise the other side as well. When I try to raise it, the roof falls. In so doing, it falls cock-eyed so it did not land on its walls straight. I give up. This has taken four hours and back to worse than I started. If I spend another eight hours? Well, in eight hours I can frame a whole new place, or at least someone could who knew better how to build. When having time for this lifestyle I simply put in another eight hours. What else is there to do? Work till it gets done. The days of all the time I wanted are gone. I now have more money, and less time.

I decide 'speed' is fun! My Viking is happy at thirty miles an hour on the open trail. There is a nice back rest to lean against. It has electric hot grips that warm my hands. Engine heat is directed at my face. There is heat around my feet. A windshield stops snow from getting in my face. A space age halogen light brightens up the black twenty-four hour nights. There is a pink sunrise off in the distance that begins to show the frost on the grass sticking up out of the snow. The short spruce trees in the swamps look like bottle brushes. An owl flies off, a moose looks up. All the things I am familiar with are here.

On the return trip to Nenana I bend a ski going up the river bank. I make it to Nenana all right. Many of my storage bags have snow in them, so I have to unpack everything. I have to rewind ropes, wash the thermos and camp dishes and lay out all the cloths and tools to dry. I have to repack survival goods. I have yet to look over the snow machine—fix the ski. Tighten the gun rack on the handlebar. I used to simply do all this, and not think about it. But here I am, not having a day of free time to do all this. I have my book to work on, an email business to run, committee meetings to attend, art to prepare for a bazaar, phone calls to make. Normal civilized 'stuff.'

Anyhow, it is nice to get out on the trail, spend the time out. Not a lot of fur sign. I do not want to trap with the animal population down. It's pretty outdoors, but the trips now cost me, not make me money.

My diary ends

I go out into the wilds, and the trips go like clockwork. No adventure, nothing to talk about. Each trip costs me $100. I do what? Trips used to be my living, and lifestyle.

I say to Josh when I see him, "I'm reminded mostly of the 'old times' when I go out. When there was more room, when there was more fur, when I had the cabin full of everything I needed. Now gone in the fire. Going out now is like camping. If I go camping, why not go to some new places? Explore wilderness I have never seen before." Josh has no such feeling to relate to.

He asks, "How has it gone with selling the trapline to those kids?"

"So far OK, Josh. I'm getting a total of $15,000 for 200 miles of trail and ten line cabins. I get to keep some trapping area to fool with. The fifty miles out to the cabin, and some of my nearby side trails within ten miles of the homestead. In this way, I do not have to observe their activity. I've been sharing my maps and answering questions on how to find traps, cabins, and trails. So far the kids have not caught much, and are still learning."

"Miles, I have run sled dogs all my life. That is what I do. That is what I will always do. Race dogs. I told Martha that when we married." Josh is in his late 60's now, and this is still a basic truth about him. He is not burned out. He thinks of little else besides his sled dogs. But happy? I'm not sure. There is a lot of talk from Josh about how the competition uses drugs to win. How unfair that is. He can't win because it is hard to beat the drugs, but he will keep trying. He isn't in the top five anymore, not even in the top twenty much anymore. Racing is now costing him money he doesn't have.

"It will all be different next year, Miles!" He says that every year. Meanwhile he depends on white man's handouts. "Got a leader coming up, Miles, too young yet, but by next year will be in a winning team. That was my problem this year, I didn't have the right dog up front. Makes a big difference, Miles!" I can only smile, wish him luck, suggest victory is just around the corner. I certainly want him to believe in himself, and have the inner drive it takes to be a champion. Josh had been given a special ball cap at the race banquet last year. He snorted disgustedly when he showed it to me. I did not get his point.

My puzzled look was answered with, "Look what the cap says Miles, 'Former champion.' What's this 'former' crap?" Josh has a point. When you have that right stuff you were, are, and always will be, a champion. And, in truth, if you once won, then you should be forever a champion of that moment. When you win a trophy, it is your trophy to keep. *It's only a hat, Josh, geez.* It would be respectful to just print 'champion.' But yes. The title goes to the swift, the strong, is always in flux, and competitive. The life of the Alpha male is stressful, and constantly being challenged. It's not for everyone. I agree, being a 'has-been' is not fun.

What I see is, Josh isn't training like he used to. He can't. He's too old. I think he is scared of the speed now. He fell off the sled a few times, and is not admitting it scares him. He can't handle a hot winning team. I'm not going to say anything about that. I hear now and then, "Geez, Miles, my dogs are a bit too hot!" The winner can never say that. There is no such thing as a team that is too hot.

Twenty years ago, he said, "My dogs tried to get feisty with me, but after 100 miles or so they slow up." My point hangs in the air. In terms of choices we have, make, or do not make. We can do what we have always done till we drop. Or we can adapt, change, find a new game we can still do well with, living in reality. It's sad to me, few want to hear about Josh. He talks dogs, leaders, training methods, and most people walk away. Even dog people. Because it is all outdated methods and stories of interest. The focus has changed. Mushers do not race by feeding dogs fish anymore. It's all high tech balanced diets. It would be like me still talking about the glory of trapping 200 mile lines, ten years after I last made a profit, or had a fur adventure that was worth hearing about. No one traps with sled dogs anymore, nor runs economical slow snow machines, even on the trapline. There are few unbroken trails in uncharted country. Few have to cut trees out of the way each trip. Today it is all about traveling a hundred miles an hour. I can't walk fifty miles on snowshoes anymore, it would be foolish to pretend I could. It is easier to look, and see Josh, than myself.

When asked what I am up to? "I am carving opal, doing casting, making knives that are cutting edge, deserving of respect. I'm still a present time trader/dealer at the two big shows I do. I still get my moose, find mammoth tusks, and engage in other activities that suit what I can still do." I realize some of my lack of the old 'Ra, ra let's go get it' is nothing but chemical changes, not unhappiness. The hormones change. The adrenaline and other such chemicals that regulate our moods, are not being produced. Thus, my feelings may have little to do with the outside world, and everything to do with the world inside my head. It's not the world's fault! Nor is it my fault. It's just 'life.'

Library Report
By Miles
The library has a web site up and running now at mtaonline.net/~library. One day maybe we'll have a domain name, and soon it will be found in search engines, and can be found as a link to click on, the Nenana homepage. One advantage to the community might be travelers who find us. They have books they read they wish to donate to us, or do a paperback exchange. We get something new to look at!

On April 17th, the library had a book signing for 'Alaska Stories-by a Little School Up North'—put out by some of our talented young local writers with the help of Cindy. Each writer signed their story. A great group picture was taken by Russ. There was food and a wonderful turn out. Hopefully, it was a great experience for the writers! Then just two days later, the Library put on an Easter event for our children. Everyone who showed up ended up with an Easter basket full of goodies. There seemed to be quite an attraction for the story reading after (was it the connection between the Easter Bunny and Jesus?)

A tape was donated to the library that might be of interest. 'Heartbeat Alaska' made a video of Nenana during tripod weekend that was aired on TV all over the state —paid for by the Nenana Native Council. The tape looks exceptional, high quality, and is a great statement on our community. You will recognize many locals interviewed. Al John talks about the old days. Marion Browning talks about local dog racing. There is a good scene with Jeff Coghill waving his arms directing the raising of the tripod! Josh and Martha talk about the Iditarod, as well as several of the racers. I talk about my art.

I like some of the footage of the community from the hilltop, and the snow machine running down the riverfront. This can be checked out of the library and is well worth seeing, not only to see your friends who were on TV—but this is a historical document we will treasure in years ahead. So the library is not just about 'books'—we have videos to check out! We encourage you to donate your videos so others can enjoy them.

This report I write shows up in the local Nenana paper. I regularly sum up what has been happening at the library. I'm on the library board. I get an email from the librarian, and help the library with a web page and understanding the internet.[1] The librarian is full of questions.

"Miles, I don't understand how this works. I thought anyone could be found on a search engine. How does one get noticed on a search engine? How much does the Chamber pay for their site? I know you helped build and now manage the site. How often do they have to pay? Are they recognized in a search engine? Just wondering"

I give a lengthy reply, and explain to the librarian how it all works as far as I understand.

A reply arrives to an inquiry addressed to the folks talking about exploring for gas and oil in our valley.

Good Morning Miles.

Thanks for spending the time to ask some important questions. For now, I am your best contact. I head up this project on the Doyon side, and am in charge of all natural resource development projects on Doyon lands. I am also assisting Andex in their efforts to secure an exploration license on State of Alaska lands at Nenana. On the Andex side…

Roughly into three parts: (1) exploration (seismic, winter roads and pads, and drilling), (2) development (more drilling, and construction of pads, facilities, pipelines and maybe some roads), and production (operation and maintenance of facilities). Each stage can present its own set of challenges and opportunities. Relationships and processes between developers and local residents that are established in the early stages can be shaped and adjusted to address new issues as they arise. I think it fair to assume that we have some influence over many aspects of the project.

At this point, I think the best way for me to respond to your specific comments is to provide answers in the body of your note, and hopefully your email program will work in that format.

I have an interest in community affairs concerning gas and oil exploration in the Nenana area. Specifically, out the direction I used to trap. One aspect concerns me. There is talk of a gate across the trail. Many locals use this trail to access trapping, hunting, berry picking, firewood, etc. This trail is the only winter access to some homesteads. The various trails across the river were cut by locals, and have been in existence and used for generations. The trails have legal, recognized historical preservation status. I do understand that we, as a society, are consumers, so need this oil and gas. I understand society is not going to let a handful of savages come between civilization and what it wants. I'm not thinking of stopping anything! I'm more looking for a way that does not interfere with the end goal of extracting gas and oil, while at the same time, not recklessly, needlessly, destroying history trails and access. There is a town meeting with a presentation. I ask the Doyon representative:

"So who will have a key to this gate?"

The reply, "Anyone authorized."

"Is that likely to include any local trappers?" My concern is this is a public trail, with historical use over many years, getting blocked by a gate.

The company argument being, "This is a 911 security issue involving a sensitive area that needs tough security."

The local argument is, "There is a specific use permit issued that does not include land ownership or total control of land use. You will get a lease to explore on 'our land,' that we own and have access to."

The Doyon reply goes, "And we have good lawyers and we will win…" Rather than what I had hoped the reply would be, "We plan to work with local needs for the land." It's a huge vast wilderness they are exploring. It is a lot to expect total control over. In my opinion, responsible locals could make good guardians of the remote lands, as we know everyone who usually goes out there, and could keep track of 'suspicious behavior.' The concern I assume, for the oil company, is sabotage, or rival companies spying. I have a reason to be involved. This is my old stomping grounds for over twenty—five years. Getting involved takes time. There are meetings, reports to read, comments to make. Staying informed is not easy.

No other trapper shows up nor cares, saying to me, "If anyone tries to run me off my trapline, I'll kill them." I know if they say this to an oil company they will lose, it is they who will be taken out with a swat team. However my perspective is as a white man who was born and raised in this oil company culture. Many of my trapping friends have never left Alaska, and that big world out there is just pictures on a TV screen. There are a handful of us that would be affected by access to the wilderness being cut off.

"So what, and big deal!" No, I am not going to make it my full time effort to find a lawyer and investigate this situation. As the head guy says, they have lots of money, a good lawyer, and always win. Not because they are right and just, but because they are powerful. It would not be wise to step forward as a declared enemy.

Awards Banquet
By Miles

The Nenana Valley Chamber of Commerce and the Volunteer Fire Department combined to put on a banquet awards ceremony and dance at the Community Center, March 29th. This was a special time for those who received awards. (list awards)

Nenana Unlimited with two new great local musicians added—our music teacher(name)and his wife(name)on drums. Mary sang some, but for the first time we saw her on the dance floor! Miles requested 'In A Gada Da Vita'—the music got to some hard rock and roll! Those who stayed till later, twist and shouted till after midnight!

We give a hearty welcome to the new music group! This is a special time to give thanks and recognition to those who deserve our thanks—that we sometimes take for granted. At this ceremony, let them know we do notice their work, and reward them. This was also a fundraiser for the firemen and the Chamber, and as such we did raise some money (name amounts?).

The Chamber puts the feed and awards on. The Volunteer firemen handled the dance and drinks. The two groups worked together well. We are sorry not more of you could attend, and hope to see you next year! (Dawn-pictures on a disk to be delivered.)

The rough draft is submitted to Dawn at the newspaper. She fills in the blanks, names, numbers, that I am not good at recalling. I do not get paid to write, but hope this is a help to the paper and the community. On my mind is that Dawn is one of the people who wanted to take credit for donating a lot of free time and work towards Art Train. When in fact, at one point tried to extort me for money, expecting to get paid, then ran off with some Chamber of Commerce money instead. The Board decided to overlook this indiscretion. I'm learning better how to be a team player. Nothing will ever be exactly how we want it, nor will the group have the same ethics as the individuals in it.

There are other articles to write for the news. This is a rough draft I submitted. I'm still the chair of the Chamber of Commerce.

Friday, May 09, 2003

Resolution Passes! Free Water Sewer for All!!!!By Miles of Alaska

Did I get your attention? Uh Huh—everyone is now entitled to a free month of water and sewer. All you have to do to get it is to pay for 11 months in advance. The savings may only be marginal when you look at the interest on the yearly amount paid up front, 'but,' it eliminates getting upset every month with the bill. Now you only have to get upset once a year!

I write out the details.

Stay tuned for the follow up story—"Free, free water sewer! Hear all about it! You heard it here first in the

Nenana Messenger!…"

I was responsible for this resolution. I'm attending city meetings regularly. I contribute articles for the local paper concerning the library, the Chamber, and events on all our minds.

Nenana Web Domain

Nenanahomepage.com—that's all you need to remember

For four years Nenana has had a web home page. Now we have a domain name 'Nenanahomepage.com'. At first there was quite a struggle.

I explain and give some details.

Being up online is great, but what good is it if you can't be found, or cannot put your own community spin on the site? Once found by search engines, you better be pretty darn sure this is your forever site!

I am responsible for the Nenana home page website now. I was originally in partnership with someone who knew more than I did. I explain to Will, "I'm not sure what happened, Will. I used to be just the picture taker. Maybe write a few stories. This gal would correct and edit my words, since I tend to not spell well, nor am I careful about details, and tend to mix up my facts. I thought it was a good arrangement, where I am an ideas person, an innovative thinker who fails to follow through in top notch form. But never out of words!"

"Yes, Miles, but maybe a lot of people think they are, or want to be, the ideas person. Not many want to be the flunky corrector, operating in the background. They want to be in charge. You know, too many chiefs and not enough Indians." I pause to consider this.

"Could be, Will. Someone once told me most editors are frustrated writers."

"Was that statement made by a writer?" We both laugh. At any rate, my partner seemed to lose interest, or got burned out, or had other things to do. For sure, people come to us when something is wrong, and few come to us to thank us for our volunteer work. Likewise, few step forward to chip in. The news lady, Dawn, tells me all the time she can't get anyone to submit a story, or tell her the news, even for free advertising. When it comes to events and such, she has to go to all the organizations to dig the information out of them. It's a lot of work and frustration.

"Right now, Will, the Chamber is paying the $29 a month for the community web space. It's still frustrating, as the Chamber of Commerce struggles." I explain we have trouble having a quorum for meetings. "Few members pay their $50 a year dues without twisting their arms. Those businesses most demanding of our time are likely to be the ones who have not joined the Chamber or paid their dues." Even so, the Chamber slowly makes progress, and does some good things. Without us, Nenana would not have a web page. "We got a sign post up so we can all hang a placard on it to advertise our business at the entrance to town. We make and put up banners for big events like River Days, Tripod days, 4th of July and such. We are responsible for the Christmas program, and buy the gifts, have Santa give them out. We have a welcome committee for those new to town, with gifts and help offered, so they feel welcome. I'm proud to be head of the organization."

"Hey, Miles, wasn't the other day your birthday?" I forgot, as I look out at the river in memories of the past, and all the years on the river.

"Yea, May 7th. How old am I now? I forget, let me get my fingers out." We both laugh again. "I think I'm fifty-one, somewhere in there!" *Not in my prime anymore, but not old yet.*

"Except for your back, how's the back after the operation and all that?"

"Well, I'm considered permanently 10% disabled, but it's OK. Mostly I can't bend over all the way to touch my palms on the ground or even reach the ground without bending my knees, and I do not have the back strength I once had, but it doesn't hurt. I've been on high blood pressure pills, but so are most people my age I know. Ha! It sucks, but what am I going to do about it?"

"Your new life has more stress, higher blood pressure, I think." I frown at the thought, even if it might be true. No way to test the truth of that.

"I can't really go back to my old lifestyle you know. No sled dogs. My trapline and homestead burned, plugged in here. In Nenana. My new life has its rewards. It is nice to feel like I am contributing something." Will is not so sure anyone cares, notices, or that anything I do affects anyone, one way or the other. Will and I watch some tourists walking around Nenana on the dirt roads, whispering, investigating, what to them is oddness. One takes a picture of a four wheeler on the road going by. They end up coming our direction and engage us in conversation.

"Is there any homesteading in Alaska, still?" They would like to acquire some free land. I explain it is not a yes or no question. In response, I explain it this way,

"Let's say I to go to New York City, and go to the nearest skyscraper I came to, go up to the twenty-seventh floor and walk in an office. I'm dressed as I am, in dirty jeans, a torn shirt, grizzly bear claw necklace around my neck and Mountain Man hat on, with blade of grass in my mouth. I ask the first person I come to if there is some prime office space for rent, cheap. What would they say-and do?"

The tourists try to imagine this scene and ponder what a reply would be. Before they give an answer I say, "I'd be lucky if they let me use the phone or the restroom, right?" I go on about how I think it would be.

I'd guess most likely they would look up from what they were doing, take me in at a glance and say, "Nope—Nothing available here," and go back to what they were doing. Not even bothering to check, or even care. The tourists nod that yes, I am probably correct.

"Well, if this person from New York shows up in Alaska in a suit and tie, all clean, manicured nails, briefcase in hand, city accent, and asks about homesteading, it's about the same thing." Sort of hinting—*like you guys, for example!* So the answer is, "There might be homesteading. But you have to know the right questions, know who to ask, what to ask, how to ask, and be one of us." If I went into the land office and said, "I hear there's a parcel or two up the Kantishna up for grabs that didn't get proved up on. That'd be on the Kantishna C-2 map, near Bearpaw."

Chances are, someone in the office would say, "Oh yea, the paperwork is all messed up, but…"

And I said, "Well, I used to trap through there and it'd be nice to have a place in the old stomping grounds, maybe we can work something out?" I pause and look to see if these tourists are paying attention. "There's a good chance I could end up with a piece of homestead land, if I really wanted it. But likewise, I could also go down-river, pick out almost any nice place I liked, and build a cabin. Locals call it their fish camp. Or trapline cabin. Part of a subsistence life. I doubt anyone would say anything. But if an outsider tried it, they'd get run out."

There is a confused look among the tourists and one asks (again), "Is there any homesteading or remote lands available in Alaska?" Never heard a word I said.

I smile back and reply, "No." Will and I watch them amble off, still staring at everything in disbelief. Mumbling about 'the middle of nowhere.' So why does anyone who feels this way, have an interest in getting some of 'nowhere' for free?

"If they got a homestead, they couldn't find it," Will commented. Such people more and more turn to the internet and look Alaska up to decide what we offer, and if they want to come visit us. I often feel like we are the zoo, or we are all in a circus. *Oh well.* But I do not wish to help out these weird people as much as I once did. Why did I bother to try to answer their question honestly.

I feel inclined to simply say, "No" walk away, or make the sign of the cross, and walk on the other side of the street. I sigh, "I do what I can, Will. I'm the buyer for the Nenana Culture Center Gift Shop again. I quit for a while, but was asked back. One reason is to try to educate people, both our own Natives and tourists, about a different culture. There is also something else I get out of my position. Here, check this out." I hand Will a printout of a document stored in the computer. I'm a curator of a museum. This gives me certain legal rights I had not thought about much, till recently. There are more rules to follow each year, concerning the transportation of many of the materials used in wilderness and native craft.

Museum Employee
1998-through 2001

Miles Martin is the art dealer and on the Board of Directors for the Nenana, Alaska Totchaket Historical Society and Museum, a non-profit organization. The purpose of this organization is to preserve, show, and educate people about the interior Alaska culture.

Totchaket owns and runs a nonprofit museum- gift shop. As the head buyer of local art, Miles's duties include purchasing, displaying, and promoting interior

Alaskan art. Such duties include purchasing materials to be used by Athabascan Indians and youth workers in the creation of traditional items for the museum and gift shop—whose sale is not for profit but to help run the museum. Such items might include old trade beads, amber, animal products, and any other material traditionally used—traded, with interior Alaskans.

Other duties include the promotion of interior Alaskan culture, through the exhibition of display items made by Alaska artists, as well as lectures about Alaska subsistence lifestyle and showing of appropriate items as would make such a lecture educational and interesting. Such pictures, materials and art objects have historical—educational significance.

Among Miles Martins' duties is to promote, lecture, and seek out sponsors for our organization, and increase tourism and good feeling between cultures. This may include finding markets for our gift shop items, finding groups who would like to visit our community, or simply educating other cultures about our lifestyle. Miles can be expected to travel in his duties in this capacity, and can be expected to have with him various Alaskan art objects, materials, display items, and lecture props.

This organization expects Miles to conduct himself legally, and represent Nenana faithfully. Our organization does not have a lot of funding so we give Miles as much freedom to pursue the goals of our organization as we can. If you have any further questions concerning these issues feel free to contact Totchaket through the manager

Signed,

Sue Marvin

"Miles, is this still valid, looks outdated to me." I glance at the date. I forget how long I have been the museum buyer. I'm not a good paperwork person.

"I guess it is still up to date, if not, I can get another one, or someone can get hold of the organization if there is ever an issue. I needed this going to Tucson with some Native art I had, and materials destined for Lower fort-eight Indians. I carried animal products most people are not allowed to have, or are highly restricted, like bear claws, endangered animal parts, animals that are protected and such. Or, legal, but a lot of officers are not lawyers, and only understand 'no.' Some kind of paper might be helpful maybe, save a lot of time."

"I see you have a 'Nenana pride' hat on, Miles. What happened to the 'White Pride' hat you joked about?" I tell him the story about the hats at a village store.

Not to mention any names: "The store owner got in some popular hats that said 'Indian Pride.' It's a common hat among the Natives, tee shirts, bumper stickers, etc., to help Indians be proud of their race. Athabascan kids wore these hats to school, and made a big deal about their superior race and color. Some of the white kids felt insulted, hurt, put down. They wanted their own hat, so they could also be proud of their race."

Will nods that he understands. He adds, "Like the van I see here in Nenana that reads, 'Native Council' on it. Well, what happens if you or I had a van with, 'White Council' on it?"

"Yea, it would be like putting, 'Ku Klux Klan' on it, make the front page of the New York Times and be lynched, it's a lifetime in jail."

"Got that right."

"Some local whites asked the store to have a hat that said 'White Pride,' so the white kids could have the same pride the Natives have. The same rights to be proud. The store owner agreed, and ordered the hats. The kids wore the new cool hats with, 'White Pride' on them. They got suspended from school for discrimination." The hats were deemed illegal. So the store owner stopped selling either hat, and sells 'Nenana Pride' hats. I support that.

"What was that you told me about discrimination laws, Miles? You were insulted at some wildlife meeting or something, I forget."

"Yes, I'm pretty sure I told ya' about it, you don't remember?" I went to an Advisory Board meeting for Fish and Game. I wanted information, wanted to participate, wanted to try to change the rules within the system by being part of this legal process. Or at least, have a better understanding of why the laws are the way they are. I may feel more inclined to follow those laws, for the good of the planet or whatever, if I could hear the reasoning behind them." The first thing I notice is, every single person on the committee is an Indian. The second thing I notice is a 'f—k the white man' attitude. I was asked why I was here, told to go back where I came from- whatever country that might be. My behavior is polite. I am concerned this committee sets the fishing laws for all of us, yet is only looking out for the Indian. This group is supported by public funds, tax dollars, so equal representation for all groups paying seems in order. I say, "Divide and conquer. The government has been doing that to you Natives forever. Today you get rid of the white fisherman—homesteader as your enemy. Tomorrow it will be you. We need to stick together. It is not me who is your enemy." The subject at hand concerned what I believed to be an illegal subsistence fishing closure on the Kantishna River.

I was told, "Good!" and laughed at, "It's not closed for Indians!"[2] I recall Will knows one of the natives.

"Feet, from Minto, you know, the really short guy we met on the river once? Well, he flat out threatened me! Told me he would sink my boat." I found this to be odd behavior at an official meeting that is recorded with minutes, and goes in official white man government records. I explain briefly how I received a copy of the minutes of this meeting, and I saw in the fine print on the back, "If you feel you have been discriminated against due to your race, write to this address." So, what the heck. Rather than bad mouth the group publicly, why not respond reasonably, and simply state the facts. See if anything gets done. Find remedy within the system, not listen to those wanting violence, revolution, or vigilante responses. What I hoped for in a reply, was that the committee would be reminded they represent everyone, and need to remember that. I hoped to have equal representation as a result.

I share with Will what I was told. I got a reply in writing, and show him. "In order for there to be discrimination, you must be a member of a minority race" I interpret that for Will, " It's not legally possible to be white and be discriminated against."

Will responds, "Until or unless whites become a minority race." I pause and give Will's reply thought. "Correct. But, Will, I do not think this is helping anyone, not even the Native cause." We both feel there is the 'divide and conquer' aspect to the situation we have discussed a lot over the years. I refuse to buy into the discrimination. Because I feel I know what is going on, I will not make the Native my enemy. That is the road to the destruction of both groups. Playing right into the government and big business hands.

"Whatever, Miles."

I change the subject. Even so, I am human. How can I not be affected by insults and threats? Worse, laws get passed based on the attitude I am seeing, protecting one race. Natives already have their own tribal government; no, their race is allowed to participate in, or even attend, even have their own land like their own country. If Natives are allowed to also dominate the white legal process, what will white citizens do? "Will they do as any race does that is excluded from the legal process? Declare war on the oppressor? Just read your history."

Will reminds me of something long ago,"Back in the '70's, Miles, we found out the Indians in Huslia were shooting down airplanes, sinking boats, burning white man buildings like the schools. We never believed it was possible, without making the news!" I recall that time period of disbelief.

The Natives laughed and said, "Whose news!" Of no interest to the outside world apparently, not politically correct, as the white man moved in on the Indian's oil. The Indian had a right to be upset. Still. I was just as upset as the Native. I too love the land, and I too depend on the land and its health. After all these years, I feel I have proven myself, and it hurts to be treated so disrespectfully. Back in the 1970's, I thought it was cool that such news was too remote to get reported, like being at the headwaters of the Amazon, and discovering head hunters. With the real possibility of ending up in a stew pot. What came of this kind of knowledge has been a slow change of 'how things get done and dealt with.' It seems obvious if head hunters put me in a stew pot, and the outside world has no knowledge, wants no knowledge, does nothing, I best adapt to the way people take care of themselves in this part of the world if I want to stay alive, and it is not by dialing 911! Will has his John Deere hat tilted back, his plaid, engine oil stained shirt hanging out of his suspendered Carhartt work pants. We get started on the subject of remote lands.

I explain, "The trail from Nenana to the Kantishna River is 50 miles long. Partly run by a bulldozer many years ago, but not all the way. The section bulldozed is a railroad right of way. It is me, along with neighbors Tom and his wife, who connected it all, and kept it open." What needed connecting was existing right of ways, old trails, ponds, creeks, that all went the direction we wanted to go, that we blazed and opened up. *Now new homesteaders, trappers and hunters follow this trail and use it as public access. Eventually, it will be a road. I thought it had been classified as a historical trail with a right of way. That was my doing. Even though I lived alone and seemed not to contribute. I had my role to play, a purpose. In my mind, deserving of respect. Allowed.*

"Miles, it's not just you and your life getting regulated to death!" I forgot how it is for Will. "I have been put out of business. Problems with regulations for years. Or restrictive to the point I can't run a small business. I have to work for someone else now!" Will has a love and knowledge of working on cars. Years ago, he made a living getting on Tradio and listening for cars for sale, buying up old junkers, fixing them up and reselling them. He'd get some free if he picked them up. So Will built a special tow truck to fetch cars that do not run. He had a garage at his home, with all the tools to change out parts and such. He'd put together running cars he could afford to sell for $300 to $500. It as a niche market for those who do not have any more money than that to invest in transportation. My ex and I got one of these trucks for $350. As promised, we never had to put more money into it. Will knew to the nearest 100 miles when it would fail. Extremely good at what he does. Even gifted. Will's passion in life.

Will goes on, "I had to get a permit, a business license, and insurance. No one could help me out on a job without me paying Workman's Comp. I had restrictions on registering custom builds. I could no longer splice frames. It just got to where it forced me out of business, Miles. The government must hate free enterprise and small business or something." He pauses and adds, "Then the government cries business people are going overseas! It's pretty easy to see why!"

So maybe my complaints are part of a bigger issue. "I'm not being singled out." This is a sore spot for Will, so he rambles on without stop. Some of it borders on paranoia and nonsense. Yet who knows where the line is between bonkers and sanity? We all draw that line at different places. It's hard to fight something we do not all agree on. Conspiracy theories and such, followed by, "The government does that on purpose. It would not surprise me if the President is a communist." I let Will ramble on without interruption, just nodding to let him know I heard. We exchange stories of people we know who tried to make a go of running their own business, or make some extra money at something they are good at, who got stopped. While the public gets told it is for our own good, and safety reasons.

"Yea right, Miles! Do you really think the world is safer now, than it was fifteen years ago?" I think this issue comes right down to how and why our government was formed, and why we separated from England. One huge question was—"Is the average person capable of running their own life, or should someone else run things for the majority of idiots?"

I understand it was decided by our forefathers that people should be given the chance to decide their own lives, things like how to raise their children, what is safe and not safe. Many people who worked on the constitution thought only land owners should be allowed to vote and run things. It was a big debate.

Past flash

Will is driving me around helping me get supplies for the winter in the 1980's. One of the stops he needs to make for his own business is the DMV to register one of the trucks he built from parts. We walk in together and stand in line. Will with his folder of papers. My slow talking, farm boy looking friend. Outweighing everyone in the room by 100 pounds, in his suspenders and John Deer hat.

Will says in a slow farmers drawl, "Here is the title for the front of the frame. Here is the title for the left back of the frame." Another set of papers, "Here are the papers for the engine block, and here is the title for the ..." He's laying it all out in order.

He gets asked, "So is it a truck or a car?" There is a line to fill out on a form. Will blinks a few times. It never occurred to him to wonder what it is. It goes on the road and hauls people. Four wheels, two headlights. Like that. Will gets through that part finally. But there are fifty other questions, and this has already taken twenty-five minutes. The lady at the counter gets annoyed. There is a long line.

"Well, you can't register this! What are you thinking!" But she cannot come up with a reason why. Yet. She's mulling this over, searching for a reason this is not possible to do. We can't figure out how much it weighs, that has to be written on line twenty-seven. Two hours later, Will has his papers, but it was not easy. He is not the same happy guy he was on our way here! He was excitedly telling me what he built! How cool it is, how useful, how he adapted parts, welded that, and took this off a '55 tranny, that off a Chevy, this other thing off a Ford, because he knew it had the same hole pattern. All over my head. I smile and nod, just to hear my friend being happy, excited, and seeing the lights on upstairs. My buddy Will, now dragging his feet, eyes on the ground not saying much. No, he isn't hungry anymore.

I tell Will about this lady I am trying to help out. Sort of a related subject. Paperwork. "She's from Germany." One of the local dog racers is known for getting free help from out of the country, talking pretty girls into coming to Alaska to learn to run sled dogs, with free room and board. He may offer to pay a little bit. Almost always there is no pay for some 'reason' he comes up with. The girls last one season, maybe two or three. They are legally here—'maybe,'—but under dubious conditions. They are not in a situation to complain to anyone. They are guests in our country, maybe cannot legally work. I do not know the details. I only know this gal is a slave, knows it, and is not happy about it.

"I'm trying to help her out, maybe get her a green card by offering her a job or finding someone to hire her. But no, not marry her." She and I talk about jobs in general, what people can do for a living and have a choice about. Working for yourself comes up, a common topic of conversation for me, as I get into conversations a lot with people who hate their job, or feel stuck, unhappy, and see no way out. This tall, young German blonde tells me she enjoys working with leather. Related to my line of work, since I deal in furs, know about tanning, and have sources for leather. I have made my own clothes from leather I tanned off animals I got myself. She is interested in all this.

She describes the ideal job that would put her in heaven. "I would make purses of leather, stamp the leather, add fur trim. I would make vests and mix colors of leather in the latest styles the young like." She gets all starry eyed as Will does when he talks about car parts, and I talk about building custom knives. My heart just goes out to her. I ask her why she can't just do this in Germany!? Why does she have to come here to do this and make life so difficult?

"In Germany this is almost impossible. You have a job. It is your job. It is the only job you will ever have. You will never end up with two jobs. In order to be allowed to sell leather goods, I must get certified. Attend years of schools. Prove I know how. Pass many tests. Pay many fees. Prove I have a reliable place to work that is safe, with up to date equipment that is certified, passes inspection. After many years, maybe I get permission to do this. Meanwhile, how do I live?"

"Wow! Bummer. How awful. I could not imagine such a horrible life. Unable to do what you love. I would not wish to live anymore. Yes, I see why you want to come to the USA! Here, you simply make leather stuff! Begin by setting up a table on the street, maybe in front of your house, in a parking lot with permission of the owner. Set up at a local bazaar or swap meet for a $10 fee. That's it. In business! The public decides if you are any good or not, not the government!" Oh, how the pretty German wanted to come here to follow her dream!

"I am looking into it, Will. So far it is more complicated than I thought. I figured she could stay with me; I have room in the house. She could work with leather I have. I donate the leather and fur, she makes stuff, sells it, and I get a percent. I got no real out of pocket costs with her staying with me. I grow a garden, so another mouth to feed would not even be noticed. Eventually she would stumble onto another situation, be able to afford her own place, or meet someone running a major leather business she could be part of. But I could help get her started!"

"With a little nooky on the side."

"Exactly."

"Nothing in life is free."

"Exactly." I pause, "She mutters something in German under her breath I do not understand."

"Probably what a great kind person you are."

"Exactly! That's what I figure, Will. She smiles anyhow. She's one of these open minded Germans. They have a much healthier view on arrangements over there in Europe then we have here. Much more practical." We are off track. In truth the focus is on honestly wanting to help. If help means she stays someplace else, or, 'us as an item' is not in the cards then 'oh well,' that is just a wishful aside. That she'd be grateful and —well you know.

"Anyhow, Will, I bragged about how great our country is and the freedoms we have. How, yes, you can have a dream and a reasonable chance to accomplish it. How easy it would be to give it a shot if you decided you wanted to work with leather. You would not need anyone's permission." Will and I wonder if 'things' are changing. To protect the public. What if the leather was not tanned right and the customers got sick? Or the furs were off endangered species? Or proper taxes were not getting paid? Or it was a scam? How would the public be protected? So we register, inspect, approve, keep an eye on all activity. We are protected. But at what cost? We end up like the Europe we left behind and had a revolution over, fighting for freedom. What was all that for if we decide that yes, Europe has the right idea? Permits, fees and permission, all supported by taxation. *Without representation* Will and I talk about stuff like this, tea, and parties, such matters as this.

My past flash ends

I SHAKE my head to clear it. No, I was never able to help my German friend. If I offered her a job, the level of permits and conditions never ends. I'd need insurance. I'd have to offer a wheel chair ramp, fire exit, chemical station, fire sprinklers, and on and on. I did visit her when I went to Germany to visit Helm. Took a train to Kiel where she lives. Super tankers are built there—interesting place…Anyhow…

Still learning about websites. I write an email to one of our local experts.

Hello Annette

Well—I talked to Dawn, who is 'supposed' to be partners with me on this web page—the one who started it. The page was dead at one point. Dawn was not very interested. Now is less than interested, and wants the page to be taken down. It seems to be a dead horse. I do not feel comfortable or qualified to take care of the community home page alone. It's supposed to be a community effort.

Yes, I went to see the Healy homepage you forwarded. Yes, it is very nice. But what am I supposed to say? It appears to have been made by professionals in Florida. I assume they did not donate their time. Because of how much it must have cost, I can only assume the community came up with some money—a grant—some way to pay someone. We do not have such money. The style used is not what I can do. I think that our existing Nenana page is more 'us,' and is interactive.

The comments I get on the page, have to do with how I can do more. How I can improve it—change it, correct it. I already spent a month's wages on it and 100 hours of time. I'm not interested in how I can do more. To do more and better I need a better web program. I need a new digital camera. I need to upgrade my computer. Someone has to maintain the Domain name. This does not get into the hours of work required to keep links working, get people to notify me when their link is changed. Pages with links that do not work, do not end up in a good spot in search engines, so people who do not bother to keep their page current affects the home page. To overcome this, effort has to be made to get listed in the search engines, which costs money and time. All of us need to keep the pages current.

I feel I should not have to defend the site, make an argument, state my case, prove anything. The proof is in the pudding. There it is. A few in Nenana understand web sites, have an interest, know what they cost, and how much time they take. What I'm asking the community for is about one tenth what it would cost to hire someone to do it. I'm not going to argue about it. If the community does not think it's a deal, (because it is not a good page or what they want) can't afford it, doesn't want it, the reason I can only speculate on, and doesn't matter.

Dawn tells me, "Probably there will be a lot of people in Nenana who think your work is too informal—artsy—disorganized for a nice homepage." I do the best I can with what I have. I see no one else stepping forward who might do better.

People outside Nenana who contact me through the home page tell me they smile, like it so homey, and small town. They find this quaint, and attractive. My opinion is, this describes Nenana. We are not offering class. I feel we should not try. *What is wrong with who and what we are?* There are plenty of places to visit or settle that out-class Nenana. How many places to visit have an Indian form of government, offer wildlife viewing right off the road, right in the village? How many places have a café where locals keep their own coffee mug on the wall and fetch their own coffee in their own cup and you can visit, talk to trappers, homesteaders in an unstructured setting? I could go on. The web site has local pictures maybe out of focus, a word here and there misspelled, things not lined up perfect. A tad like a child's imitation of a poster. Cute.

It looks as though the community will end up without an internet presence, and not enough people think that is a great loss, nor care. I feel bad if so. I care about my community, and think we need a web page if we want tourism. Or if we want people to find us and move here, attract good school teachers.

"The proof of what I mean is, the gal who runs the Senior Center, Valerie, got the job because of my web page work. She emailed me and asked me to tell her about Nenana. She'd never heard of the place." It sounded nice, so she came here to check it and the job offer out. She looked at the community pictures, picture of the school, the river, the Chamber page, the library page. All of which I maintain by myself. I wrote all those words, took all those pictures.

I was supposed to get help through the Chamber, but that help volunteer runs Apple, and apple program and mine, seem not to be compatible enough to be interactive. So far, we do not have the knowledge to make it work. So here is an important person in our community who is here because of an internet presence. Several school teachers also told me they went online looking for information on Nenana when they got a school job offer. The web page made a difference. A nice laid back simple life with no stress. Happy children playing in the street, no advertising posters along the roads, no need to dress up.

New people who moved here say, "Like the lower states were a hundred years ago."

"This explains where the web site situation is." I explain to community members who ask. I am in hopes that someone will offer help.

An internet customer compliments me on some sheep horns sent to a university for a class in how to make the old style spoons from horn, as done a thousand years ago. I know how. Done it. The horn is softened by boiling, then scraped and shaped. I was interested in how the project turned out.

I was told, "Where else would anyone get such a material from! The internet is so great! Bringing such an interesting subsistence person as you in touch with a university! You will go on our list as a supplier!"

> **Hi Miles**! I bought sheep horns from you last year and promised pictures of the finished products...we still aren't finished. (Did Karen send a photo of hers?) Just wanted to say hi and let you know how nice I think your new website looks! Take care, I won't forget the photos, but it will probably take quite a while.
> **Best regards, Janet Yang**

I see the note at top. I use a bookmark and file by first name to leave notes to refer to, as reminders to go look in a previous file if I need to.

Hello Janet!

Yes, I am curious how the work with the sheep horn turned out. It might even be interesting to have a section of my website where there are some 'before' and 'after' pictures.

"What you can do with my material—this is what Janet did!" kind of thing. Do you do this for fun or do you sell the work? If you sell, do you have a web site? Anyhow, I emailed Karen (wasn't she in the same class or something?) that I got some nice sheep horn in not long ago from the Arctic—well preserved and large. I have eight. So—if you need any more? Did you say there might be ongoing classes? Anyhow, let me know if you need more—I could do a price break on more than three, if the class puts in a joint order.

Later! Miles

THE CLASS SPENT a total of $1,000 on wild Dall sheep horn. Now only a year later, a restricted item. Not illegal, just more conditions. All I have to remember is, the horns have to be separated to be legal. The purpose of this is to ensure horns are not sold as trophies, and sold only as a craft item. The concern being there is a lot of money—big money—in trophies. Some poor people might be tempted to kill sheep just to sell the horns and wipe the already dwindling wild Dall sheep population out. I make sure I do not deal in trophies.

Yes, the horns are from hunters! Hunters who find where sheep were killed in winter snow slides, or ate the sheep and have no use for the horns. Sometimes hikers find winter wolf kills and save horns, or old timers have had them for years in a garage, and sell them at a yard sale. I have a source for horns that are too damaged for display, so could be cut up for art projects. I get some from a hunting guide. While his clients are hunting, Pete picks up horns and puts them in the plane. Pete is the friend at the land office who helped me out years ago. He and others I know support my views, and the repurposing, scavenging wilderness garbage for crafts and education.

The first level of restrictions is just annoying, not a concern. "Cut the skull, separate the horns!" Ok. Next step is record this and prove it. This involves pictures in the mail, paperwork keeping track. Later come fees, and permits that can be, and sometimes are, denied with penalties supporting whole series of levels of government employees, the legal and prison systems.

My thoughts get back to my community. *Yes, I understand class. I was born into it. Class is not something you can easily learn. It's more about breeding. I know what class is, what it offers, and what it does not offer.* I nod and reply to myself, "To many Nenana people I know can never experience class, yet long for it, and see me as one who does not represent where they wish to be or end up. It is beyond their comprehension, I was born into what they dream of, and voluntarily walked away to have what they already live." *They do not see the value in what is right under their own nose.* "Would they really die to sit at the opera in a suit and tie?"

Another email:

Hi Miles, you are right, you cannot put a value on nature and being in it. I have hunted Brown bear up the Mochatna river and Moose in British Columbia and when I get back home, I look at people and think, you don't have a clue what life is all about. The pace of their lives is so fast they don't know much about what life is all about. I miss those days in the wilderness and long to go back.

By the way recalculate your total. I would like to pay what you said, but I think you shorted yourself. Pretty cool being able to talk to someone so far away. Gotta love computers. I got waylaid on finishing that piece, trying to get some antler Christmas pieces to stores in the next couple weeks, but I will send Pic's of mammoth carving as soon as I can. Let me know when you think the order will get here. Thanks

David Bodine

Dave is not in a hurry. I can get his order out when I am not busy. There are no tracking numbers, and the word 'scam,' has not been put in the dictionary yet. Small time suppliers deal one on one with customers. Customers become friends. *A Donovan song!* Yes! "Do you remember when" *Fishes were caught for to fry.* An over-all message of days when people stopped to talk, sat on the beach around fires fishing, they had time, *Do you recall? Miss those days?* "Written way back in the 60's!" *So, yes, we not only remember, we are doing something about it, choosing such a life.*

Another email and another and another, for a total of twenty-two emails today. It takes five hours to get through them. One takes a while to reply to. This is an ongoing interest in living as I do, with me helping out. I get this request often.

Miles

Thank you very much for that. I want to reassure you of some facts. Firstly: I appreciate that a man's hard won solitude is a precious thing-and I never want to impinge upon yours. Secondly, I am aware that I am asking for a lot as I am a complete stranger to you. How I would want to play it is to just leave you with the idea-let's both think more about it.

I like your cabin suggestion very much and I feel that it strikes me as making quite some sense. If I could build you up a good cabin it would make me feel that I had gone some way towards earning the right to learn from you. I am not a builder and I would want to do the job right for you. Could you recommend someone who might be able to come out to do the job? I would labor for them at no cost in wages. It would be interesting to get a handle on how much it might cost concerns the generator-do not worry, I would not put 2 in 1 oiled gas into it! I have a small farm here in Scotland and use a large lumber chainsaw regularly for my firewood.

I will not be loading my own ammunition, but will bring in buying stuff. I will not be firing off loads of the stuff anyway. Nevertheless the issues you raise are very serious and I am going into this with both eyes open. It is very important to me that you do not feel beholden here in any way. I am very grateful for your response and would like for us to just take the time to potentially work something out that keeps you happy, does not waste your time and also helps me to learn the basics. I am a fast and determined learner and know when to be quiet and to respect other people's space and privacy.

I spent my formative years on The Hebridiean Island of Mull. In Scotland the culture is not about brashness. Anyway-if you could get those building costs to me it would be helpful.

Please remember that you are not committed in any way here. Let's just take some time to think through things. If we came to a plan of action I would come out to meet you first. No matter how good the deal-if you find me a pain in the neck (to put it politely) it is not going to work! Look forward to our next contact-and thank you very much, for coming back to me so swiftly.

Kind Regards
Guy

Next email

I am a collector of skulls as well as whale material in that I am a neurosurgeon and am interested in unusual skulls. Any skulls from whales or walrus or vertebrae. I would also be interested in mammoth tusks.

Charles Rawlings

Hello,
I am looking to sell some beautiful ivory pieces. They are already carved. My friend died and left me his ivory.

Hi Miles,
Nice work. I have a store in St. John's, Newfoundland and I'm interested in mammoth tusk that I can cut into smaller pieces and sell in my store. I'm also interested in wholesale pricing for your jewelry in mammoth tusk. I'm assuming there is not a problem shipping this in Canada?

I'd love to hear from you soon as we are gearing up for the tourist season here.

Thanks,
Nikki McGie

Mumbo Jungle
HEY MILES,
Did the money get there? I sent it last Friday like I said I was going to do.
LATER,

The usual variety of emails makes the business interesting. *Imagine living in a place called Mumbo? Do you suppose people there mumble?* A long reply to the guy who wants to live like me, and wants me to help him be my neighbor in the wilds, so he can pump me for information and learn from me. I know or assume he means well.

The mind wanders *Not just business email. There are some personal emails going on!* I have a file of women I am writing. Some come and go. I think it is over. Then hear again, then hear from someone new, then I hear from no one. Right now there is Bev, Vickie, Jodee...and speaking of which, here is a new email from Jodee.

No miles
i am not there...i am still here...and still recovering...:((here—colorado. sorry it didn't work out with vicky...sorta...lol yes i met the pilot...a cutie but a no go...i am wayyyy too bold for him...lol...he is a lot like you but doesn't smile or laugh much...and i love a good giggle...:-) but he is nice and will be good for someone a little softer than me...

And the latest goes in her file. I glance over our previous correspondence before writing. Guessing it was over a year we have been friends. Maybe we both thought off and on, we could work out a relationship. I'm not as optimistic as I once was. I drifted off into a fantasy world. I accept that fantasy as reality now. Who could ever plug into that? Still, I smile, and sort of wonder, sort of hope, as I read over some of her past words …

hi miles....
cool pic...wish i was that fox...you holding me by the tail...lol...but still alive of course...yep...still in colorado...well..i wish you would accept my friends list request so we could chat live...i won't overwhelm you or consume your life and/or your sleep you know...:-)
laters, xo

This refers to a new method of live chat on the internet in real time. It's a new idea. However, there are various complications. One is that with dial up slow internet connection, it's probably not going to work. Then something about dropping my computer security, while something I do not understand is installed in my computer. I have not accepted all the new aspects of loss of privacy in this upcoming computer age. I'm not about to drop my security to let a company in, I am trying not to let in, 'some big business I know nothing about.' This is exactly why I want security to begin with Da!

I'd also prefer to think about what I want to say first. Jodee is about my age, but looks younger. Long blonde hair, thin, good looking. She seems outgoing, honest, feisty. One picture she sent is of her wrestling a big alligator in Florida. A staged picture, but a real alligator. Makes her look very athletic and outdoorsy. I look at more of her words.

Almost everyone is looking for love—who wouldn't be?!!!Why haven't you found someone yet?

The main reason might be that I spent twenty-five years alone in the wilderness and had other priorities beyond a woman. Taking care of sled dogs is very time consuming.

Jodee? Well, for all her talk, she does not seem ready and willing to move. She asked me to make her a piece of jewelry, but would not give me her address. I assume she has had trouble with stalkers, or guys she could not get rid of. Someone who does not trust me enough to tell me where she lives is not someone ready to commit to.

Highway Excitement by Miles

Dawn and Miles represented Nenana at this year's 'Highway Companions' annual meeting in Talkeetna, May 7th and 8th. This is a meeting of people from communities who have highway tourism on their mind. We let each other know about our community, and what we offer so others can pass it along. We exchange ideas, facts, and brainstorm. There are guest speakers who are people we all need to have an in with. The DOT, the Railroad, the park policy makers, heads of tourism, marketing groups, the Milepost magazine and those who talk to thousands of tourists every season. This is a great way to get a handle on the big picture. Did you know, for example, that there is a fast growing interest in bird watching! People are paying lots of money to come all the way to Alaska to see a bird? (Boy! Have we got a deal for you!) Did you know the average Mobile home driver to Alaska is forty-six and makes fifty-six grand a year (fascinating!) Did you know 50,000 cars went through Tok last season and 70,000 people signed the Fairbanks guest book? Did you know the guy to talk to about scenic road grants has two pet goats-and one poked him in the eye?

We heard of several grants Nenana might qualify for. There is a web site to go to that has updated road conditions for travelers, and lists construction areas, forest fire reports, even accident updates. We can put a link on our web site to this. Copper Center made a brochure that is mostly a great big map of the state. He said we could have a zillion of them—for free. We talked to and got to know really important people like Dan and Murph and Toni and Karen—and can connect the dots from them to their jobs—the head of tourism—head of parks—DOT-The railroad …

I get interrupted. Life goes on. There are things to do to make a living, like dinner! Moose meat again. I seem to never get tired of it. Well, when I have 500 pounds of meat, it can end up being two pounds a day for a year. There is fresh lettuce from the garden, but no tomatoes yet. Not till about fair time. I make a lot of stir fry because it is easy. Chop up a bunch of stuff and toss it in my iron skillet. There is a single element electric stove now. Potatoes, onions, moose meat, and my own parsley, chives and turnip tops. I toss in some pepper, fresh garlic and fresh chopped ginger, then set a lid on. Takes about five minutes. No, I never eat anything out of a can, nor ever in my life cooked a frozen dinner. Maybe frozen pizza, but always add fresh stuff to it. All the bean meals are my own pressure cooked beans. I freeze the extra for instant meals later.

There is no washer or dryer for clothes. I go to the laundromat, and hardly notice the change going in the machine. My 1916 log cabin home looks like a hobbit house, tucked in behind huge lilac bushes.

This is the year I finally got Fish and Wildlife to send a representative to the Highways Companion meeting to give a workshop for those in tourism, educating us on legal crafts we can sell, and under what conditions. We get to ask specific question we have all wondered about. We find out that whale baleen does not have to be signed by a native or turned into a craft to be sold, just cleaned. However, there can be a shipping, exporting out of the state problem. An individual who has a receipt from the shop can carry it as a personal item not for resale across Canada, or to most countries.

Issues our shops have heard of from customers involve loss of receipt, customs not knowing the law, or someone lying and trying to resell the baleen later. Now we know what to pass on to the customer. We learned that anything fossil can be sold, shipped without restrictions, no receipt, proof, or permits. Including fossil walrus ivory. This information dispels rumors going around contrary to this. I feel good to have someone in the know come and talk to us, and get the truth out. Instead of discussing among ourselves, arguing, wondering, acting on rumors, now we have it right out of the horse's mouth.

Crazy Lawson, one of my neighbors stops in after I eat. He sees my left over dinner and comments on eating well, leading to growing, hunting our own foods. Lawson lives in Nenana with no running water, in a one room home that used to be a boat. Crazy reminds me of a back hills mountain recluse. He is tall, skinny, long beard, wearing a worn out floppy felt hat. What stands out the most is the patch he wears over one eye. Crazy is a subsistence person who believes in taking care of himself. He is the type who knows how to snare rabbit, make his own fish net, his own snowshoes, and does not like to be told what to do. He's a stoner, so appears not to be very bright, due to the fogged mind, slow far away speech.

"Miles you need a partner again at the boneyard?" The first time did not go well, and a second time was not much better.

I joke, "No, you'd find all the mammoth tusks and I'd feel bad." The conversation turns to regulating how we live and our rights to take care of ourselves.

Crazy tells me, "You know the government does not like us to be self sufficient. The government wants us dependent and needy. The government wants us all someplace where it is easy to keep an eye on us. Being alone out in the wilds, without being able to keep tabs on us, combined with being able to live, even get ahead, is not good for the government."

I have heard this before, and from a lot of people I know. I add, "I do agree subsistence is not wanted, and eventually will disappear. It has now become an Indian only issue, I feel this is about 'divide and conquer,' as has been done for a long time." Crazy knows what I mean. In the past there was a large group of subsistence people that included white homesteaders along with the Indians.

"Miles, subsistence is being legally defined as 'poor,' so it means you qualify for welfare, food stamps, energy assistance, fuel oil programs, weatherization help, and such. It's hard to turn down free stuff."

Crazy asks if I heard about Salina?

"Yes, Lawson, Salina Alexander, I know her all right. Gifted Native artist, very good businesswoman, sober, hard working, and smart. One of the finest examples of her Athabascan people. Got arrested for selling bear claws in her jewelry." Up till now, it was only illegal for white people. This is the first time a Native gets arrested for craft items using animal parts. Of interest to me, because I predicted this would happen. I talked to her after, and she told me she could not afford a lawyer to fight it, so was forced to plea bargain. She was disappointed the Native Corporation would not back her up and provide a lawyer to fight for Native rights. She is someone who included me, when using the term 'we.' She feels the native corporation is making political deals with the white government, not looking out for her people like it should. By pleading guilty, Salina does not have to go to jail, but pays thousands in fines and a new legal precedence is set. In this way the rights get eroded, one part of subsistence at a time.

"Yes, Miles," Crazy adds. "Because the corporations depend on federal grants, and can't go against those who have it in their power to cut the funding source off. That now includes Native corporations."

I'm reminded of an email I got from a fan. I relate a story to Crazy, "You know how to tame and control wild pigs?" Crazy wants to know what that has to do with the subject at hand. I tell him to be patient. Someone new in the USA, from someplace like Guam, is asked how he likes his new freedoms in the U.S.! His reply was to ask the one questioning, if they knew how they domesticate wild pigs in Guam.

So it goes like this:

"First, you begin to put food out in the woods for these wild pigs. At first, they are nervous and do not touch it. It is easy food, so eventually they come to the easy free food source, as birds come to the feeder. Soon all the wild pigs in the area are coming to this one food source.

After a week or so, you put one wall up near the food. Again, the pigs hesitate, stay away a few days. 'This looks different!' The pigs do not understand, but it seems harmless enough. So they ignore the one wall and feed again, nothing changes, so it must be OK.

Then another wall goes up! The same deal, and a third wall goes up, and it takes a little longer. Eventually, the pigs go in this three sided contraption to feed. A fourth wall is made with a gate. This takes the longest to get used to. However, now the pigs like this feed, it's free, they are getting fat, lazy, and dependent. So they walk in the corral and the trapper pulls the gate shut. The pigs are not happy at first, but, 'Oh well.' They calm down. Someone is feeding them. Life is good.

They are now domesticated pigs." *Till it is time for the slaughter.*

Crazy does not need the story. He has his own version. So we change the subject —sort of—but not really. "So, Miles, do you still get to the boneyard for ivory?"

I'm reluctant to offer up any facts or information. This is not like the old days. Crazy might even be working undercover as a snitch, looking for a reward, part of a plea bargain if he got caught at something. *Probably not*, "but why take a chance?" He knows he should not be referring to a specific area we used to go to, now illegal to fossil hunt in. I have to get to new areas now, and not going to tell Crazy about the Cosna. If I say "Yes, the boneyard," he might offer to go with me, and to avoid that…Well, Lawson, I get down there now and then, but more to hunt and fish, visit people on the river I know. I have been going there for years. Over these years I have met a lot of people. I have permission from a lot of miners and natives who have subsurface land rights. As you know, this is the legal way to get fossil ivory. Not off public lands, as the bone yard is. So in my many miles of river travel, and my knowledge of how to find fossils, I check out these places. I still find tusks here and there in these legal places." I add as an afterthought, "These people give permission only if I travel alone and give out no information."

Crazy does not believe me. We have known each other a long time. Long ago, maybe as friends. Crazy is the sort you'd stereotype as running a still in the Beatles song, 'Rocky Raccoon.' (Whose woman went out with another man and Rocky didn't like that and shot out the legs of his rival.) I zero in on how knowledgeable he is concerning backwoods lore. I get my poplar pitch mixed with bear grease salve from Crazy. *Good for cuts and rashes!* I do not hate or totally disrespect Crazy, I see it as simply plugged into reality, and accept it. Crazy will not leave this alone. He is not getting the hint.

"Like where?" he asks sarcastically.

I am not about to give specifics where I go. *This is what I mean, getting demanding and unfriendly.* It's a multi-thousand dollar business. Big money has its own sets of problems. If Crazy tells others, someone might decide to follow me. I reply, "As you know, it is legal to get ivory off a patent mine, but even so, the university can shut down an area as an archeological site if there is anything of public interest. No one wants their land confiscated and turned into a museum's dig." I review what we both know, and have talked about over a lot of years, and agree on. Yes, I have heard of issues coming up. All of us in the business have.

Several employees at Fort Knox Mine have talked with me, done business with me over a lot of years. I'm convinced employees are told not to keep any fossils, or tell anyone what is found. They are ordered to bury tusks and say nothing. Bulldozer operators have told me they turned up tusks, even complete skeletons, and have run them over and buried them, by orders of the mine owner, their boss. I consider this a crime that angers me. To destroy something of such value, in such large amounts, while our country cries for a better economy, more jobs, more resources. I'm hurt and disgusted. Museums cry how these fossils are rare, desired, need to go on display and not sold.

"I'd love to keep one, Miles! Or supplement my income by selling fossils. It seems a shame to break them up, destroy them, and rebury them. But it's not worth getting fired, getting caught." Crazy has similar stories, as well as our local buyer, Tusk. It's considered 'common knowledge' among 'us' local residents.

"Lawson, I had a Fort Knox worker sneak a tusk out she found, and get it to me. She hired me to restore it. She could not bear to have such a piece of history destroyed." Fort Knox takes the university threat seriously. So does Jack in Eureka. "He told me he had to go to court once, to prove the fossils found on one of his mines are of little archeological interest." All of us know how much time and money court costs. That guy we both deal with, the bank owner in Fairbanks, the big collector whose name we never use, has told us some of his sources have been cut off due to the university.

"Whatever, Miles. It's old news, tell me something I do not know! We all know the university is not about the preservation of knowledge, good will or education. But control!"

Yea, whatever. Crazy has his silly grin and that eyepatch. I may or may not agree, what does it matter? People who keep talking like this end up as 'persons of interest' and anyhow, my observation is, good things do not happen to complainers.

"Lawson, the only way I am given permission by land owners, is if I promise to keep my mouth shut about where, who, when and such details. So if people think I still go to the boneyard, it is to my advantage. They will not try hard to discover any other place I might be going, since it is illegal to get ivory there, they will not want to follow me or get involved. I then become one of the few sources."

"Well, Miles, the joke would be to get arrested based on such a rumor! Ha!" I do not laugh with him. I think again, Crazy is someone who would turn me in if he had proof. I wonder, *Could I get convicted on no facts, just a rumor?*

"Maybe, but how far can that get if it's simply not the truth? So I'd be OK if it ever went to court." Sometimes I have my doubts. Like the Salina case. Arrested, but no trial. *How many cases these days ever get to trial?* "There are hardly any trials. There is plea bargaining." Pleading guilty to more than you did, so you can get a tiny fine, told not to do it again, and in return the government gets a new precedence set, closer to making what they wish to accomplish, legal. Meaning I may never have the chance to clear myself, if arrested. Crazy knows this happened once before to me. I was charged with selling a $5 bear claw, an owl claw, an ivory box I made, all turned into art, facing up to fifteen years in prison.[3]

For now, I do not know a better way to handle this present situation. It's the first thing I get asked about whenever I have ivory. "From the boneyard, right? I heard of that place!" If I simply smile and say nothing—what's the harm in that? If I say, "Well actually, No. I have another legal place I go…" They are all ears, want details, and word is out, "There's legal places to get mammoth tusks Miles knows about!" Followed by local questions, who do I know, where do I go, who has seen me, and where. Lots of curiosity. Maybe even in the public news.

"How can I do what Miles is doing and make that kind of easy money!" I've already met people who told me they invested in a boat for no other reason than to duplicate what I do. They bought the exact boat and engine I have, so they can be like me. *Twenty grand in ivory for a day's work is great incentive.* If these people want to go someplace illegally, they risk getting caught, so not in competition with me anymore. It's a bit like prospectors being reluctant to let anyone know exactly where the gold is, or how much gold, or your favorite fishing hole. *Or, heck, even big oil companies keep their cards close to the chest when it comes to new finds! We all send people off on a wild goose chase. Or if the news media and public wishes to wrongly speculate, why not play along?*

"It's difficult to separate fact from fiction, from the truth, from possible, from not likely, from total fantasy."

"And the government likes it that way, Miles, you bet! The more we wonder, do not know, and are afraid of what might be possible, the better for the Gestapo government. It's all about fear!" I hate to buy into that totally, but I do see one thing I agree with. If everything is going fine, we the people tend not to need big government. So it is not to the government's advantage for everything to be fine. Government grows and gets bigger, the more problems there are.

The masses tend to panic and say, "Please government, help us, protect us!" from crime, floods, rapists, drunks, guns, bad food, global warming, and on and on.

"Thank you!" When the government has a plan in place. When the media tells us of some scary event, statistics show evil is on the rise, the government shows up to the rescue, demands more branches of the government to cover new levels of protection. When money is tight, it is the services we depend on and need that get threatened. 'No money for fire protection, ambulance, need to cut these off to meet the budget cuts!' It's rarely about cutting their own salary, getting rid of the personal jets, packing a lunch, or eating at less spendy places for travel meals or sharing rooms.

Crazy adds, "No! it is all about someone else making a sacrifice, Miles!"

I am just not sure to what lengths the government will go to actually create chaos and fear. In the same way I have suspected Norton Anti-virus of creating computer threats and the next day, selling the cure.

It is, in fact, about time to plan another trip for mammoth tusks. *Not that I'd tell Crazy.* I feel somewhat like Clark Kent, or Indiana Jones. By day, some flunky boring life, sitting at a computer like a drone. Blending in with the sheep. Little does the world know, I smile at the thought.

Seymour does not have survey work for me this season. None. We talked off and on about quitting. I should totally depend on my artwork now, and raw materials business. No more paying into Social Security or unemployment. No guaranteed cash from an employer.

There is a rototiller for the garden, and the greenhouse is more fixed up. An automatic water system is perfected, so I can take off for weeks at a time without the garden going bonkers.

City water is easier to deal with than when I had a well with low pressure rusty water. There are five crab apple trees that I hope to graft edible apples to one day. I call all this part of my subsistence life, 'depending on the land.' Part of the boating trip is to look for berries and catch some fish, also part of dependence on the land life. Over the years, I know where wild edibles can be harvested during different seasons of the year. I have favorite mushroom patches, and a place to get wild mint for tea. The boat gets me to these places. Two chest freezers keep half a year's food. In winter, the power is shut off, but summer months I have to run the electric. It might be cheaper to buy food...but like the wild pig story. *Is easier always better?*[4]

I enjoy the reward of growing, the pride of doing it myself. The confidence that comes with having done it. It's not a dream—wondering if. Some of it is 'boring' in terms of, "And what did you do today Miles?"

"Weeded a garden." Wow. Still, I smile. I love the smell of the dirt, the birds going in and out of the birdhouses I built. We have violet swallows. *They eat their body weight in mosquitoes every day!* There are three nesting pairs in the yard. Juncos show up, and some chickadees. Ravens hang out at the tops of the trees. What characters! Ha! How entertaining!

Just yesterday, I heard banging on my roof. I paused in wonder. I hear a similar noise at the other end of the house. I'm more puzzled. "Bang, bang," pause, "scratch, scratch." Sound repeated at the other end of the house. This happened three times. I go out the front door with a frown, string up at my roof-top. Two ravens— one at each end of the roof—jump up and laugh, as they fly away."Made you look!"

The other replies,"Haw Haw!"

I answer in their language and wave. "Clack, Clack."

There is a reason Natives call this one the trickster. They can do damage and steal things. I suspect they know that, because ravens and I joke with each other, but not do damage or hurt each other. Why is this, when other people tell me trash cans get knocked over and invaded, food stolen, on and on. Never me. *Is it because I talk to them in a happy voice?* My mind goes back to survival and food storage.

There are others in the community with similar interests. At the Wellness meeting I go to each week, we exchange seeds we saved from last year, and share garden knowledge. The community being self sufficient is part of our discussion. In case there is an earthquake that cuts off the only road into the community or wipes out the bridge. We have in fact had forest fires, floods, and earthquakes, that temporarily cut us off.

Federal grants are getting smaller. It is good to look to ourselves for help. There is a community rototiller, a big one, and a community garden we can all share. There are shared seeds, free water and tools left for any of us to use if we have none. I did volunteer work on the community greenhouse so we have a permanent covering on it. We all chip in. That is a good part of our community. We take care of each other— sort of—well more so than many places!

Some argue indignantly they accept no hand outs! Pay their own way in life! Look down on those who do not! Insult those who live off the rest of us! I try to kindly point out what they say is not the truth. I ask, "Can our community of 300 really pay the teachers and the bills at the school? Do 300 of us really take care of the post office and all its costs? Or maintain the roads, or the airport runway? Or our own electric power?" *I think not! Dream on!* "That is all being paid for by tax dollars from larger communities subsidizing us. If not, for sure outside money." I personally do not care for this, would prefer we learn to live within our means. It would mean a drastic step down in most of our lifestyles! We'd have a one room school, with one teacher for example. We'd have dirt roads. The post office could be as in some villages, the store or library. We'd all have wells and septic systems, or pay for delivery and pick up. Few of us would live that way, and step that far down. But that is what it would take to get what we pay for, and live within our means. When money gets tight, and those in the big city say they do not want to subsidize life in rural areas, I think they have the right to say that, and are correct!

"I have no right to demand even a dime of your money." It's offered, we gratefully accept it. That works. *Usually with strings attached.* "Is it good to demand this standard of living, depend on it, as a right?" I think about these things as I pack my boat for the river trip. On my mind, because here I am creatively figuring out how to pay my own way in a world with few job opportunities.

An example just came to mind. Nenana talked about holding drag car races on the runway, like we did in the old days as a community fund raiser, to attract racers from Fairbanks. Our community is in the unique situation of owning our own airport and runway. "There is no legal qualifier drag strip anywhere in Alaska. No drag strips are long enough. So if an Alaskan racer wants to qualify for serious racing outside, there is no place in the state. Nenana could offer that! Our runway meets the requirement!" It was the subject of many city meetings, the formation of a subcommittee resulted, with expected races calculated to be worth $30,000 a weekend. A lot of money to a community of 300. This amount is promised us by the Racing Lions in Fairbanks, looking for a place to race.

But the FAA said, "No. Nenana accepted grant money to repave the runway. If you hold drag races, you must return the multi million dollars spent, because drag racing will ruin the runway." It never ruined it in the past. Landing planes does more damage. An average of one plane a day lands on our runway. Money could be set aside as part of the cost to maintain the runway, fix any damage. But no.

We know a drag track was offered to Fairbanks, and the racers want this to get built, but has hold-ups. Nenana would take business away if we built the track first. Nenana could build and run the track cheaper due to lower land value, fewer restrictions and permits, like not being in a borough or having city taxes. Racing Lions is interested. Nenana is not in a position to outmaneuver the bigger Fairbanks. One more aspect of a small community life is lost.

"No drag racing on the runway!" We used to mud bog out in one of the swamps. This used to draw a huge statewide crowd. Now it is called a wetland that can't be disturbed. Fine. Some duck might get excited. But the entire interior of the state is wetlands, an area the size of Texas. We mud bog on 100 feet of it, and it helps us pay our bills big time, and be independent. I would address 'Joe public,' if I could, "Instead of mud bogging and supporting ourselves, you, the taxpayer in the big city. subsidize us, the hick community that can't take care of itself. Protecting one duck family is costing millions. Does that make sense?"

Are you an idiot, don't you get it! I've lost respect for the public. The average citizen is brainwashed, and scary in its decision making. I can think of better ways to spend millions of dollars. I struggle to be happy in a brave new world with such thinking in it. Were the British correct, citizens are incapable of governing themselves and only royalty and the educated should run things? *Which is already happening anyway?* "Are you referring to the fact big companies can come destroy wetlands all they want?" J*oe public swears it does not happen?* "We know better, seen firsthand what gas exploration is doing in the area, right now, as we speak." *Ra Ra the big boys need oil! The heck with a poor community trying to pay it's own bills.* No I am not going to dwell on this. To what purpose? Me and who else will change the world? "Ha!" *Yes, be happy, enjoy life, count our blessings. The beauty of Nature is still out there!*

NEW to my gear on the boat is my laptop computer! *Ha! Survival gear not of the 1800's.* I have a small inverter for my twelve volt outlet that makes power for the laptop. I can work on my book, on email replies to customers out on the river, with swans flying overhead, sand under my feet.

I pack some art for the village stores in Manley, Minto, Tanana, and Ruby. They usually buy a couple hundred dollars worth. Not a ton of money, but it might buy my gas. I have an electric cooler for fish I get. This all ends up being fifty pounds of goods. *Quite a bit more than the old days!* "However, in the old days I was often over-loaded, trying to get supplies someplace." *Building materials, all my food etc.* I hardly ever traveled empty, or close to light, so that has not changed a lot. I substitute the homestead supplies for comforts. I feel a little guilty, but remind myself, in the 1800's mountain man life, I'd be dead by now. There would have been no recovery from a broken back. Modern surgery fixed it, and modern medicine fixes high blood pressure and diabetes. *The good news of this day and age is, being able to still get out on the river in comfort as a free man.*

I started off in the 1970's with a ten horse engine, then a twenty-five horse, then a fifty horse and now a sixty horse! I'll have 100 gallons of gas on board, to cover 700 or more miles of wilderness. *In my early years, such a trip took all summer.* As gas is siphoned into the tank, I get back to my thoughts about subsistence and self suffi-ciency, compared to the city and costs and such. My thoughts go to the post office, since I just checked the mail.

The postmaster is telling me about changing a light bulb. "I can't do it myself! The post office sends someone from Fairbanks, a 100 mile round trip, to bring me a bulb. Then he is the specialist authorized to change it." We both speculate what that cost!

I add, "Yea, and maybe the guy has to eat here, and even can't make it back, and has to spend a night in the lodge." We laugh how it might cost $1,000 to change a light bulb. Meanwhile, the post office cries to the public about hard times, and rising costs, the price of a stamp is going up again. The inefficiency being passed on to the public rather than getting fixed. I have little sympathy.

The post office also sent its own crew to paint the post office. We were not allowed to take care of that locally. The store could have donated paint, volunteer locals would have painted. Zero cost to the public or post office.The high class post office with all its computers and high tech stuff, seems to me to be overkill for a community of 300. No wonder the post office is hurting for money and going bankrupt. Could any of us run our business like this and make it work? In earlier days I can recall, in small villages, we got our mail at the village store. There would be some small amount of government money to help the store. The rent, insurance, heat, electric, employee costs would all be covered under part of the store costs and absorbed. Thus affordable. The community was actually happier gathering at the store getting our mail, compared to a government building full of government rules. "No guns, no loitering, no getting anyone else's mail, no putting notes in others box, no favors. All about following big city Federal rules that do not apply here."

The postmaster says, "I heard in the news, US scientists figured out how to get a ball point pen to work in outer space in zero gravity! That was quite an accomplishment that took a million dollars."

I read that article too, and add the rest of the story.

"Yea, while the Russians solved the problem with a pencil." I do not want to hang around exchanging government waste problems and jokes. I have enough to do running my own life efficiently and getting it to work.

So, yes, I like taking care of myself in the woods. None of this nonsense is going on. Boating keeps me sane, keeps the blood pressure within reason, gives me hope for the survival of the planet, allows me to forgive mankind for its mistakes, and encourages me to be as good a person as I can be.

All gassed up, have my thermos with hot stew for lunch, my fishing pole, my ivory hunting tools-like my tonker stick. It's a ski pole with steel tip for poking things I think might be a fossil. I can tell by the sound of a tap. I have hose clamps to clamp a tusk, so it does not crack. An ice pick, Elmer's glue which a put on a wet tusk to seal it. There is a tarp and plastic bags. I carry some climbing gear, but do not know how to use it, and never needed it. I have my rifle because last time I had to shoot a tusk in half that I could not reach, and the visible half fell off the cliff. I'm not sure how many tusks I have found in my life. *More than I can count?* "No, just not dwelling on it." Maybe five to six—maybe eight or so. *It's better to be vague anyhow.* "Yea. It's better not to recall." *Naturally I tell the IRS about the cash with no receipts, and pay the appropriate taxes to support…bla, bla…*

MANLEY HOT SPRINGS is a favorite stop on the way to the Cosna River. I get to Manley by river, but it is also the end of the road through the mountains. I spent a year or two here with my houseboat long ago, and have been coming here ever since. I met Karen and the kids here. I used to dog mush, and pick up my mail here. I have some good memories. Mike, the postmaster used to give me a hard time, but he is old, a different person these days. *I'm told 'happier' because he has a better woman now.* I sell a few of my books, and some art to the store. I trade a book for a meal at the lodge.

I could stay with Seymour in his guest cabin, but prefer not to. I'd want to cut wood to replace wood I put in the stove, and I'd use his propane, need to change the bed sheets and clean up. I feel more comfortable staying in my tent. Seymour is away right now, anyhow. I know where the key is and am invited, but the tent I set up is in sight of the lodge. There is a $5 camping fee. I do not mind paying, since there is an outhouse, a campfire, wood pile, a nicely kept mowed lawn in a very scenic location on the hot water slough. This campground is next to the boat launch, so I can park the boat and visit with others I know, who have boats. I discovered over time I get treated better, with more respect when I walk into the lodge compared to 'long ago.'

"I'm spending the night at the campgrounds, here's my $5, thanks!" Because it's a loose situation, and no one really checks, many locals would use the grounds and not pay. It's more for 'tourists,' to pay. I could get away with not paying, but am more respected for contributing.

I overhear some visiting tourists at the campground, talking about being disappointed not getting any fish.

"You guys want a couple of pike? I ate a burger at the lodge and the fish will taste better fresh, I'd rather not hold them till tomorrow." I did not tell them I have a cooler, but in truth, the cooler is overfilled with fish I got at Rock Creek.

"Wow, thanks a lot, for sure?" All excited. I hope it gives them a good memory of their trip to Alaska, and its friendly people.

There is a place nearby I sometimes find mammoth tusks, but I have to go up a creek a long way. I also usually ask at the lodge if any miners are around. I know most of them, and can ask if they have a tusk to sell they got at the mine. The standard going price is $25 a pound. I usually offer $30. I can sell it for at least $60 a pound, but sometimes as much as $100 a pound in Tucson at the big show. I have to remind myself of the high cost of getting a tusk to Tucson, and cost of setting up to sell. *This can be into thousands of dollars.*

I can think of no one around here who thinks it is wrong to get tusks off the river or off a gold mine, and sell them. Locals have been doing it about forever. All of 'us,' are survivors who know how to make a buck. There has never, to my knowledge, been an issue where someone ruined the land getting a tusk. We find them in the mud visually. No one digs for them except miners looking for gold, with fossils being a side business. *It is true though, no one else but me from around here is targeting this as a business.* "Others simply stumble on a tusk and sell to the local buyer, Tusk. Or now, to me."

"There's no environmental reason to find fault with mammoth hunting, Miles! The government has gone nuts!" One miner tells me at the bar in the lodge. There are five others in the bar.

I do not drink, but it is common here to eat your meal in the bar while visiting. The community is not big enough to have a separate place to eat. A record moose rack is on the wall behind me. A huge black wolf hide hangs near a barrel wood stove. Old antique mine equipment, and fossil finds lay around on window sills and ledges. It's a tourist attraction, and looks much like a scene out of the TV show, Northern Exposure. There are a lot of elderly, retired people in rich looking homes, mixed in with miners, trappers and natives that come and go from here.

There is no form of government in Manley. No taxes, no police, no fire protection, no road work done.

Seymour once commented, "We, as a group, decided we'd like a community well house for water. So we passed the hat and came up with enough money to build us a building and put in a well." Not complicated. "It is in fact possible to exist and function without Big Brother's guidance."

Manley Hot Springs is not within any borough, so no community taxes of any kind on any level. This alone makes Manley a unique place. I think there are seventy residents here. Mail is picked up at the store. The school is small, with two teachers. The runway is dirt, and several friends, including Seymour, keep their planes tied up on the runway free of charge. Float planes are tied up in the hot water slough at the docks they built themselves, no fee. There are zero 'no trespassing' signs. No 'keep out' or banners advertising along the roads. Seymour makes the point, "People do not need to be watched, regulated, protected, ordered around, taken care of, Miles. The average person is descent, hard working, sane, honest, willing to take care of themselves, help others, and smart enough to make their own decisions." He pauses to make a comparison he thinks about, "Where in civilization, the government teaches citizens, we are all stupid, unable to make decisions, need help, protection, rules, police, instructions, signs telling us where to go, not to go."

I get his point. I see the difference between one option, the choice to live here like this, and other choices to live other ways someplace else. "But change is in the wind, Miles. I see the direction the world is headed." I understand what he means.

"Nenana used to be like Manley, within my memory." He only nods. I feel good here, relaxed, comfortable, somewhat safe. "A lot of my kind of people here." I'm thinking to myself, *If I ever had to go to court I'd want someone on a jury from here. My peers.* I'm guessing my blood pressure drops while here. *Nenana is a nice place as well, for different reasons. Nenana has access to both the wilds and civilization. Life costs less in Nenana. I have internet, easy trips to Fairbanks, health clinic, lower home costs…*

"Hi, Miles, haven't seen you in a while. Have a good trip on the river? I see you got a new four stroke sixty horse." One of the elder Natives from here, I have known many years, addresses me. Frin sits next to me.

His wife has Eggs, cooking today at the road house. He is Athabascan, and does 'this and that,' vague answer to"What do you do for a living, Frin?"

"Some guiding, taking tourists out on boat trips, trapping, mining, commercial fishing." A shrug of the shoulders, meaning, 'whatever comes up.' A respected hard worker of many talents. Frin is also on the Federal Subsistence Game board. I admire him a great deal.

"Had a good trip, Frin. This sixty is quiet, good on gas, lots of power. It seems worth the extra cost." We talk boat engines for a while. He reminds me once again, the story of how he found a complete saber tooth tiger skull!

"Eggs sold it at a garage sale for $10. Didn't know what it was. Yea, worth about 10 grand." We both laugh. Life can be like that.

Frin is a good person to ask what is going on, with the various changes in the game laws. "I don't know, Miles. I give up. I have asked the Board many times to define subsistence to me. I have not been given a good definition. If we can't define it, how can we regulate it?" Seems like a good point to me. He has told me before, but maybe forgot, as he repeats. "The 'sub' part of subsistence means 'beneath.' But this is not a lifestyle that is beneath other lifestyles." Frin may well be the only one on the Board who lives the lifestyle. Maybe the only Indian on the Board. He's fed up with not getting anywhere. I'm guessing there is a lot of politics going on. He suspects the same, but does not add any details. White man forked tongue stuff. This is not the sort of negativism Frin dwells on, he is more positive, offering more solutions than problems. He says again, "Well, you are a subsistence if anyone is, Miles!"

He is referring to the idea that this is becoming a 'Native only' issue. He's maybe the token Indian—token subsistence person, allowed to be on the Board to look good. But anyhow…

"Doing good fishing, Frin? I passed your place coming up the slough, and saw a lot of kings hanging." The king salmon run is on, and Frin is putting a lot of traditional dry strips up for the year.

"Yes, pretty good run this season, Miles. The law only gave us two days of fishing, but I have enough, maybe 2,000 fish." Yes, 2,000 fish in two days seems good. It used to take me a month with nets when I fished for sled dogs. I never targeted the King though. I caught chum, dog salmon, and the late fall Silver run. Frin can't sell any of this though, it is a subsistence fishing opening. Sometimes called 'personal use,' a little different from subsistence, in that, any local can get a free permit to catch salmon for their own needs. There is no limit on the number of fish. The limit is placed on time allowed to fish. I feel this method of control favors the rich, who can afford faster boats, and more efficient harvest equipment. Subsistence people, who tend to have small boats, using nets instead of wheels, will catch far fewer fish.

In a community without any police or law? It is not polite to ask how it all works. It takes a serious offense to get any law down here from Fairbanks, a four hour drive away, and not in anyone's jurisdiction. A little of this happens, a little of that. There are local ethics to go by. No need to get into details. *The big city with its government, permits, rules, regulations, is far away.* What matters here, is morals, protecting the environment, but balanced by the facts of life, of need. Most important, not to be wasteful. Bottom line being, anyone can look around this area and think, *Wow what a pretty place! So filled with nature, everyone in a good mood, a place that is living the good life that works.* Most viewers would compare this to where they live in civilization. Summed up, *Not like this.* Conclusion, *So what works and what does not?*

I MEET WITH A MINER PRIVATELY. It is understood no one wants it known exactly where mammoth tusks come from *because of the fear the university will be interested.* "Yea, Miles, I care about my gold! The heck with the ivory trade! That's pretty small potatoes to me. Ivory sales is a little diesel money for the dozer. I go through 100 gallons a day at the mine. Anyhow, I am not going to risk my gold over a tusk or two! Dang university anyhow. This is not about educational needs, but land grabs and power plays!" I have heard this before from many miners, so am not surprised at this line of talk. We have had a longtime understanding. Many, even 'most' miners see tusks, and just run over them, bury them, all broken, and say nothing to anyone, complying with the law. *I will not reveal who, where, when.*

"I can play a shell game with the tusks." I buy a little, trade a little, find a few. I cut most up because they are so damaged they cannot be made to look like a natural complete tusk. There is no legal requirement to tag them, record them, keep any records, or get any permits, etc. Once cut, and put in a common box, who would know what ivory came from where? It's legal to protect my sources. I'm asked how the rest of my business is going.

"I admire how you think and do business, Miles. You make a living dealing with the odds and ends the rest of us here toss out. I guess bones, teeth and claws that are common here, are rare in the city, and have a value, huh? Nothing I'd want to mess with. But glad you do, and are able to support yourself." At the core of a lifestyle all my peers believe in, is not supporting deadbeats. I have to think about that. *It certainly used to be so!* But the outlook seems to be changing, or maybe just my perception. As the economy fails, it seems to me the rich are getting richer, the poor, more poor, and the middle class is getting divided, moving either up or down, and disappearing.

"Or, Miles, consider there are more rich then ever in our history! The middle class is disappearing all right. It may have been the middle class you sold to in the past. Those still connected to the land, reality, ethics. Money was not their God. They respected animals and the environment. Did not believe in waste. They were close enough to being hungry to understand it. The new market has their nose in the air, never missed a meal, and cannot comprehend ever doing so. They have zero connection to the land. It's all about perfection, prestige, money."

"Maybe." I have no answer. This view seems to stereotype the rich. In truth, I have met some rich, ethical, together, good people. It is often the poor who are not educated, maybe more likely to have a narrow view of the world, and are often less connected to the land than the rich. "I meet inner city poor who have never seen a live tree before, not in their whole life." The conversation winds down. I yawn and dismiss myself. I do not have far to walk to the slough and my tent.

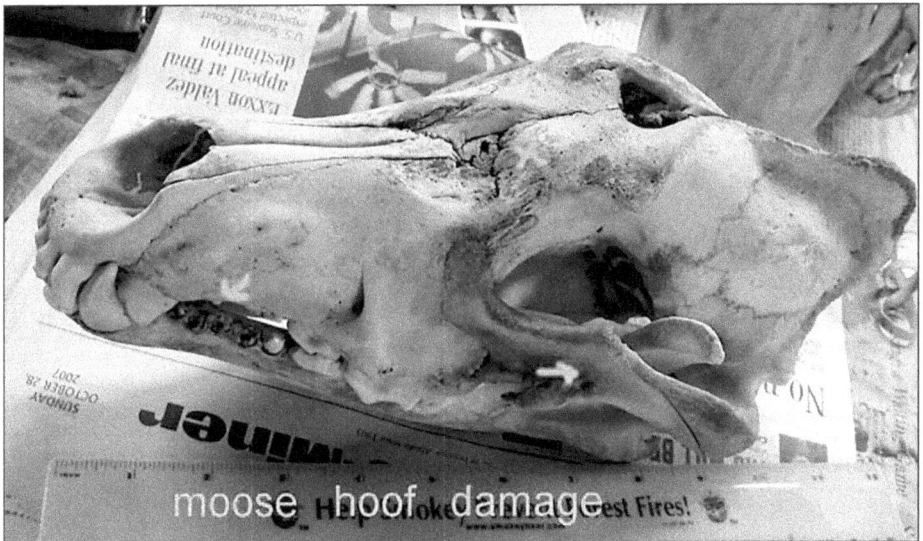

Wolf skull. Got kicked in the head by a moose and survived long enough for damage to heal.

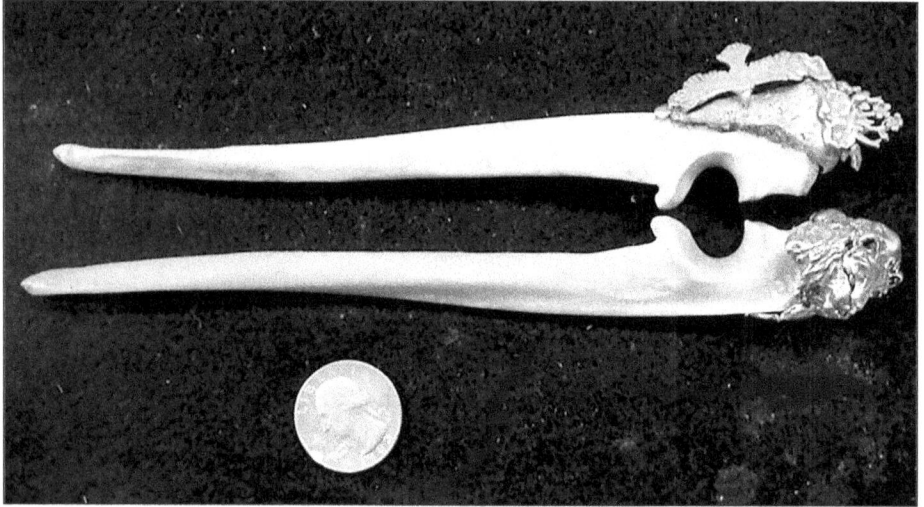

Hair sticks made from the bone that goes into the hoof of a moose.

CHAPTER FIVE

COMMUNICATE WITH THE EX AND SON, TOURISM, HEAD OF CHAMBER OF COMMERCE

In the morning I pack up the tent before having breakfast in the roadhouse. A handful of early rising fisherman in rubber boots covered in river silt are exchanging local gossip. After eating a meal served by Eggs, I head on out the six miles of slough to the main river, and on into the wilds. There are no roads beyond this point, a thousand miles to the ocean. Tonight I'll be in the native village of Tanana. More books and art are sold here. I have known the store owner in Tanana a long time. Paul, the husband, is one of the Starrs, a family name going way back. I knew Paul, and his father Al, when I was at Lake Minchumina for the winter trapping. I'd stop in the Starr cabin to visit, almost forty years ago. Now, he and his wife own a store. Bushy Charlie is still here, and some others I also knew many years ago. Paul looks much the same, with the face of a carved cigar store Indian. He is quiet, and does not say much.

One of the natives I know has some moose antler to sell me. Another has some grizzly bear claws to gift. I am used to a local dialect among some of the Natives.

"Yea, bear came fish camp, tore tent two nights row. Third night in the tent, bear get in. Shoot him." This is a typical story. I'm pretty sure no one kills bears just to acquire body parts. I hardly ever get claws from the same person twice, for one thing. So no one is trying to establish a business killing bears.

I reply, "Yea, I want to keep it subsistence. I sell parts of animals that were taken for food or self-defense by subsistence people, as much as I can." Now and then, guides I know end up with surplus body parts. A hide gets spoiled, some horns not big enough to mount, etc. I get a lot of wolf fangs from the tanner. The real ones get replaced with plastic in skulls he mounts. The real fangs usually crack, or are hard to take care of. In a rug, who is going to look with a magnifying glass at the fangs?

I buy some extra gas with the money I got from the books. Gas is $2 a gallon more than in civilization. It's easy to go through $300, just in gas, on one of my trips. This is one reason there are not very many people who live like I do, traveling like this. I tell my grizzly claw supplier, "Guess I'm glad, or OK with the high costs. It means only the serious are out here in the river. Gets rid of the competition!" The Athabascan laughs. He is used to complaints, not good words concerning high costs! We both have noticed, with fuel cost increases, fewer people on the river. The game populations have moved to the river. We both comment on more geese nesting on the river banks these days.

A stash is made of extra fuel, as well as antlers and other things that I can pick up on my way back home. This saves on weight I have to haul. I hit a rock pulling in to shore with the propeller. As bad luck would have it, a fin on the propeller is missing a third of its mass. I have to change propellers. *There goes another $150!* A cow moose with newborn calf is bedded down in the nearby willows, and jumps up when I pull in. I smile at seeing them. Nice blue sky, bright yellow sun, reddish willows, snow white capped mountains in the distance. A very post card view. *Or Van Gogh painting with the splashes of colors.* It is scenes like this that have a lot to do with loving to just get out on the river and enjoying it. I stand in shallow water, barefoot, with pants rolled up, changing the propeller, glancing at the view.

Frin, from Manley, has land on the Novi River. The Folgers have land not far off, that fish cop Gary is a Folger. A few have Native claims with subsurface rights. It is legal to get tusks off of these lands along the rivers I travel. There is, in fact, a mammoth tusk way up the cliff. It looks too dangerous to try to get. I do not know how to use my climbing gear, just have it for emergencies or easy stuff. I take a picture of the tusk in the mud way up the cliff. It makes a nice picture. I sigh that I can't get it. I tried to figure out how the climbing gear works off the roof of the house. Going down is easy. I could not figure out how to go up. It's supposed to be easy. Someone told me how to use two ropes to go up. My German friend Helm knows how to repel. Others tell me, no, "You can do it with one rope and an ascender and descender." You'd think just looking at the gear it would make sense. I get asked if that bothers me, in general, to not be able to get tusks and having to leave without them!

"Miles, how can you look at something worth $10,000 and walk away!"

Well, we look at stuff like that in stores, and do not buy it, right? We go home without it, don't we? City people go to malls just to look sometimes, I assume. Stop in jewelry stores to see diamond rings they can't buy or have, right? I see moose and do not shoot them.

These fossils have no value till they reach the market. Does a fisherman catch every fish going by? Is it wise to dwell on the ones that got away? Isn't success and happiness in the direction of counting your blessings, and looking in the net at what you have there? So goes my thinking. Other tusks elsewhere can be too dangerous to try to get! I could die trying. "Even fish in the net sometimes wiggle out and fall back in the river while pulling the net in." Is that a disaster? "Be happy with the fish we get to market!" Will we be so greedy, and will money be our God, to the extent we will be depressed over money we could have made maybe, but did not, because we saw something not under our control or ability to get? Would we drown in the river jumping in after the fish that wiggles loose? So goes the conversation with myself on this subject as I stare up at this tusk.

So yes, the 'one that got away' makes an interesting story, a nice picture, and part of a fun, exciting trip. If I'm addicted to adventure, the thrill of the chase, I just got my dose of adrenaline. *Money is not my God.* I leave. As I eat up the miles, to the drone of a happy engine, I think about such things. If money could be made by someone just handing me a tusk in town, and I hand it to someone else, I think I would not be very interested. To never go on an adventure and get paid, or to have the adventure, and make nothing, even living close to starvation? I'd choose the adventure. I've proven that with action, with choices I made in life already, so that's not just empty words. I've turned a lot of high paying jobs down in my life.

"Can money buy happiness?" *A tusk, is that a tusk?* I turn the boat around, come back against the current, a slow three miles an hour as I stare. This time it is not a tusk. But many times I was not sure, tested it, and find it was in fact either a tusk, or fossil of some kind.[1] One time something looked like a one inch piece of bone, hardly worth picking up. It does not come up out of the mud. I pull and dig. I have hold of the very tip of a bison horn, attached to the skull that is 4 ft. across. A 40,000 year old Steppe bison.

I crane my neck to look backwards behind a chunk of mud I was keeping an eye on. I only get a half second look, as the boat goes on by this narrow cut. In that cut are two blue matched mammoth tusks. Not huge, but in good shape, pretty, worth $7,000 for the set, even still wet and muddy.

The sound of wild trumpeter swans interrupts my thoughts. *There they are on a sandbar in the distance.* My camera is always handy, so I get it off the dash, do a 'zoom in,' and get a nice picture of a family of swans with tree roots in the background on an otherwise barren looking moonscape. The swans face me with long stretched out necks, being very still. I can tell they are wondering what I'm going to do, and if I am a threat or not. But I go right on by, far enough away not to scare them overly much.

I eventually make it home. I tell no one I was gone, nor later, if I was on the river much this summer, or if I had a successful summer or trip. Or if I found anything or not. *We are living in ending times.* Sometimes I can't get out of saying something, giving some answer.

119

"Miles! I saw you go by the fish camp on the river. Looks like a new engine! What was under the tarp? It looked like a heavy load!"

"Oh, you know me, out and about, 'stuff,' headed for the homestead!"

Someone else, "The local ivory dealer said you sold some ivory, so guess you had a good summer! Good for you!"

"Bought a little from a miner in Manly," or, "Yes, the boneyard is looking the same as always," or "Got a new ivory spot up the Kantishna." Rumor is, I'm quite the story teller.

"Miles of full of crap, he never went up the Kantishna this summer!" *Did I say Kantishna instead of Cosna? Oh my, how forgetful!*

"But Miles told me…?" It is said I am making jokes—not being serious.

Others say, "No, weird," or "The village idiot."

I nod, "Yes, yes that's me!" It's all about being safe. Saying I got stuff when I did not, saying I did not when I did. It's like crying wolf. It's just Miles again.

"Who knows!" It's all about, what can you prove? *I'm legal, I just do not trust my government, trust that my government is legal.* Before going in my shop, I look to the right. I look to the left, scowling, seeing if anyone is around. I turn the music up in case there was a listening device planted in the shop while I was gone. I believe what I am doing is legal, and what the government is doing is not. But *Ha! How does that work? The government almost by definition is the law and is legal! So where does that leave me?* Anyhow…"hmmmm."

MORE EMAILS BACKED UP. The forever emails and the computer that *runs my life. Both a blessing and a curse.*

MILES! I WANT TO KNOW IF YOU HAVE A PIECE OF RAW IVORY, 4.225 LONG X 1.51 WIDE X .356 THICK. THANKS!

I pause at the question, wondering how to reply. I already know this customer will not be happy with my product or service. And I know why, but think he does not. He thinks it's a simple request. I review my saved replies in my mind. *Where did I put the saved reply that suits this occasion? What did I call it?*

Oh yes, here it is under 'Buying strawberries.' Huh? Well maybe I am the only one who knows what that means. It's a story I made up to illustrate two different ways of thinking…

Maybe people see and perceive things in different ways?

I say to one person, "Describe getting strawberries to me."

Person A replies:

"Well, I went to Safeway on August 5th at 9:00 AM. I bought two pints at $1.75 a pint on sale. I parked in lot C, took them home in my '86 ford 250."

That is their memory. What we might call 'the truth, reality and facts' of 'buying strawberries.' If we ask person A,"How did they taste?" They look confused, disoriented, it's a trick question.

"Why, was something wrong with them? They tasted OK, I guess, like strawberries, I assume." I might wonder how you can buy strawberries and not know how they taste, why did you buy them, if not for the taste. Did you really buy them?

Person B is asked to tell of their experience buying strawberries.

"I saw them. Big, red, ripe, and there were lots! They smelled like jam. My mouth watered before I even tried them. I closed my eyes and took it all in. I got them vine ripened, out of this world!" This is person B's reality, and set of facts. The world through their senses. If we ask person B:

"And when did all this take place? What parking lot did you park in?" Blink, blink, confused look.

"I do not know. I do not care. Why, does it matter, is something wrong?" We could say to person B:

"How do we know you got strawberries if you can't tell us when or where, or what they cost?" What would the IRS say for example?

I assume then, some people think in names, numbers, dates and times. Others think in sets of sensual experiences. The world is made up of bean counters, and artists.

This is how I explain it to customers, *if they even care.* I'm someone who replies, "Are you nuts! I wouldn't know to the nearest foot what size the pieces are. I'm someone who built an entire cabin and never measured anything, nor knew how big it was till it was done."

This has me day dream about various legal issues. The law assumes we keep track of, know, understand, and can prove, by the use of names, dates, times, with the records of such. The assumption of the law is we are all type A. This is what goes into court records. To relate a sensation, and not connect it to correct dates and numbers is to be a liar. If my ivory is so much as a sixteenth out of whack, customer A type is likely to go ballistic and call me a cheat, trying to pass on an inferior product. *Probably eligible for a refund as well!* I'd rather just say, "Next!" with the advice: "Go find a numbers cruncher." Also, my pieces are odd shapes in the raw. Anyone who asks for these exact dimensions, and expects this product to be called 'raw,' is not going to be happy with the price. As an exact dimension is no longer raw, but a worked finished product.

I build knives, just as this customer does, and I have never measured anything. I draw the outline of a blade freehand. I lay my hand down and call that a good length for a handle, and draw that. I cut out the steel. I go to my materials with a visual image of the shape of the handle. I grab material I think might fit. I lay it on the handle, trace the outline, and cut it. If it doesn't fit, I adjust either the knife steel, or the material, or go get another piece of raw fossil from the pile. I do not know how big the knife is, till it is done, and then, only because I have to describe it to sell it, numbers are expected. I do not know why. It would never occur to me to ask how long the blade or handle is when buying. I'd pick it up, see how it feels, decide by looking at it, if it will do the jobs I need it to do.

I want no legal issues with customers. More, I simply do not want them to be dissatisfied with my product. I sell magic, dreams, provenance, stories, beauty, connections between worlds of the past and present, and lifestyles. That is what you are buying. If you can fit that into 4.225 long x 1.51 wide x .356 thick. Go for it! I'm not even interested in trying. I find the task amusing. But neither the customer nor the law may find it amusing if I accept the money, and I can't deliver.

Hi Miles,

Thanks for the reply I'm Ynez Slaymaker, journalist for "AK This Month" a statewide entertainment guide. My editor has requested I write an article on small town fairs with the focus on Nenana Valley and Deltana.

I'd like to talk to anyone who could tell me about the Nenana Valley Fair and the people involved; what's the attraction/highlight; who attends; who participates; is there anything unique about this fair; how does the community get involved; and things along those lines.

My reply to this email results in a radio spot for Nenana all across the lower state. The next email is someone with fond memories to share, and wants a response on their comment.

Good Morning,

I have some really fond memories of Nenana when I was a small child. My Grandparents, George and Alice Johnson, owned some property there and I used to go and spend summers with them in Nenana.

I have always wondered how Nenana had grown (or if it did at all). One day I was sitting here at ye ole computer surfing the net and that Nenana thought crossed my mind, and here I am… etc etc Sincerely,

Hallie Horey

I take the time to write back, and tell her I think some of her relatives still live here, and give some contact information. The Chamber is still running a community website. I am supposed to be working with Annette from the local towing company coordinating the site. She is more of a computer wizard than I am. But so far we have not been able to share data. The next email concerns wanting trophies.

Wild Miles

Need a set of huge antlers for the wall, figured you'd be the man! Willing to pay a grand if they are exceptional.

My reply,

I have seen moose antler sets close to seven feet wide in my life. I do not shoot such a moose nor buy such antler sets. My market is for the craft people, and spiritual items. I'd rather not sell trophies. I get material from Natives and subsistence people eating the meat and we tend not to go after the ones with huge racks, as not being as good eating, and hard to pack out. Sorry!

It is getting harder to keep up with all the changes in laws. I cannot trust any of my sources to tell me the truth, and I do not know how to look laws up. Lawyers do not especially want anyone else to have access to and understand, the law. *That puts them out of business.* There are few lawyers who specialize in wildlife laws. Selling trophies may not be considered subsistence sales. This might be something you can google, but not give a court case number or anything to take to court to argue with. I can picture telling a judge, "Well I googled it!"

Hi Miles:

I'm following up on your request from a couple years ago to keep you informed of any developments regarding gas exploration at Nenana.

Planning is underway for a seismic exploration effort west of Nenana next winter. A public meeting is set for Tuesday, May 25 at George Hall in Nenana; starting at 6:30 p.m. Representatives from the exploration company, Andex Resources, their seismic contractor, PGS Onshore, and the State of Alaska will be present. Andex and PGS will describe the program, take questions, etc.

I will be there as well. Hope to see you. Please help us get the word out about the meeting.

Regards,
Jim
James Mery
Senior Vice President
Lands and Natural Resources
Doyon, Limited

And here is a contact of interest, as Nenana is still discussing holding drag races. There is talk of buying land and putting in a drag strip as a source of revenue, since it is likely we cannot use the runway as hoped.

Hi,

I hope this is the right mail address for the chamber of Commerce of Nenana. I am in charge of automotive chassis developments at Delphi Corporation, Europe, and am looking at winter test facilities in Alaska to be used this fall '05 (sept-october timeframe).

Someone has told me that there was several years ago a Proving Ground that could be hired in Nenana. I think it belonged to the US Army??? Can you please tell me whether there is such a possibility in your area, and give me the contacts?

I would appreciate your help very much.

Regards,

Thierry Annequin

Manager Vehicle Testing & Prototyping

One aspect of this testing grounds is 'something remote' where test results are less likely to be observed by the competition. On another subject, An article is written for the Nenana messenger.

Public Meeting—Police Department

By Miles Martin

A public meeting was held in the Civic Center, facilitated by Traci Wiggins from mental health. The purpose of the meeting was to have a public discussion and come up with a plan, or understanding, about the budget as it concerns the police department. There are some details I glance over and focus ahead on.

A lot comes down to trust. Does the community trust the City Council—those we elected—to look out for the best interest of the community? That seems to be the bottom line.

Our Mayor summed it up best with,"All this talk is fine, but the bottom line is, we do not have the money to support the police department as we have been doing at the level we have been doing it."

Several people, Ned in particular said, "When you're out of money that's it, you can't spend what you don't have." Others pointed out the council managed to come up with twenty-five grand for the Parks and Recreation Department to pay children to pick up trash.

A few said, "If the children are busy, that is less time they have to get in trouble!"

Even so, the timing of saying,"There are zero dollars to go on with the police budget," and at the same council meeting, saying,"Hey, let's give the money to the kids to clean the park!" appears to be a slap in the face of the police, and has some asking,

"Is the money the real issue?"

The report goes into more details, but I just scan it and set it aside. There is some Chamber of Commerce news…

The newly formed '**Nenana Valley Open Market Committee'** is a work group part— of the Nenana Chamber and has a meeting an hour before the Chamber meeting at 7 PM at the Senior Center, on March 18th. The objective is to have an open market established for Nenana this summer near the Taku Chief. Anyone interested in this should attend or keep in touch with the Chamber. We hope to offer *a place to sell local produce, art, and garage sale items,* but how and what is still being discussed. Several Nenana people have been interested in this for several years and it seems to be starting to come together.

I'm glad to see this finally get started. Some locals want the market to be more of a farmers market, others want it like a flea market to sell used goods. I favor being open about it, and sell whatever works for the community. As the economy struggles, the Chamber looks toward the economic opportunities that might help our community. Offering an outlet for small business, truck farms and craft people, seems like a good direction to go. It's a little late in the season, but we try out a weekend, and get an OK turn out. One lady sold out of eggs and homemade bread. I made $400 selling my custom jewelry to tourists that stopped. A local ten year old, sold cut dry flowers and made $50. I smile thinking of her optimism. This is a great incentive and learning experience for the young.

I volunteer to write for the community paper because I believe in information instead of rumor when making community decisions. I believe in participation.

"If you have an opinion, be part of a solution, not part of the problem." While I have issues with our bigger government, I do believe in the basic concept of the intention of our constitution. Local government, our local system, I trust more, because I personally know everyone involved. Have not been scammed, ripped off, lied to, or used locally as I feel has been done by the bigger government. *If I know everyone I vote for it is hard to run a bogus promotion. We all know what you stand for.*

As WINTER SETS IN, I get a letter from my old girlfriend, Karen, who I lived on the Kantishna River with for four years. I learned a lot from her about gardening. She always knew the Latin names for about every kind of plant. She is still good looking, loves the outdoor life, running sled-dogs and all I believe in. I miss her sometimes.

Getting a letter has me thinking about my being alone so long. Well, a few off and on 'situations.' Nothing long term and meaningful. *I must be hard to get along with.* There seems to be a lot of female friends in my life, rather than romance. The Turquoise lady in Tucson for example, the one with the exquisite buckets of turquoise....

Hey Miles of Smiles,

Howdy buddy, so good to hear from you and I'm so sorry it's taken me so long to respond, but frankly, since July or so I've been in a coma, almost except with migraine headaches, blurred vision and high blood pressure and Miles, I'm just getting old.

Gosh darn it, and I'm not going to go quietly into that dark night, so I started setting up my garage for lapidary work, you know, two little trim saws...

This single life is sometimes not all it's cracked up to be and frankly it's for the birds, but the alternative in Apache Junction could very well prove to be detrimental to my existence, if not fatal to theirs, so I'll do this one for awhile...and you my friend...anything new on the horizon of love? Do you have any new pen pals? I checked out the Singles thing on Yahoo and then another one where they sent me at least twenty photos of single men [MY AGE & OLDER!!!!!! yuck!!!!!!] every week or so. I can't be that old—not yet...It upset me, so I stopped looking at the pictures and just deleted them. How sad huh?

Hey, before I end this novel I wanted to see if you are interested in any Sugilite. One of my customers sent me some and then another fellow out here is going to send me some gaspeite and I just took over this old guys rock shop business because he was afraid his wife would take it all in the divorce so he just loaded all of it up in my truck and Jeff's truck and we gave him some $$ and away we went. I may even learn how to grind up turquoise, azurite, or even malachite real soon here, because he was doing that but didn't try to find a market for it, but I'll dig around a little bit if it looks like it may work. Because one of my customers is a wood turner and they have a never-ending need for xxxxxxx-small to dust rock.

Okay Miles WAKE UP!! And thanks for the picture it is too cool...and I'm glad you're doing so well right now, I hope that continues for a loooooonnnnnnggggg time to come-

Take care now Miles and YOU HAVE A NICE DAY TOO!!!!!
Turquoise P. .

I should see her in Tucson, and get some of these new stones. She wants wolf claws. No. She likes the heat, couldn't stand Alaska. We already talked about that. No. I'm not moving to the heat. I recall Turquoise being the gal with the long perfect legs I helped out. I loaded pails of turquoise into her car while my buddies admired her buckets. We have actually known each other off and on almost a decade now. Another woman...

Things are well. I'm not bringing up Zim now because at the last minute he had to take four more entrance level classes. Oh life can change so quickly. He will be up for the Month of May, a month long Glacier class, and then back down here to get his stuff and driving the Alcan instead. It will save a bunch of mula. Been busy, leather work, teaching cello lessons soon.

Much Love Rising Moon

Moon knew me way back when I was living in Manley Hot Springs on my houseboat in the slough. I apparently had a big impact on her when we met. I only vaguely recalled meeting her when she confronted me several years later. We ran into each other again in Fairbanks. She says, "Miles! Good to see you. I knew we'd run into each other again! It's like destiny!" She tells me I live the exact lifestyle she dreams of. She lived alone for two years in a remote cabin with her baby. She had constant dreams about me, and could not get me out of her head. Like I am perfect for her. A romantic, touching, flattering story for sure. She's a few years younger. A very attractive Native woman with long black hair. Round, smooth face, good happy smile, penetrating eyes, and seems to know how to dress well and look good. I was available at the time. We discussed getting to know each other, to see where this goes.

"I'm an artist like you, Miles!" She does sand paintings and some jewelry work. "A lot of leather work, Miles!" Her son is interested in being a silversmith, and here I have all the tools and knowledge. He seems to be a bright teen, eager to accept me as a mentor figure. But right off, Moon wants me to join her, and follow her around. She likes to travel—like out of state. She dresses very high class, silver and turquoise high end class.

As I get to know her, I wonder where her money comes from. Sex, money, power, maybe religion, are the great driving forces that make or break relationships I think. Believing this, I want those questions answered. The, "How are you supporting this lifestyle you live," question seems to stand out most here. Because the bottom line would be, "Can you be happy on my, or 'our' income together in the lifestyle of our choice?" I did not think her art paid the bills as she says it does. If two people are not in the same reality, that can be an issue. We get along in every other way.

We are both attracted to each other. Over time I grasp, she gets a lot of money from her parents. They are older, and maybe wealthy. Former rock star band players who did well in the 1960's. Her father wrote music for the band, Momma's and the Poppa's. If she is dependent on her parents financially, and they hold the purse

127

strings, I need to know about that, and what effect and hold it has on her. *Would the parents money control my life as well as hers?*

We see each other a weekend or two, maybe a week long, and not see each other for months, since we live in two different households far apart. Like many beautiful women, she is used to getting her way. But that can be OK. Having a lifestyle and occupation in common is saying a lot. However, so far, we have not worked out how to get us to the next level.

WHEN I GOT MARRIED, I believed in forever. I'm not the one who wanted out. But! We can't control anyone else, nor make them do something they do not want to. We all use certain words, and it brings images in our head. Sometimes we assume everyone else knows what we mean, and gets the same images when we key in with a word like, 'family.' We all get moony eyed and sigh, "Yes." It never occurred to me that a woman and a child is a family. I'd frown and say, "And my role then is?" I'm more open minded these days, make sure we all agree on what words mean.

Meanwhile, back at the ranch…Is there anything I can contribute the last year of my son's critical formative years, before he is on his own to fulfill his own dreams? This is his last year in school, the end of basic education. He can then legally be on his own, able to say, "I don't have to listen to you!"

The ex agreed this is now out of her hands. I should have him this time without her control. No saying, "Send him home !" Again. Leading me to wonder, if I had raised him, how his life might be? Different than it is now for sure! But 'better'? Probably not, just different. Yet from my standpoint, it would have been nice to have seen if my ideas about parenting work. To see the results.

About everyone has only good things to say about my son! How smart, what a good guy, kind, treats others well, and such things. That's great! But it has nothing to do with me. I didn't raise him. He's a stranger to me. I doubt if I have spent more than 100 hours with him in his life. I feel closer to Joy and May I helped raise with Karen. But no. We weren't married. The kids and her have come into my life and gone. I get a Christmas card from them once a year. Maybe I just do not bond well with others. Something is just missing…

Past flash

My son Mitch and I are at the homestead on the Kantishna River on one of his few week visits from California. Maybe 1995, give or take five years. I feel we have a lot of catching up to do! *Guy stuff!* I teach him how to throw rocks. Skip them, try to hit stuff. It's a boy thing. We make our own arrows for a bow we build together. He asks about guns and reloading. I show him how to be safe with the BB gun. He must be thirteen years old, give or take five years. I show him how to use a hammer, nails and a screwdriver. Handy stuff, if you are a guy.

We seem to enjoy each other's company. Give this a month and we'd bond. Give it a year and we'd be two peas in a pod. I focus on the guy stuff since he has spent his life with Mom. *No way she would teach him how to throw a rock!* A lot of catching up to do, so this is like a crash course before his mother takes him away from me.

We have this arrow we made, but the bow broke. It is the 4th of July. I tell him how it was for me this time of year when I was his age.

"We had fire crackers! Not what we got today, that go snap crackle and pop. We had stuff that went 'Whump' and shook the city block. Lit up the sky. M-80's I think we called them."

"I wish we could make a rocket or something, Dad," So sure, we are handy men, we can build us a rocket all right. You don't have to buy it.

"I'm Green, you know, from the Red Green show!" No, he doesn't get it, not one of the programs he watches. The show that tells ya how to make and fix stuff using duct tape! Together we found a stove pipe in an 'unorganized heap of stuff you gotta have'(junk) pile. *That mothers will never say you need* I got some outdated reloading rifle powder.

"Son, we probably need the slowest burning big caliber rifle powder like 4895. Not the Red Dot for pistols." I make sure he is paying attention. "Stuff ya' gotta know if you ever want to build a rocket. Lack of knowledge could be hazardous." We both nod our heads in agreement, as I thread a cap on one end of a pipe, after drilling a hole in it for a fuse.

"And we need an over wad!" He doesn't know what that is, "To go on top of the powder and make a seal so when the powder burns, it builds up pressure!"

"Cool!" *I'll show you cool all right, kid.* Being a guy is a blast (pardon the pun)! I calculate an amount of powder I think will work, based on being a responsible adult. We do the over wad bit, drop the arrow down the uncapped end of the pipe. *Kind of like a cannon.* With all the moves and behavior of performing a magic trick. I show Mitch all the steps, and why each step is necessary. How to be careful and safe, too. Not to do it alone and all that. We prop this bazooka looking thing up against a piece of driftwood on the river bank. A hundred miles from the nearest other human beings. I have him light the fuse. We both scream and run in excitement. To a predetermined big tree to watch from behind.

It all goes as predicted. A big 'whump,' a ball of flame, a cloud of smoke that would gag a maggot. We are both screaming and jumping up and down. Looking up, way, way up, we see the arrow up, up and away, out of sight, to 'Never Never Land'. Now, I might not choose to do this under other circumstances. If he was different then he is. I'm trying to teach him being a guy does not have to be an awful experience. *I suspect his mother hates men, not just me.* It's nice being a guy! I'm not sure my son knows this. Girls pretty much don't do this. Don't want to. Will not. *This is stuff you can only do with your Dad.* Or some other important idiot, but the secret is, 'A guy.' Stuff your mom would never do with you, that's important to know! *Gosh darn it, you need a father around, kid!*

I didn't say that. But that's kinda' the general idea. I had noticed Mitch arrives from his mother almost always, quiet, depressed, submissive, and polite. No sparkle in his eyes. He often leaves jabbering, looking around with intense open eyes and full of energy. That's the main thing. But he tells his mother what we did. And it's all over. I do not get to see him again for another ten years, maybe twenty, or whatever. But maybe that lesson is worth about ten years of good memories. Who knows?

Another time it was the frog we caught together and wanted to keep as a pet. He was blabbering non- stop. Not the frog, my son. We had plans for a cage! He wants to look up everything he can about frogs! He can't wait to show his friends! I've been there and done that. I was a kid once and I remember! *Mitch does not know me enough to realize I could write that book about how to raise a frog. That's ok, let him get to know me and figure it out.* Mom comes to pick him up, sees this frog. Sees how happy and excited we are, and puts a stop to that right now.

"Turn that poor thing loose right now! What are you doing!" Like pulling the plug in a bathtub of happy suds. It all goes down the drain. The spark in his eyes, the babbling, the joy. Once again, the meek submissive eyes on the ground, zombie. She glares at me with hatred. Taking her son away, where he can be safe. *Rockets and frogs, who ever heard of such nonsense!*

My past flash ends

MAYBE THE GOOD NEWS IS, my ex may have understood. And set me free. Well. In that she told me once her own parents' story.

Only—it'd be nice to have my son, and not be just a baby sitter under her rules. Though I notice, as more time passes, Mitch is less adaptable, after sixteen years under Mom. It might be too late to introduce him to the wonderful world of guys. But never give up! After all! My parents tried their hardest! Beat me, punished me, instilled guilt, every trick in the book. All undone in a few hours after seeing Alaska! I described in Book One as, "A duck that finds water for the first time." I knew I was a duck, and I knew I was born to be in the water, the weeds, and to fly!

My son is not me? No. But he is the one who excitedly said, "I want to catch a frog and keep it for a pet!" And, "It'd be so cool to send an arrow into the sky like a rocket!" When he was a baby, he sat next to me and duplicated everything I did. He crossed his legs like me, got the same expression, copying me while he was still in diapers. When I went out the homestead cabin door to feed the sled dogs, Mitch would quit breast feeding and cry to get down, crawl over and up to the window sill, to stare at the world outside, the world of sled dogs. He was, everyone who met him said, 'just like me.'

And no. I did not necessarily want to push him to be like me. If he ever said to me, "Dad, I just love school and I want to be (whatever)," and there was a fire in his eyes and he was awake and alive. I'd smile, "Good for you, son, have at it!" I'd help him, ask how I could help, even if it meant we would not have as much to share. But meanwhile, what is wrong with doing stuff together in his formative years that turns my crank and has us bond?

I drift off to thoughts of a bunny hugger I met and liked. Another artist. We have been writing over the past couple of years and she's becoming my friend. She lives in Maine. On an island. She paints so well, she has done duck stamps for the state. She says, " Yes, I like to take animals in and take care of them. My house gets so full of animals I do not know what to do sometimes!"

I wrote back, "Cool! A perfect match. You bring them in the front, I'll shovel them out the back!" She did not find any humor in that. *You know, ying and yang, being in balance and all that.* It sort of worked, that concept, for Karen and me. I was hard on sled dogs. The team and I put in a lot of miles, hard miles in deep snow. It was Karen who kept the best eye out on them, brought them in the house when it was needed, tended sore feet, put medicine where needed, babied them, a lot more than I ever would. I, we, had a much better team for it too. Neither of our ways alone would be great. The dogs would not mind her, would not work for her.

She said once crying, "The dogs treat me like the poop scooper!" She'd get frustrated, lose her temper, yell and scream at them. They'd yawn and lie down. As if to say, "Let us know when your temper tantrum is over, and maybe we can get something done around here." No respect. Karen was very upset that I could just snap my fingers. Or step out the door, and get every dog's instant, full attention. With a quiet, soft command, get nine dogs to behave. I never once yelled or screamed, and the rules were consistent. All these thoughts when thinking of women, children, relationships. *Oh I forgot, if the dogs misbehaved I shot them.* "Minor detail."

I get my mind on something else less mind boggling, answering a guy named Frank. He is asking about Nenana, tourism, the economy in Nenana. He has actually written a couple of times through the Chamber of Commerce. Frank has land he invested in years ago, a homestead he has not seen, so wants an update on the value of his land, and the ability to live here.

Hello Frank!

Well, if I had any advice it would be to go for your dream and not have that dream dependent on anything anyone else is going to do or not do. As for Commerce in Nenana. Geez, we have all kinds of issues in our community. A majority of the population may not even want commerce in Nenana. Some are not affected—like the ones on welfare. Many work in Fairbanks. Many are Indians who have Indian money coming in. The attitude among many is this:

I pass on some local thoughts and answer his questions. I do notice that locals who want work, have it. But Frank is not looking for a job, he wants to know if we are a rich bustling industrious community. While everyone who wants works has it, we are a community that has not changed population or economically in fifty years.

Well, I'm just rambling. **Later! Miles**

WHILE STILL IN the Chamber email, I need to deal with another aspect of tourism. Princess Tours, who handles over half of all tourism in our area, is tired of the Nenana experience our local Eagle offers with her tourist trap monopoly here in town. Or at least, those at the Princess head office tell the Chamber this. Princess says they like to work with local Chambers of Commerce to coordinate tours. Eagle makes handling tourism in Nenana easy, but at the expense of being a scam, with imported items labeled as local. A monopoly, a sugar coated disguise, made to look like a community effort, representing a quaint little village. I sigh and ponder the ways of the world. Eagle is not a member of the Chamber of Commerce. She has not given up, saying, "When the Chamber decides to get a gambling permit and puts me in charge, let me know, I'll join."

When I get discouraged, I feel like the entire tourist industry is 90% scam. All about the quick money. An illusion offered visitors. Being financially driven, to be competitive, those in the industry who survive, must offer the most for the least cost. Money is most people's God. Interesting in that I come from the wilderness world where this is not so! I take my position as the head of Chamber of Commerce seriously. I work hard. I care. I am in a position to make things happen, if the community wants it. I'm doing the best I can to help create an environment where business can thrive.

With this in mind, the Chamber contacts Princess after a Highways Companion meeting I went to, representing Nenana. I remind locals, "This is an organization whose concern is tourism up and down the highway. All about working together to enhance the tourist industry, and hopefully encourage more, and better tourism, leading to more profits for the communities involved. We meet once a year at one of the communities who is a member." I do not go into details, But! We all get an introduction to the community where we meet, with a "fam tour." Basically, a free promotional tour. Local business contributes free boat rides, a night in a motel, whatever that community can offer. In return, we are able to make recommendations based on personal experience when talking to tourists at our various visitor centers. Guest speakers in the tourist industry are invited to come speak to us and answer questions. The head of the tour train, cruise ship tours, Princess Tours, those who write tour guide books, etc.. In this way, we can understand their business and what is expected of us, if we wish to be included. I explain this a lot of times to whoever will listen.

For example, we, in the interior of Alaska miss out on a big portion of tourism with the ocean cruises! Thousands of tourists get off a ship and descend on a small coastal community, dumping a lot of money. However, the coastal community does not offer all of what the tourists desire. Some side tours, or some Interior characters and color could be put to good use. Tourists want to hear a good gold story from a miner, dressed like Felix Pedro, who discovered gold in Fairbanks. They want to meet a real trapper, homesteader, interior Indian, and generally, all we stand for. Even pay us!

Maybe we can send some characters down on the train to greet the tourists and give talks. None of us would know about this if we did not have these meetings. Interesting. At one of these meetings, I talked to one of the head people with Princess Tours. Nenana is recalled. Many of the bus drivers complain about how Eagle runs things. I hear from Princess, "She sometimes jumps in the middle of the road and physically forces the bus to stop. Playing her accordion, she gets on the bus with a smile. Our drivers tell her with a scowl, she has fifteen minutes! And she stretches it to an hour." I understand. I have heard it before, and seen it for myself. Very aggressive, not quality products, but the driver can't make a scene in front of the tourists. Most drivers wish there was an alternative, even another way into Nenana besides the main drag, so they can bypass her! A few I suspect take kick backs, paid extra on the side to let her run the show, run into overtime.

This sounds like something the Chamber could get involved in. I email my contact person at Princess Headquarters in Seattle after a Chamber of Commerce meeting.

Hello Denise!

Things did not go so well for the arrangements in Nenana for the short tour and rest stop. The driver seemed to have no information and stopped at the Visitor Center, which would be the thing to do usually, but in this case, with no information or contact name the worker at the Visitor Center sent the bus across the street. The tourists got their break, with the owner of a tourist trap gift shop, not a Chamber member. In the big picture of the total trip for them, all was probably well. But the arrangements the Chamber made were of little use.

Our local restaurant had a pot of coffee, hot rolls and an extra employee on hand. Two guides were prepared to do a quality quick tour—volunteers who set aside this time weeks in advance. I'm left wondering now, what it is that is wanted so this doesn't happen again. I talked to the driver later. The driver didn't have a clue who I was, or that there was a tour planned, a coordinated stop arranged. The shop owner who usually handles the twenty busses a day stepped up to the plate, did the usual routine. This routine is very generic, fast, easy, but did not include snacks, or a tour. It was just a pit stop on the way to someplace else selling imported items.

We understood time is important, but that you also wanted a short, but quality experience. We feel Nenana has a great deal more to offer than is now being seen. You seemed receptive to the idea of having the tourists see a real fish wheel working, some genuine Native crafts- with a possibility of seeing them being made at a cultural center. A snack stop can be at a great mom and pop place where the locals stop in that shows the real Alaska. This can be short, but quite different.

The Nenana Chamber is trying to have greater vision and look at the big picture, believing if we give the visitor a quality experience, this will lead to good things. It is just not very workable to stop in front of a tourist trap and expect more than getting trapped. As I said, twenty busses a day fall for it. We sincerely hope you want something different for your tour. I'm putting the restaurant directly in touch with you. Maybe this way the driver will have a place, a name, and directions (easy to find, we have only one main street and a few businesses on the main drag.) Hope you are having a good season! **Miles – Nenana Chamber of Commerce**

A reply arrives a week later

Miles, I don't know how that can be that the driver didn't seem to know of anything happening in Nenana. He had information in the folder about it, except for the number you gave me yesterday, which I couldn't get to them. The number is included in the folder for the next group, so I hope that happens. Not much I can do from here. Next time the driver calls in I will ask him about it. I'm sorry it didn't work out and the restaurant and volunteers were discouraged.
   Denise

I'm guessing Princess does not have time to work things out with one remote bus stop out of hundreds of stops she manages. Eagle is just crafty. Those of us in the Chamber had not been thinking with a devious mind. I'm sure in my own mind, Eagle knew of this plan, and worked something out with the bus driver.

"Play dumb, stop at the visitor center, I have them in my pocket, they will send you over to me." In return for $100 tip or whatever. Tourism is not the only business in Nenana, but one I personally understand a little.

It looks to me like there are advantages and then disadvantages to a small community where laws are loose, and we have lots of freedoms. Such places attract people who can be a big fish in a little pond. It has been said by many people, that

Eagle would not do well in a big city, with the kinds of methods she uses to do business. Her hired help takes 'made in China' stickers off and puts 'handmade in Alaska' stickers on. Even 'Authentic Native Made.' In Nenana, who cares? The few who do, can be made to shut up and mind their own business. We leave each other alone. Or, if we care enough, take care of problems ourselves, vigilante style. Places are capable of mysteriously burning down. None of us in the Chamber have that kind of mentality. But Eagle does. Along with others who run things and make big money. They all tend to follow rules of some kind to survive. They all leave you alone 'if.' I have more doubts now, if the Chamber will ever be allowed to have any clout.[2]

Teaching school kids how to make rings of wax and how to cast them.

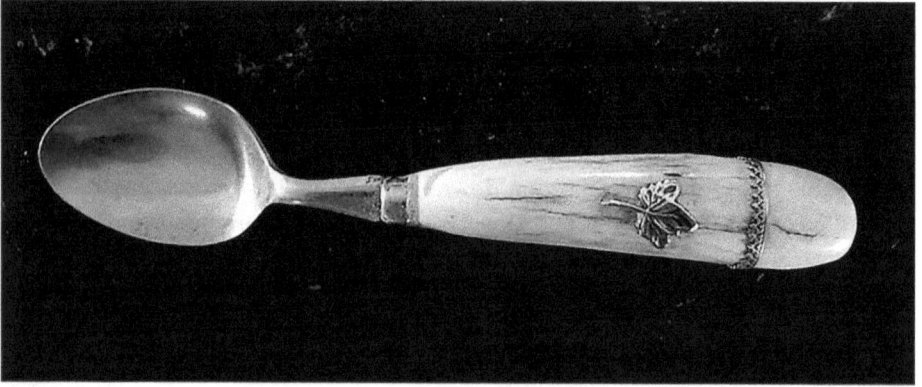

My spoon breaks- I fix it with a moose antler tine.

Photo Section

10 mile lake—a deep snow year.

Baby bird sits here every day waiting for the sprinkler to come on.

U.S. Fish and Wildlife Service
United States District Court
Violation Notice

CVB Location Code: ALSB

Violation Number	Officer Name (Print)	Officer No.
W0780188	JILL BIRCHELL	SA0459

YOU ARE CHARGED WITH THE FOLLOWING VIOLATION

Date and Time of Offense (mm/dd/yyyy)	Offense Charged ☒ CFR ☐ USC ☐ State Code
04/20/2004	16 U.S.C. 1372, 50 CFR 18.13(c)

Place of Offense

NENANA, ALASKA

Offense Description

Knowingly sell marine mammal parts to wit: On 04/20/2004, Miles MARTIN did sell two white walrus ivory pieces for $55.00.

DEFENDANT INFORMATION Phone: (907) 832 - 5442

Last Name	First Name	M.I.
MARTIN	MILES	W

Street Address: 5TH & C

City	State	Zip Code	Date of Birth (mm/dd/yyyy)
NENANA	AK	99760	05/07/1951

Drivers License No. | D.L. State | Social Security No. 091-_6

☒ Adult ☐ Juvenile   Sex ☒ Male ☐ Female   Hair BRO   Eyes BRO   Height 504   Weight 160

VEHICLE DESCRIPTION VIN:

Tag No.	State	Year	Make/Model	Color
				UNK

A ☐ IF BOX A IS CHECKED, YOU MUST APPEAR IN COURT. SEE INSTRUCTIONS (on back of yellow copy).

B ☒ IF BOX B IS CHECKED, YOU MUST PAY AMOUNT INDICATED BELOW OR APPEAR IN COURT. SEE INSTRUCTIONS (on back of yellow copy).

$2250 Forfeiture Amount
+ $25 Processing Fee

PAY THIS AMOUNT → $2275 Total Collateral Due

YOUR COURT DATE
(If no court appearance date is shown, you will be notified of your appearance date by mail.)

Court Address
CENTRAL VIOLATIONS BUREAU:
1-800-827-2982

My signature signifies that I have received a copy of this violation notice. It is not an admission of guilt. I promise to appear for the hearing at the time and place instructed or pay the total collateral due.

X Defendant Signature

Fish, Wildlife citation- Note the charge is selling white ivory. This is not a crime. A crime is to do so without a permit. I had such a permit that I was never asked to show.

138

Cabbages grow well in Alaska this one is 30 pounds.

Dogsled I built years ago by hand is on display.

Custom capped grizzly claw, these claws can get big!

Duck display made of fossil ivory and opal on crystal base.

Fishing clear creek in the rain.

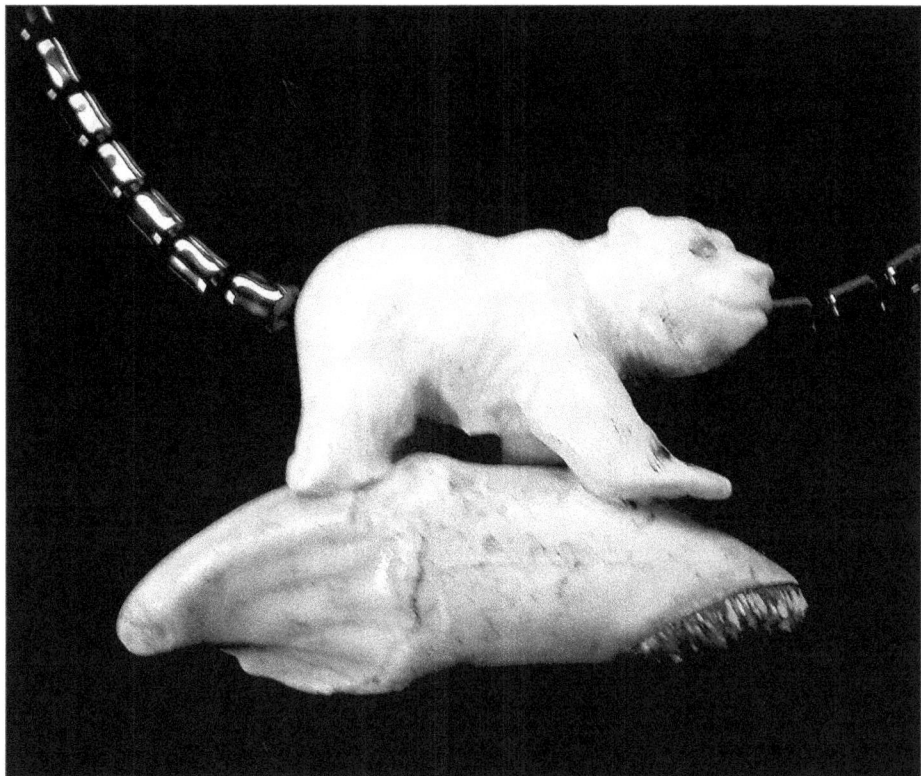

Fossil necklace- carved fossil ivory-cave bear tooth and opal.

I am invited to view a secured area- oil or gas is here under the land I subsistence live on.

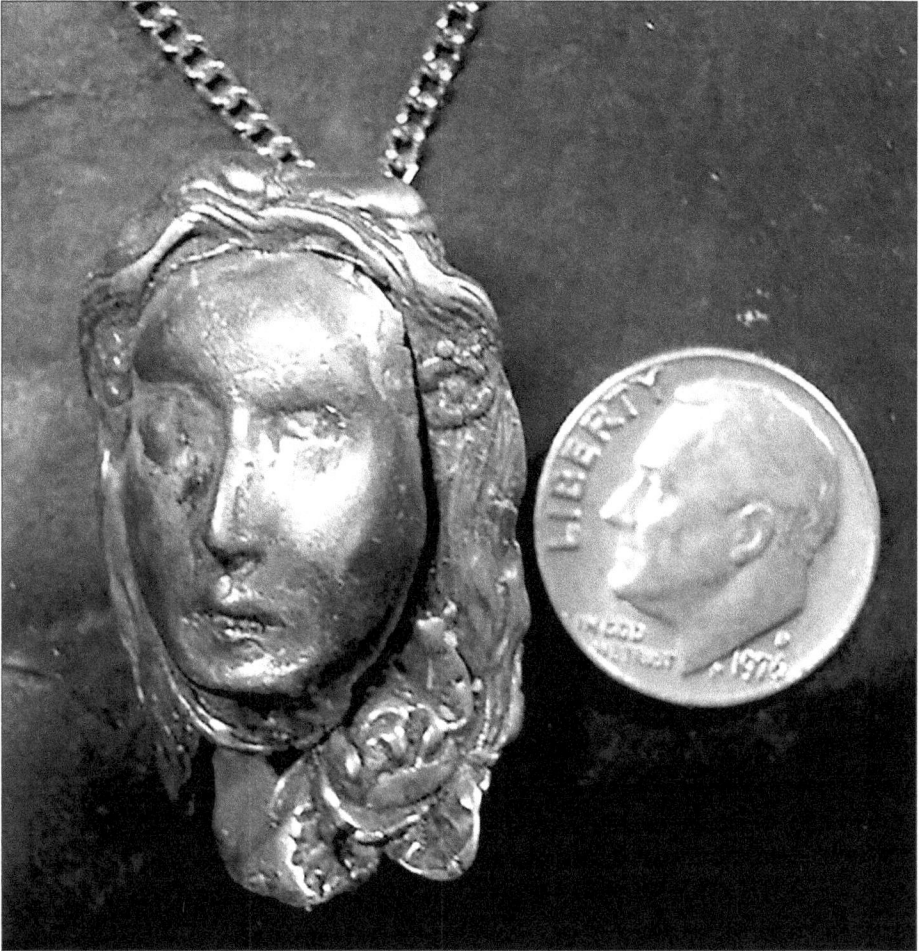

I hand carved, custom cast this face, with an opal eye.

I turn lynx claws into necklaces and earrings.

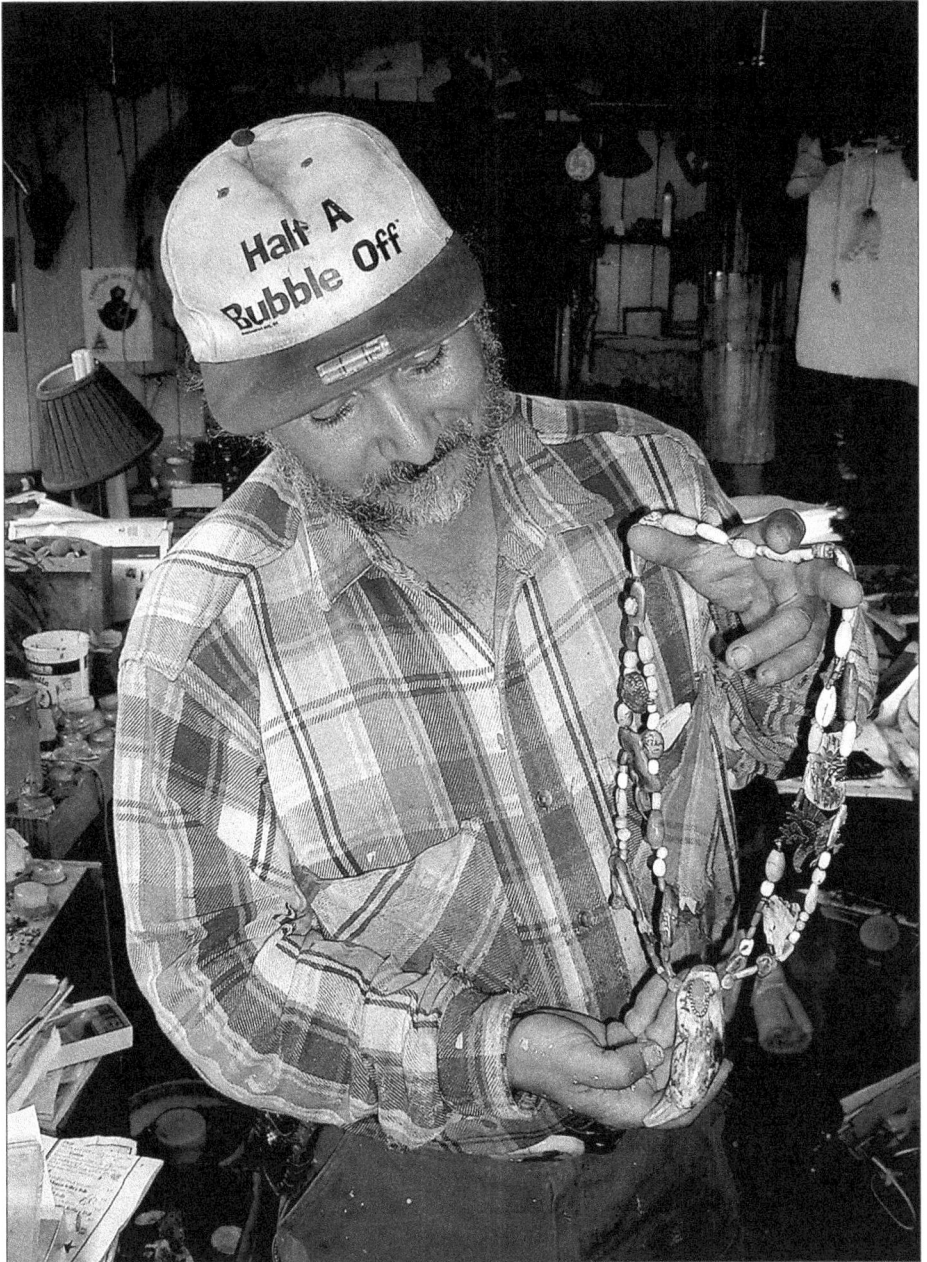

I might be half a bubble off, but this necklace I made sold for over three grand.

Me observing a forest fire at a place called lunch lake.

My custom howling wolf caps showing the variety of wolf claw sizes and shapes.

My garden hoses, water supplied through a broken window in the house.

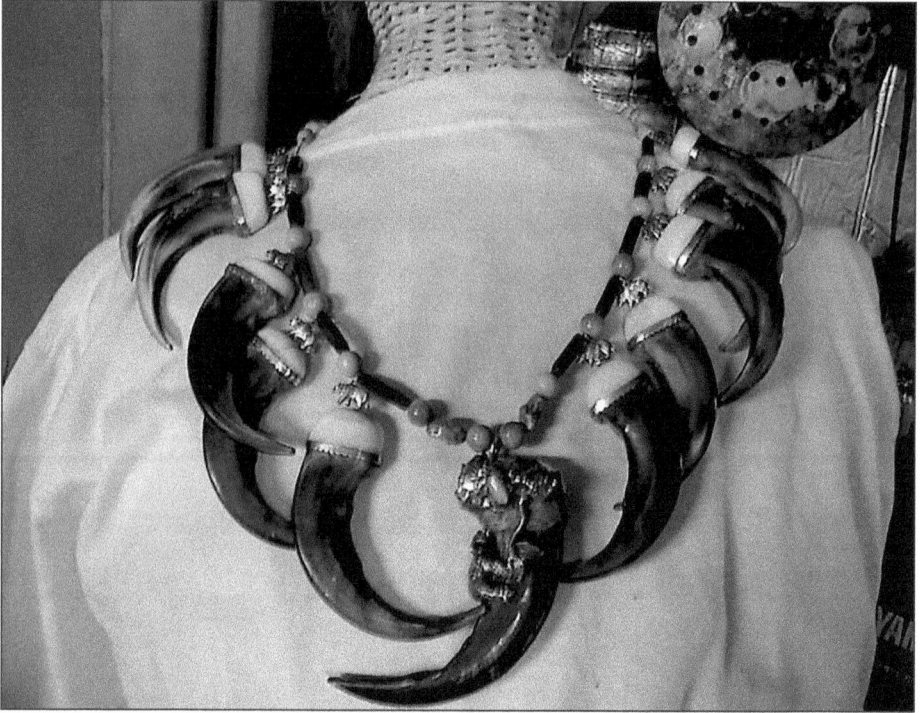

One of my grizzly claw necklaces made from the customers claws. In most cases illegal for me to sell.

Survey camp on the Cosna River.

The man who had my Nenana home before me, back in 1932.

That's a mammoth tooth in its jaw bone.

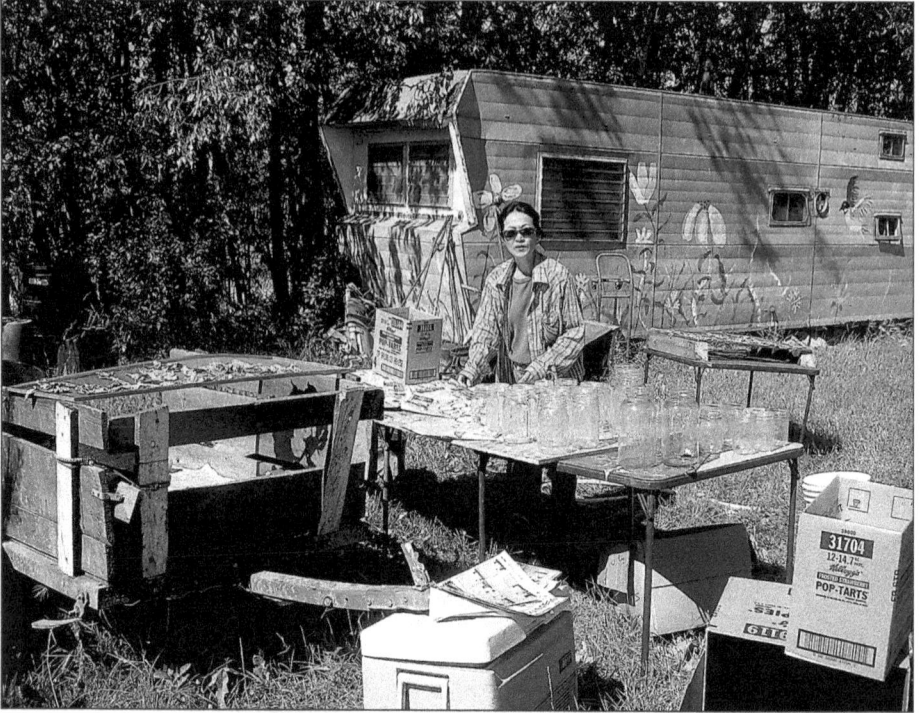

Little Duck, getting ready to can the garden. Temporary outdoor facilities set up for a few days, can over wood fire.

Using a-dehydrator woodstove I designed for vegetable drying box. Made of nothing but stove pipe fittings.

CHAPTER SIX

FIGURING OUT THE NEW COMPUTER, TUCSON FOSSIL GEM SHOW

I review some old paperwork I forgot about. I have always wanted to focus on the good stuff. Forget the bad stuff. Let it pass. I've done a good job of that. *Huh. What's this? Do you remember this?* Down the road, the issues this citation I'm looking at become more important. I got in trouble over two small pieces of ivory. Worth a total of $55. I sort of recall when I see the citation now in front of me. An undercover agent buys the ivory. But did not ask if I had any legal papers for it. I did. I do not automatically show paperwork to every customer. It interferes with sales and often changes the subject.

I hear from the customer 90% of the time, "Blankity blank government anyhow!" I have learned not to go there. Why? Such a subject can go on a long time. While such a conversation is going on, I am not making sales. Other potential customers tend not to want to step into a political toss the tea in the harbor discussion.

I study and think I understand the law. What is important is that the ivory is legal and I can prove it if I need to. If a customer has a problem, they can use the receipt and come back to me for verification, proving the transaction was legal. They should be able to easily say, "Well gosh golly, I got it of Wild Miles, any problems?" No one knows until I am contacted, out of the customers hands. "Bye, have a nice day." End discussion, especially if they agree.

This citation states I will pay a fine over $2,000, unless I want to get a lawyer and go to court. I believed in the legality of the transaction, so got a public defender. I did not meet this person till two minutes before my case was heard, in the hallway on the way in. My case was mixed in with traffic violations. I show the lawyer the charge and he repeats, "Yup, selling ivory." Looks at me with, "And your point is?" I give what to me is an obvious answer, he as the lawyer, should know more than I do.

"That is not a crime." I pause to see if he gets it. He does not. I go on. "The crime is to do so without a permit." I pause again to see if he gets it. I say further. "I have a permit, right here in my hands to cover that ivory." The lawyer was flustered. Not what he expected.

The judge, if I recall, was not interested in anything I had to say. The judge let me know the maximum fine and jail time if I fight and lose. I am not sure what a 'felony violation,' means.

"Doesn't felony have to involve crossing state lines? Is there something called a state felony?" No one will explain the definition of the charge against me. "Why is a felony being tried in a traffic court?" I'm about to be be reprimanded for asking to many stupid questions not relevant to the crime, and wasting the judges precious time. His coffee break is coming up.

My public defender tells me,"If you do not shut up you could get five years in prison!" The byword of the day is, 'Plea bargain.' I'm offered a deal. If I recall, a $700 fine. The lawyer has only one answer, "Take it! Be glad!"

I said, "No. I'm in the right and I'll win!"

The public defender says,"Well, I am a public defender and as such, my job is to get you the best deal I can, and this is it. I have done my job. If you want to fight this then hire a lawyer." In the ballpark of $20,000 for a lawyer. He continues, "Look, it's no big deal, it is a violation. Pay the fine, it's all forgotten. A little money a little paperwork, it's done."

"But I am pleading guilty to something that it not the truth!" I'm puzzled. *It's all about the truth, right?* "Well, obviously I cannot come up with twenty grand, cannot move to town to be in and out of court. I'm between a rock and a hard place." As far as I am concerned, I have no choice. At the time I was quite upset to be pleading guilty to something that is not a crime, *and not knowing what felony violation means.* "And why is a felony being tried in a state traffic ticket court?" *So am I a felon now?*

"Poof" it never happened. The mind is an amazing thing. I move on with only positive thoughts. I learned nothing. I was not angry. Because it never happened. Except for this annoying citation in my file. "Oh yea and I suppose I was out $700," *I do not recall.* I assume. If you don't see it, it's not there. Grin, So is the converse true, *If we see it, it's real?*

THE GROUND I live on was chosen in 1916 as one of the prime spots to build. It is a natural high ground above the surrounding tundra. Other owners around me who arrived later had second rate choices, and had to haul in gravel to raise their land up to build on it. No one especially thought about where the water would go as they built up. I do not think anyone had malicious intent, or did not care. It just was not on their mind. In most cities you need to do an environmental impact study dealing with wetlands. It's a pain. Permits, inspectors, approvals, waiting periods, public comment periods, fees. It's a nightmare, I'm sure. I myself hate all that! *Let's just be nice to each other! We wouldn't need all this with the big stick!*

How nice to come to Nenana and do what you want. Build how you want, where you want, by any method that works! So no one wanted to, or thought about, putting in drainage culverts or ditches. The slough that used to connect my land to the river so a canoe or boat could be kept with access to the river, got filled in and built on. All around me ground got built up.

Now my land is the low spot all the water runs too. Now it is my land that is second rate. Every spring there is two to three ft. of water in the yard, including under the house. My bottom cabin logs are rotting as a result. It makes it hard to get the greenhouse going in that critical spring time period when it is under water, along with the path to it. The garden itself is under water. A shame, because this was once the best garden spot, and driest, valued land in the whole area!

If I mentioned it, there would be a puzzled look of, "And your point is?" In the spring, I might pay someone to come with a machine to dig a ditch across my yard over to the pond next to the property, to help drain it. The pond is all that is left of the slough going to the river. *Being a river guy, it sure would be nice to have river access from my property!*

"Wow, that would be such a dream, and add so much to the property value in general, water frontage!" Those who had the house before me, tell me of the old days, with a boat dock, and going swimming off the bank. Everyone who owned this place has been 'poor'—among the unprotected nobodies. The movers and shakers with the bulldozers, changed the world to their liking around us.

So, yes. I can see how rules and regulations get started. What we do affects others. If we were all considerate, with good intention, there would not be an issue, we wouldn't need all these rules! Or maybe 'considerate' is a relative term, or defined differently by different people.

The city came by when I was out surveying over the summer and hydro-axed all the ornamental trees along the road out front, which was my hedge. Trees had been here for fifty years or more. A whole 100 foot row of fifteen foot tall lilac bushes. Mowed down without a word to me about it. A wood storage shed shoved aside with the bulldozer off its foundation. Because?

It's not on my exact property. It's on the road right of way. I knew that. The home was built before roads were put in. When the city roads were set out on a grid, a jog was put on the road to go around this property, out of consideration for the original owner. The actual plotted right of way is two feet in front of my door. The road jog gave me fifty more feet of front yard I did not own. This is recognized. I went to a city meeting to bring up the subject, and propose a solution.

"As a surveyor, the land out front gets surveyed. I buy the extra fifty feet so I own it, and the city can get the extra yearly taxes while the road stays where it is." Nothing would change except I'd be paying extra taxes.

I was told, "OK, but to do this you have to have permission from the other two property owners on the street—to officially declare where the road is now, the right place where it will stay." I went so far as to get neighbors' approval. If I paid for the survey, they'd love to own the land they now maintain as a front yard.

Even Seymour was contacted, "Sure Miles, I'd give you a deal on the survey. Mostly we could do this if I had a job nearby to help cover my travel cost."

The Mayor tells me, "But why bother with a survey? The road has been where it is since 1916. We aren't moving the road!" This sounds logical. The road being driven on is not on the road right of way, but on city park property. I assume this loose arrangement will remain the community policy. I relax. *This is how life is in a small community, the rules get bent to accommodate reality. To help us all get along, we work with each other and not sue each other, how nice to see.*

Months go by. There is a new plan to expand the park's ball field across the street to a legal size. I am not notified. The contractor simply bulldozed the right of way in preparation for work. I get a puzzled, "But it's not your property, why is it any of your business?" I could have moved my wood shed, dug up the lilac trees and moved them, if I had been told. How about a simple 'being considerate.' It comes down to what courtesy means to you. The city could have easily dug up my **trees** and transplanted them onto the property line.

"Trees worth a grand each if you had to go buy them and get them delivered."

As my buddy Josh says, "Geez Miles, who cares. It's a bunch of trees! The world is nothing but trees!" As if I am an idiot to worry about a few bushes! It was my fence. My buffer separating me from the road. My privacy. Now it is ugly bulldozed root wads and rocks. Josh is correct. Who cares? It's not my property. I do not want to get known as a complainer, tossing a monkey wrench in city plans. It does not occur to some people that plants can be pretty, desired, ornamental, worth something. Now I will have to plant new trees and wait for them to grow. In this climate that might take twenty years.

Josh cannot understand the white man. "Very puzzling," he says. He talks with more of a Native accent when he gets excited. "White man buys trees to plant after clearing trees from the land! Clear Gods trees to plant man's trees, then cries!" Josh's priority is his sled dogs! "If I catch anyone trying to touch them or feed them,

I kill them!" I'm guessing there would be puzzled people wondering what the big deal was if you pet his dogs, give one a snack, and Josh shoots you. Josh has his dogs on land that is not his. How would he feel to have the city, without notification, move all his dogs and dig up his dog lot? So many of us have sets of rules we live by, and assume a normal person would understand and agree with us, common sense, obvious. It does not occur to most of us, that what we are saying is not relevant, or of concern to the rest of the community. Unless we are one of the sheep. *There is no greater insult to the likes of Josh and I, to be called ordinary, one of the sheep, part of the herd. We pay a heavy price.*

FROM MY DIARY

Thursday, November 11, Headed out to the Trapline—a letter
Hello Dear!
I am in the cabin warming up still. Getting here was a bit of an unplanned adventure. I set some traps along the way and had some of my hot meal in the thermos along with hot tea. I was dry and warm. The trip was routine. A few windblown trees had to be cut down as usual. I took time to use my machete on the worse overhang branches. I got to the Kantishna about 3:00 pm and would have been to the cabin within half an hour. But the river was not frozen enough! It looked too bad to take a chance. There was no snow on the ice. So the river had just froze last night, with a lot of open leads.

I have an alternate old trail I used to use a long time ago, that came out on the river closer to where the cabin is. I'd just have to cross the river, not run the river, and go in behind the island. But the trail is a few miles back, and a few miles longer, rougher going, with more twists. One of my original dog trails from fifteen years ago. I had a lot of trees to cut, and might have run out of gas before I got to the river. This is a major undertaking that could take a whole day in itself!

About 4:00 pm I get to the river again at this old crossing. It is not great looking, but I think I can cross. I go fast, get through overflow here and there, but it was OK. Getting up the creek I am on is easy. I couldn't get the snow machine up the cut bank at the cabin, so just walked up the bank and went inside the cabin from the creek. I got the fire going, shutters off and such. I got wet clothes off (from sweating, snow down my neck, and sitting on snow on the seat). By the time I got the sled unloaded, gas in the snow machine, and chores done, it was dark. My gas container fell out of the sled someplace not far away, but I have gas here. I will find it on the way back and stash it to get it back here.

I shoot a grouse near where I set a trap, so will have that in the morning. Some tracks of various critters to catch. Tons of otter. A lot of new active beaver houses. I'm worn out, but it seems to feel good. It is nice to have a cabin no matter how humble, as camping out in the open is so tiring in terms of energy, staying dry, and figuring out how to dry the clothes, cook the food, get a pile of wood etc. This is more than I want to be doing! So glad I could cross the river!

1:00 am and up early again. Went to bed at 8:00 pm. Not tired at the moment, but every bone in my body is sore. I can barely move, said with a smile. Nothing is 'hurt' but is it all 'wore out'? Yes, I know my blood pressure is down. I love the peace and quiet. I am familiar with the quiet and the wood stove heat, the smell of clean air and the view out the window. I love the taste of melted snow with birch seeds in it.

I love the look of the items on the wall that defines this life. The snowsuit on a nail with its legs up to dry, guns drying, mukluks, gloves, mitts, trail tape, rope, candles, duct tape, mosquito coils, hammer and nails, roll of visqueen in the corner next to a Coleman generator, and all the things one might need to make life pleasant here. A mere day of deeply breathing pure air while working hard, seems to clear my lungs and brain. It is difficult to be angry at anything, or depressed or sad.

There is only life, and the natural order of things.

When I check my emails at home, I hear from my good German friends Helm and Anita by email

Monday, November 29,

Hello Miles, ware pretty busy renovating a little bit the old house. We have friends from Anchorage which are coming on a regular base to Germany. Because they are here only some days each 3 or 4 months it meets our ideas of privacy. The weather is typical for here drizzle and around freezing. Had some frosty days last week and some snowflakes down here and the first snow in the hills.

Good to hear that you are well and it seems that you are not celebrating Christmas alone. As I told you prior on the answering machine I lost the little silver bear from my claw and I would like you to send me one so that I can fix it again. Pretty busy here as well with all the Christmas decoration inside and outside the house. It seems that you do have a really nice winter weather over there now. The picture looks pretty. Will call you some time next week

Take care. **Helm- Anita**

Helm has a favorite bear claw necklace I gave as a gift. He needs a new cap for it. I remember to put that on my list when I do casting again.

From my diary

Dec. 1

Trip to Kantishna, two feet of snow and minus fifteen degrees. Tom and Lana broke trail to his turn off. Meet him at the top of the drop. The machine does all right—pull gas and supplies. Swamps and river not froze well. Got into some overflow but spin through. Use winch two times.

Cabin, OK, temp dropping to thirty—five below. This is a new small frame place that got built in a few days. My saw quits. Used emergency bow saw to get wood. Fix saw in the dark by flashlight—cut enough wood to last the night. Cabin not insulated yet, so like a tent.

Could have shot a big bull moose that stood and stared at me. Vern not out yet— my neighbor trapper. Large marten visits in evening—make a set.

Dec 27

Set snares and traps. Temp below minus twenty—five when I left, now here it is forty below. Spend seven hours getting here setting traps along the way. Saw Vern and his friend as well as Mario on the trail—so trail busy today. Lots of otter tracks—saw mink or otter dive in hole. Next day have mink in trap—next day have fox in trap where mink got caught.

It is time consuming learning about the computer, its programs, and how to make them work. An entry in my diary reminds me.

I write a dialog in my diary concerning my computer, a make believe conversation. What I think would happen if I called for help.

Monday, January 26,

My Monitor

"Dell help desk?" I pause to verify I have the right contact. "Um—I have a problem —my computer has a problem—well two new computers have a problem. Um—no, the answer to the problem is not in the instruction manual, nor on any chat bulletin board, nor can it be fixed by reinstalling the operating system, nor trouble shooting. Yes, all systems tell me how great everything is, and not a thing is wrong. The problem? Well—my laptop Dell Inspiron 1100 monitor thinks it is a Dell Desktop Dimension 2400.(?) *(He's awfully quiet—bet he never heard of this before!)* I bought them about the same time.(?) You will want to know how this came about—probably? Um— you want the short version or the long version? I don't know technical stuff so I'll explain it emotionally OK"? *The strawberry' B' personality- remember?*

My laptop met my desktop and it was instant love and they bonded. I made the mistake of not only introducing them—but allowed them to connect and bond and exchange internal parts. I realized my mistake, separated them, but it was too late.

They were in love. I had to give them both a lobotomy. The desktop survived. The laptop still has residual memories of the love of her life, and will not give it up. She thinks she has a desktop monitor. She threw away her old identity, and refuses to take it back. The symptoms are, that everything works on the screen, but the visual portion is a quarter of the screen in size. All the laptop monitor drivers are gone, along with all its support.

To explain it as technically as I can. I bought Norton Ghost, a great way to back stuff up and transfer stuff I was told, and read. I knew it would take days if not weeks to install all seventeen programs I need from the desktop to the laptop, adjust all the settings, register my name and password and email seventeen times on line, getting me on a zillion spam lists, find my desk top picture, set my font size, my click time, my screen resolution, font, desk top icons arranged right, folders set up, hand set my server and emails, transfer my address book, get all my ftp parameters installed for all the web sites I run—remember what pop up and ports I use. All the 'stuff' that goes along with using computers. Huh? Use Windows XP Transfer Wizard? Yep, my first thought too. I forget the exact problem, but recollect 'insert your floppy into the A drive.' My laptop has no A drive. So I tried to use the CD drive. Rats, no can do. A direct link cable, and learn about networking? ? Maybe just another possibly stupid idea that might not work anyhow. So! I decided to back up all my settings on the Desktop, and transfer them to the Laptop with my new $89 Norton Ghost! Aren't I clever?

All the programs traveled along too. At first that was the coolest thing—wow! It looked like a clone! But some programs didn't work (frown) and there were error reports (frown) and incompatibilities (frown) and one at a time I resolved them over the next 100 hours (About the same length of time it would take to register seventeen programs, but much more fun) and after learning how to tweak all the tweak—ables (you'd be proud of me! You thought you made it all customer proof?) Huh, why didn't I just bring it to an expert? (Excuse me while I go scream in a closet and come back, OK?)

Once I had a computer that was a year old and fine. I brought it to the experts to have it fine tuned, checked out and updated and have the oil changed and a tune up and all that. Thinking, "Why not let an expert do it instead of me, with baling wire and duct tape, right?" Was charged $400. A formatted computer that couldn't connect to the internet and didn't even know my name anymore was the result. My computer asked me who the heck I was! The expert knew less than I did. The original problem was a server problem, that had nothing to do with my computer. It cost me a loss of probably thousands of dollars. I lost a month's work on my book, my business contacts, and diary. That's when I decided to buy two new computers. Surely with three computers, one should work, right?[1]

I found out a basic problem. I had created a partition. The only way to solve my problems was to reformat. As my operating system seemed to be installed twice, in two parts of a computer not in touch with each other. (Who'd a thunk it?) I learned Windows XP has no DOS mode. Many hours of learning later I found out how to delete a partition and reinstall my operating system.(Did you notice I had re-registered my computer four times in two days? Did you wonder what I was doing?)

Four lobotomies later, it works fine. Except the visible screen size. Someplace I read about monitor problems. I did like asked, and yup, my monitor icon is a desktop and nope—that adjustment section does not respond, and says it is in default mode, and will not get out of that. My resolution adjustment will not budge. I have downloaded dills, chips, ext's (?) and monitor drivers. Nothing changes anything—except, it needed to be defragged! So! How do I get my laptop to accept the fact it doesn't have an external desktop monitor (besides throwing it out the window)? And—try real hard not to tell anyone you heard a good one today, OK? Huh? No, who cares what the serial number is, why should that matter? Huh? A week. I've owned it a week—it's brand new. "Click"

Hey! He hung up on me! *Help desk indeed*

I'm guessing hundreds of hours are put into understanding the computer well enough to work my web page, and write my book. It's nice to get a break from the computer, and do something else entirely different, like getting back out to the trap-line. A handwritten letter is written, pencil and paper! Imagine! BC—before computer.

I am writing to Moon. It doesn't matter, I suppose. The women in my life all blend together. Home and back to the computer again. Back and forth between the cutting edge of technology and the Stone Age. *Time travel is indeed possible.*

As I get older, some of my views on trapping have changed. Like the realization that in most cases, the end user has not got a clue what it is they have. There is zero connection to the wilds or the animal. If there is respect, it is for the money, not the animal. This may not always have been so. I am not sure. It takes much of the romance and thrill away, to comprehend those who wear the fur cross the street and walk on the other side when they see the likes of me, the one who respects the fur and what it stands for the most! In other words, the wearer strongly dislikes what that fur really stands for. I feel the same way when I sell art to someone who hates art, but has it as a financial investment. It does not stop me, but I am a little less excited and happy about what I do.

Sunday, January 11, 2004
The Computer
Not going so well with computers lately. Spent two grand on two new ones. And

both have glitches—the laptop is serious, not booting up even. But. 'But' I know my way around much better. I study the events history-defrag-do diagnostics—and file names start to have a pattern. It is like trapping—following a trail—studying a track and looking for the same one again. Meaning in patterns in nature, is much the same in the computer. I can scan down a list of abbreviated file names and see the one that will install the program—or delete a program, or fix it, or the one that doesn't belong, or repeats itself when it shouldn't, or code strung out too long. I can decipher HTML code a little, just by seeing it thousands of times.

Monday, January 05, 2004

Blood pressure-Trapping

Been on like four blood pressure pills for a year now. The average being about 150 over 85 with a high 70's pulse. This morning was 113 over eighty with a fifty-eight pulse—lowest ever recorded—just back last night from two days on the trapline. The first time I feel like I'm trapping since leaving the Kantishna. Am sure civilization is the root of my high blood pressure.

Vern makes a few monthly payments for the trapline, and then doesn't pay for a while, then another payment. It's far from a perfect situation in terms of who owns the trapline. Vern has been setting traps along the trail to the cabin and around my homestead, which was not part of the deal, and not paying me as we agreed. I can sympathize somewhat.

Vern Contacts me on this subject, "Miles. It turns out much of the land you trap has been selected as Native Corporation Lands. There appears to be no immediate plans to use it for anything. It's just a vast wilderness designated 'Indian land.' The Corporation does not seem interested in acknowledging trapping, trails, or cabins by anyone but Corporation Shareholders. So you have nothing to sell." Partly true, and only perhaps. *It did all happen after a sale agreement.* First, I know the Board Members of the Native Corporation. As far as I know, long time established trap lines will be honored by traditional subsistence people, of all races.

I recall, I had a misunderstanding for a lot of years. Some locals even tried to kill me. However, the elders, the tribe, the Corporation, understood and forgave. It was only a few hotheads I had trouble with.

Vern is willing to give the entire trapline back to me. Call what he paid a lease. He does not want to deal with the Native corporation. He says, "If you find someone else to sell the trapline to, you can, if you want." Not very likely, because he is right, partly. It's now been too long. I have no rights to sell. I cannot show anyone the cabins and the trials. And yes, it now might be 'Indian only' land. The inevitable could be stalled a decade I think. I saw the time coming, but assumed trails to legal homesteads would be called 'access,' and have legal rights. Meaning the state cannot offer you a homestead, have you settle in, and then tell you there is no access to it. The state in general cannot say the trail or road you put in legally is no longer available to you.

Since the time I believed that, I have become more educated on a variety of laws. Indian land has special exemptions. Federal and state laws may not apply. All state homesteads had a clause that reads, "Patent pending," with the assumption home-steaders would get a patent when the state got its title from the Feds. At statehood, the Federal Government, by law, was to transfer a high percent of land to the state. The Federal Government stalled and never complied. There was an assumption, one day the state would get this title owed by the Feds. It never occurred to anyone at statehood, that much of the land would not go to the state, but to the original Natives who would get title to land that was there's to begin with.

The homesteads would have to be honored, but not the access, as state law reads. What may happen is, the agreement can end up being, "Yes, you will have an easement to your land. It is along the section lines, a grid set up every five miles." This settles the legal obligation. Much like access in urban areas. You can't just cut across someone's yard following the lay of the land to get to your house, even if the original footpath exits from the 1800's. You hire a surveyor, and go down the property easements. Cutting straight lines along designated right of ways. Easily done in town, but would be a nightmare in the wilds, and even impossible. *"Here's a quarter, call someone who cares."* "Yes, the words to an old country song we like."

I'm guessing it would be twenty years or more, maybe 'never,' that the tribe would wish to go to court over where some yahoo white man was trapping. It's a huge wilderness still, with plenty of room. *For now.* But the future is cement slowly solidifying.

It would only take an argument with a drunk Indian yelling, with Oly in his hand, "Git uff ma lund, White mun!" And a life's work goes to the drunk.

Even a sober Indian might say, "I like all the work you have done here, I think I'll take it, thanks!" It's not a pretty future. The past has shown me that the tribal council that approves something out of logic, a sense of business, morality, kindness, will drop 'all that' to support one of their own, right or wrong. I've seen it all too often among my Native friends like Josh. I think all groups stick together to protect their own, not just Natives.

My observation is, that the state is open minded, somewhat fair, offered the land for homesteading, and wishes to honor its agreements. However, I feel the Federal government does not want anyone at all on remote lands.

The direction is in making life harder, wanting remote people to give up and leave. In the big picture the joke will be on the Indian, for he too, is not wanted on remote lands with valuable resource on it. *Study history of treaties and agreements.*

Even tribal leaders, Native corporations, do not want their people on remote lands. I talk with Josh, leaders like Frin.

"The corporations are slower than they need to be, conveying tribal lands into private Native hands." Yes, the Native as well as any race, gets caught up in politics. "Miles, to many tribal leaders are running off with our money, being no different than their white leaders, making deals with oil companies for personal gain."

The bottom line is that trapping is a huge part of being able to survive in a subsistence lifestyle, Putting an end to trapping is a very big step in stopping subsistence. I sometimes get involved in discussions with my fans, those who look up to me as representing a lifestyle. They want inside personal information on their dream lifestyle, from someone living it. In the same way football fans would be so thrilled to hear insider information on how the game is played, right from the source. More have a perceived notion about what they are and out to hear, supporting their dream.

"You might not want to be a football player if you knew the reality of what it means." That gets a frown. So it is for me.

Wild Miles, you represent a simple way of life, without politics away from a rat race. So why are you so involved in the cutting edge of Man's laws, and wishing to be involved! Leave that for a*&^%hole politicians and lawyers! Real mountain men stayed away from all that!

I reply

Of the real mountain men, not one wrote their own story through their eyes. Less then one percent could read and write, and most could not even sign their name. I can think of only one who ever got title to their land, with the rights of a landowner. I review this all in my books.

Reply

Yes! But I do not need to hear all that, I am looking for a mountain man story!

I answer

Well, this is not your story it is mine, and while written for you, I do not wish to write a lie. I too read all the mountain man books, saw all the movies, and went out into the world believing it all. This is more of a biography, written by someone living the life many only get to dream about, and I wish to offer insight into the truth of such a life as off the grid, free thinking, not being one of the sheep.

I have to pause and think how to word the rest in an understandable way.

Civilization rules and controls the entire world. There is a flag up in Antarctica, the north pole and the moon. Some country says it is theirs, and the rules of that country will apply! The rules are only applied if there is enough reason. In many cases, people living on remote lands will be left alone. However if you select good land, some civilized person wants it and ends up with title. The mountain man had to keep on moving west until there was no more west to move to. He did not spend his life in one place. Or his life was a decade, or he was among the very few exceptions. Savages, the uneducated live at the mercy of the rich. Homestead farmers moved in replacing the mountain man. Towns moved in to replace the homesteaders, and cities replace towns. Each with a progressing level of rules and regulations, contrary to what works for the previous group.

I get a homestead, put time and love into trails, remote cabins. Do I control them? What happens when it is opened for homesteading oil exploration, timber, commercial fishing? What rights or protection do I have? Who will defend these rights for me? Recreational yuppy off grid types do not support trapping for example. Few such people do not have a 'live and let live,' view. Authorities are called in, rules created, permits needed. The wild gets tamed. What is his process?

Understanding the process, how it applies to me, being able to be part of this process is a way to increase my level of freedoms. I am part of the system and understand how it works. I can be at the cutting edge of what I want, by being at the cutting edge of what I can get away with. I can be part of an accepted exception to the rule. I can help write, or argue in favor of them. If I know those creating and controlling the exceptions, I can understand through them, what I might get sway with, or not. I might win over these influential people who write the rules, by working within the system to have my rights understood, protected, made legal.

I bring this idea into the wilds, so it might be understood from the viewpoint of a mountain man in the wilds.

In the wilds, I deal with bears. One option is to make the bears my enemy and kill all I run into. This seems like the civilized notion of dealing with problems. After a decade or more, most wilderness people decide on another option. Learn how to understand the bear, figure out the bears priorities, and see if there is a way to work with this. It turns out the bears do not naturally or usually hate humans. Often negative encounters are a result of a misunderstanding. There are laws in the wilds to understand and live by. With bears, I not come between a mother and her cubs. If there is a bear feed kill, acknowledge it is the bears, and stay away. Do not camp in their trail. We can call these,'laws of the wild.' As with civilized laws, learn the laws and be part of accepted exceptions. Like getting to know and be on speaking terms with the bears in your area.

"Oh, it's you again." And, "If it was anyone else I might maul them, for no other reason then because I can!" "But you seem harmless I guess. Possibly even useful. I've eaten a few piles of fish guts you left behind, thanks." Civilized laws are quite similar. Same concept, an officer, referred to as a bear, "Oh it's you illegally fishing. Well I know you. You are not wasteful, understand your lifestyle, you have been helpful in the past, care about treating others with respect. Will treat this situation as not a problem. If you were some tourist stranger, I might drag you off to jail. Have a good day." Many locals may not know what day it is, do not want to know, as part of the perks of a lifestyle. Permits require driving 100 miles to get. Some locals can not do this, do not drive. This understanding, if pointed out, can be incorporated into the local legal system as a subsistence legal loophole. This can only happen if mountain men show up at meetings. This understanding was learned dealing with bears in the wild. Does it make sense?

IN MOST CASES, "No" Fancy word dancing. Unhappy. They want to meet Grizzly Adams, Joe Meek, some movie hero, presented by professional writers and movie directors who would not know a wolf track from a bear. Never eaten wild game, slept in a tent. Their reference material is past material civilization got fed, acquired originally from writers back east, sent out west to get a story, ending up at the end of the stagecoach line in a small cow-town. Hang out at the bar and take notes. Few knew how to ride a horse, or could build a fire. Even Jack London, Robert Service, were educated writers, not outdoor people. They created and kept feeding a myth that got created, of the cowboy and mountain man. They could not write of the intricacies of a lifestyle these real people spoken of lived. Robert Service lived in a log cabin in Fairbanks for a short time. He was not a wilderness expert. It is difficult to alter accepted history. *Truth may not even be popular or sell.*

From my diary

I saw a mink go in a hole; set a trap and caught him right off. Went exploring, saw bad spot in swamp, went to turn around, but sled held me up, back of the machine broke into the swamp, spun up blackfish—got loose OK, but lots of blackfish in snow behind me.

Playing at trapping. Reliving my youth. Enjoying old memories. I certainly no longer own everything I can see from horizon to horizon as I once did.

Saturday, January 03, 2004 Rescue Dim

Got a call from Phil, the kid I tried to save from his drug business with the local cop, "Dim ran out of gas four miles out, can you go bring him gas? He called on his cell phone". Dim happy—has a lot of fur in the sled. So much, that the weight slowed him up. He burned more gas, also lots of snow drifts and overflow he says.

I GO HELP DIM. It's nice to talk trapping with someone else who knows the life.

"We can leave the machine here, Miles, I have a spare and sled to come get this one, but be nice if you could haul the beaver in to the house." I know if we leave the beaver out even one night, wolves will steal them and not one beaver will be here in a day. One beaver is hard to lift and must be over sixty pounds. Jet black.

"Dang, Dim, worth a lot of money! Good job!" The fur buyer in Fairbanks told me the Nenana and nearby Minto Indians are the best beaver trappers in the state, and know how to skin them better then any he has ever seen anywhere. Dim is one of these experts. Dim has told me he can skin a beaver in twenty minutes. I have five hours into the job, and it's not as well done. I'm in awe.

"Well, you can handle marten good, Miles, I heard that, and seen some of your furs."

I laugh back. "That's because Martin is my name!" *I will not tell him, spelled with an 'i' and not an 'e,' so named after the bird not the mammal.*

"I heard that too, Wild Miles. Miles for the distance you go, and Marten for the fur you catch."

"People thought it was a made up name when I first arrived, Dim, figured I was wanted someplace and changed my name!" In the early days when I arrived there were still people arriving on the run from someplace else. Many of the mountain man heroes in real life went west as criminals, some wanted for murder. Mark Twain was wanted for killing a man in an illegal dual in another state. There were local names in Alaska: Soapy Smith, Swift Water Bill. In Nenana: Barefoot George, Crazy Lawsen.

"We do not see that so much anymore, Miles, has Alaska got more tame since those days?" Dim himself in the old days set a bear trap in front of a sign that read, 'This is my trapline, keep off.' His brother my have killed Gene, and was known for pulling guns on people, and getting away with it, as acceptable behavior at the time. Somewhat like the desperado days of the wild west. Shoot-outs in the bars in the Alaska villages, and all that. I get Dim and his furs to his log cabin. Woodsmoke curls up from the roof. A whole winter supply is stacked in the yard. He never locks his door. It does not even have a way to lock it. We just walk in. Dim does not have an oil back up stove for emergencies. He depends totally on wood heat. Sometimes he sells firewood to make some extra money if he is in a money bind. Snow machines with hoods up reminds me Dim also fixes snow machines for locals. He has worked on mine before. It would never occur to anyone to ask if he is certified, has insurance, or a license.

"He fixed Bob's across town, that's good enough for me!" This is how business happens. I wave good bye to Dim, and take off down the unplowed snow-packed road only snow machines or sled dogs can run.

THE ANNUAL TRIP to the big Tucson show is made. I am at the Vagabond Hotel this year. Trying a new spot.

"Yes, Eaa! This looks good! I like the atmosphere for sure." This is one of the oldest sections of town, with a big sprawling grass area, large swimming pool, lots of shade, set back away from the road. I have a table under a tree in the grass. Hummingbirds flit around me.

"Not as many people here, Eaa, but the ones who show up tend to have money. Not as many tire kickers or locals. This is a more serious part of the show." Eaa does not like the same set up I do. He decides to stay at his old spot by the pool at the Howard Johnsons. He swings his Jesus robe with a flair as he sets himself down.

"Is your friend Moon here yet, Miles?" An embarrassing question. Moon and I have been staying in touch, off and on, 'serious plans.' There had been a 'fiasco' I did not record. I went to her place outside Fairbanks. A place she just bought. She had promised this house would have enough room for a studio for me, with lots of room to do my art. I arrive to check it out, maybe move in for a longer trial period. The house is big. It is fall time. The house is not ready for winter. Not even close. Lots and lots of work, but too late to get it done for winter with the resources we have.

"Do it ourselves!" She said excitedly. Except she had not said anything before about the condition of this house, so I am not prepared. We'd freeze to death here, and her plans do not seem sound to me. There is one room we could seal off, and keep warm enough to survive, maybe. Compared to a whole house and shop in Nenana, this is a bad replacement.

I tell her, "You could join me in Nenana, and we could work on this place of yours in spring for a more long term plan." Her son has another year of school left, so we enroll him in the Nenana School.

She tells me, "I just do not like Nenana much Miles, some bad experiences there at the bar. It's a rough community." We do agree Nenana is a great access to the wilderness life we both share. Maybe we could do something with my remote homestead. Yet nothing seems quite a balance we agree on. In the end, she never shows up in Nenana. I have not heard from her for a while.

Till, in the middle of winter, I hear from a mutual friend, how she lost the house, lost her job, has nowhere to live. Bartending in some dive bar I hear. Living on the street. I am certainly glad I was not going down the drain right along with her. Everything I believed would happen, did happen. Still. She's an artist, she loves the wilds, is gorgeous, younger, and infatuated with me. I'd about sell my soul to have it work out! *Please*, I am thinking, "Just come to me, move in and kick back, regroup, let me take care of that which you are not so good at…"

A good six times now she has changed her date to be here in Tucson. She is supposed to be here to help set up and sell. Maybe sell some of her leather work along with my stuff.

"We could run a business together and call it, 'Leather and metal' *Like the song 'leather and lace' we both like. God, it would be so romantic.* Doing shows together. *I'd be in heaven* She said she was renting a truck. Supposedly is on the road, with various troubles. But after about four different major disasters, it is hard to know what is going on. I write in my computer diary, using my new laptop at the show.

Friday, February 13, Moon

Moon shows up at Mom's after about six times of changing the plans, dates and program. So I am surprised to see her at all. We talk long into the night. At first, she seems eager to spend the time 'in bed.' Then we lay together and talk. Then it was like she is not interested anymore. She couldn't sleep. She is not used to, and does not seem to like, anyone close to her sleeping, due to her past. She tells me she loves me. Tells me of her past injuries. Some she cannot remember, so has to write daily events down. This helps her remember. Not a problem to me. I understand. 'If.' Meaning, if someone I love and live with having medical issues, mental issues and needs taking care of, ok. However, if a mentally struggling person expects an equal vote in how our life should be run, I take exception to 'being equals.'

"I will take care of you, but will not knowingly go down the drain for love." One big issue I have had over the years with 'those who need help,' is they wish to be one of the chiefs. Like my sister, *"Let's get in the canoe and paddle across Lake Champlain in this blizzard, Miles!"*

Moon tries to give me a lot of advice—on how to sell, how to be accepted by others, but somehow I feel I have no reason to take her advice. She doesn't sell better than I do. She hasn't got, hasn't had, any successful relationships, any more than I have. Her art is only OK. She sold one item in her life, at a high price, but sold nothing else. I only now grasp that. Everyone, of course, has an opinion and advice, and it seems to me, the advice I should take is from people who I feel know more than I do about the subject at hand. Or does one take advice as an issue of love? In a relationship, I am not looking for advice, but acceptance. What comes first though, acceptance, or changes? Anyhow, it is nice enough to see her. We are going out dancing, which I really look forward to.

There is work to do, so not a complete diary entry. I had more to write. Moon and I have a nice hike up 'A' mountain on a gorgeous day. Holding hands, looking at the city below all in lights, is an experience unlike any I have ever had. We talk about important things on our mind, sitting on a rock among the cactus and lizards.

"Miles, how has this show gone for you so far, how much money have you made?" Since we hope to run a business together, it is time to lay it all out.

"I'm not sure. Money comes and goes. In the $15,000 range." She looks dubious as most people do, so I hasten to add, "Well that is gross of course, I have to take out all my costs!" *Implying there are many, and when we figure it all out I earn the money you expect, nothing.* I also add, "Yes money is an issue. I lost a wife and child over money. Or so it appears. I was never told why I was left, but money was a big subject I got reprimanded on a lot."

She nods, "The easiest issue to address, there are numbers that can be quoted." She acts like it is ok if I am poor. How everyone exaggerates and wants to look rich. She is used to being poor, no big deal. If I want to lie about the show money, she understands. I sigh. I start pulling money out of my pockets. I have over $10,000 on me. She is not as much impressed, as puzzled.

"So, Miles, if you make so much money, why do you dress and act like a dumpster diver? It does not make sense." *Does everything in the world have to make sense?* I think. This is supposed to be a time to be honest, put who we are out in the open.

"My life dream was to be a mountain man. This dream got adapted by this term in vogue now called Subsistence. About the lifestyle of a mountain man, defined in legal terms. By definition, 'poor.'" I have to stop and think to go beyond this thought. I speak the obvious. "Being a mountain man was the priority, and to qualify I have to be poor." However the situation is not so simple. I have given up on being a mountain man, and my goals are changing. I want to sell my art and get my books in print. Not going to happen as a subsistence person. "I like to please people and they prefer I be poor." This is not correct either. "Maybe not 'want,' but expect."

Moon offers some insight. "I can see that expectation. If it looks and walks like a duck, probably it's a duck. People like things understood, known, and in categories. They want to know what class you are in so they know how to treat you. There is little credibility when a dumpster diver pulls ten grand out of their pocket. They obviously did not earn it." I think even in this situation, Moon wonders if I am a drug dealer, or stole this money. I will not say anything, and when we set up together and start selling, she can see for herself.

It is the end of this show. There is one other show in the city with one more selling day. Over where Eaa is.

"Moon, this Tucson Fossil Gem and Mineral Show is a series of separate shows coming together in the same place at the same time, with different managements." Each show is in competition, while at the same time working together. Some shows open a day early to promote that to the venders, as a reason to come set up at this particular show, and for customers to show up early. Some have what is called 'jump start' opening three days early for other venders only. Some stay open a day or so later. Moon wants to go check out the African Village. This is a whole section of the city with nothing but African vendors selling their countries' items. We look at old trade beads together.

I find the guy I get the fossil lion fangs from each year. I still suspect they are not lion fangs, but cannot figure out what they are, if not. So, Oh well, poof, they are lion fangs. *But only to the magic people, not serious collectors or museums, probably legal issues with real lion anyhow.* One of the shows has some customers hanging around.

Moon and I set up a table to sell along this side street, as Moon wants. Without permission, we set up next to some hippies who also are not a paying part of the show. I can see Moon gets along with street people. She does what I once did ages ago. She stands in the selling space, talking to people who are not potential customers, visiting, gossiping, having a good time. As potential customers walk on by unnoticed, unable to get in the booth. I can tell from this behavior, she has no experience selling. I do not say anything about it. It's not the right time. This is the first time we have set up to sell together. She has her nice leather goods out, and I have a few metal pieces. My belt buckle's compliment her leather belts. I have some in Indian looking squash blossom buckles that suit Moon's flower tooled wide buckles meant for women.

In my booth I could ask and get $500 for one belt. Here with the hippies, not part of the show where the druggies hang out, we might get $50. One biker customer looks at the belt and is interested for his biker lady.

"Dang, fifty seems a bit steep, how about twenty-five?" I say No but Moon steps in and says this will be fine,

"We are not out to gouge people, we are all poor, just glad you like it! Thanks!" I just smile, thinking, *Taking care of the poor and needy is costing us money, not making money.*

Moon goes off for lunch, and returns hours later.

"Miles! You would not believe what happened while I was on my way back! A big semi truck all loaded with cars went off the road, across the lanes, and headed right for me! I barely got out of the way! I hit a telephone pole to avoid getting crushed! The semi truck went on by me and burst into flames! I had to hang around and fill out a police report."

174

I am very concerned. "Wow, amazing! How awful! Are you OK?" But quickly get puzzled. Her rental has no dent in it. She seems calm now, with no injuries. There has been nothing on the news about a big wreck as described. I conclude it did not happen. So now I must decide if she hallucinated, and believes what she saw? Is she a pathological liar? Whacked out on drugs? I sigh. *What a waste of such a perfect body! Mind, I mean, yes mind!* So much for all the love she feels for me.[2] Hardly any money is made. Moon is disillusioned. Well, she missed the main show, missed setting up where my goods and her goods might sell.

I paid for advertising, was set up as part of the show, not with the free street people. Those with money tend not to come by the dark alleys on the outskirt of the real show. I myself made thousands of dollars and did well. Moon has a lot to learn, a long way to go to get from here to there. Does not even realize it.

"It's not a good show, Miles, I do not like it!"

Yes, we sort of ended up going dancing. After we go out to eat, she gets mad at the restaurant. More than mad. Goes ballistic. I am not sure why. More than ballistic. She refuses to give me a ride home, and drives off without me. I figure out how to take the bus back to Mom's. *Off her meds?* This is my first thought. If everything was out in the open, understood, such as, "I get money from my parents to live on, I have mental problems, and I'm OK when I'm on meds. I do not have that much experience selling. My art is OK and might sell, but it is untested." In her eyes, am I truthful about my own situation? Truthful with everyone? I decide more important than the truth, is an agreed upon perception of it. *Truth is sand sifting through an hourglass.* I could deal with a reality we both faced together and agreed with. But. Well. Never mind. It's not worth getting into. I'm a tad heartbroken.

From my diary

Friday, February 13, 2004 **Tucson show**

Has been nice having the computer laptop to keep up with bookwork. I had to wait seven hours in Fairbanks for the plane, and was able to get the end of the year inventory entered. Nice to see Mom—show at the Fossil Vagabond went well enough, though it seems as fast as I make money it gets spent on cool stuff. A couple of people run a con on me so to speak. The deals are not as great as they could be. I get high—graded the first day at lowest wholesale price, or traded for at my wholesale to their retail. But this works out 'somewhat' in the long haul. Meet interesting contacts for both buying and selling, and get introduced to the latest fads and interests. I can see how the economy is, what sells, and for how much, which helps me set prices myself and predict trends, which is difficult from Alaska. I look forward to using these new materials I got when I get home (!) I am able to keep up with my emails!

So it is nice to be able to keep up with internet business at the same time as I am doing a show. I see a lot of potential here. The ability to run a business while traveling. I sometimes have to stall customers, explaining I am on the road and let them know when I will be home to fill their order. This potential I keep envisioning keeps my energy up, figuring out how to overcome the various computer obstacles. *Such a long, hard battle!*

"Several years now?" *Geez!* All I can really say is that I am not giving up. I will understand this and will have a successful business! One idea I have had gets more firm and a direction I want.

I realize it is hard to compete against China third world countries slave labor. It is not honest to say, "Always cheap." No. Some products are in fact superior, plus cheaper. The way to deal with this issue as a seller in competition is not to get mad but to get smart. Eaa rolls his eyes up. I ask why.

"Well it is an old wore out subject Now, Miles, you get into this almost every time we talk, it gets old."

"Oh, really?" I chuckle. "I'll try to tone it down!"

SPRING IS ALMOST HERE when I get back to Alaska from Tucson. Time to think about garden seeds, start a few sprouts on the window sill. *For sure tomato and cucumber! Yum!* After I attend a local dance, I write about it in my diary.

I address the Chamber of Commerce at a monthly meeting. We have had two missed meetings due to lack of a quorum. Dawn knows the topic, but says I need to give everyone the details. She and I had gone to a Highways Companion meeting of tourist interests along the highway. We finally talked the group into a meeting in Nenana! I announce, "Dawn and I brought this up the last time we met. We are to host this event. Maybe fifty top people in the Alaska tourist industry will have the chance to meet us, the business people of Nenana. We have things to decide!" It is expected we offer some "fam tours." I was thinking of our reindeer farm. Later offer a big feed. "Tripod weekend makes sense. We already have a lot of events planned. It would be easy to use this opportunity to show off what we have to offer." There will be dog weight pulls, races, music and such. I figure we can all meet someplace, and the business people can each give a presentation, or offer a tour of their shop or place of business. Each restaurant can offer a meal to show its business off. Each visitor pays us a fee to cover meals and a little for lodging and such.

Only a few of us seem excited. I have a concern Dawn and I will look like idiots if this is a bust. It will hurt tourism in Nenana—big time. If we can't even have a meeting, how can we pull this off? Dang. *Do we want tourism business in our community, or not?*

I add, "I arranged for a guest speaker. Someone from Fish and Wildlife will come talk to us about Customs and laws concerning purchased items crossing borders, Native made items, and animal products. Many of us have wondered if we can have, buy, or sell, whale baleen art, or if there are laws concerning grass baskets, and what not. This will be the chance to ask and get answers." I have been thinking about, and working on this for years, and am excited to have this guest speaker. We had such a speaker at the Highways meeting. *The word can get out through us, those in the tourist industry, to all the artists and gift shops.* "Not just shop owners need to know, but all of us in the tourist industry get asked what we can do and not."

Not that many seem interested. In any of it. It looks like work. *Well Da!* We expect perhaps money to get handed to us? We have to promote ourselves, advertise, put ourselves on the map! I'm somewhat sorry now I worked so hard to pull this off. Dawn, of course helped, but it was me who wrote the proposal and made the plea to the Highways group last time we met. It is nice that the Chamber pays for Dawn and I to attend. That in itself shows a level of commitment and caring since our budget is so low.

AN EMAIL COMMUNICATION from my German friends, Helm and Anita reminds me I am looking for better ways to market my jewelry and have the ability to pay my bills. I respond,

Hello Helm and Anita!

The Hannover Fair sounds like it would be fun—what is it like? I am unsure now about my trips to Tucson. I will go to buy and see my Mother, but the selling is not as good as it should be, I think. The spot I was set up selling that worked OK is not to exist next season. This hotel is being sold!

A new place for the fossil people to set up is planned. This new place is not so nice, and the show people want lots of money, and took $800 from my credit card to give me a space in a tent. There will be more fees if I cancel, or sell with a friend.

Thinking of another show along the way. The Seattle Wholesale Gift Show. Maybe also on the same trip, the Anchorage Wholesale Gift Show. I am working on a 'product line' that I can offer, that will be easy to reorder. My cast items. Making castings from claws and caps for crystals and wolf and lynx claws that I can have a lot of. So many new ideas for me!

Yes, I will be interested in news on the book. I have maybe four books left and have not had to tell anyone I am out yet, but soon the shops will want more for summer. I have been holding off till I have these new ones.

My first survey job is in a week. I will be gone till May 7th. There will be less work for me this summer, as the boss found a younger person to saw for him (which I requested him to do). I will try selling art and the book as my only occupations.

I have at least three offers to be a tour guide and tell my stories. Not for this year, but maybe next year I might try this. Tell stories, then sell my art (but only to the rich!) —ha! The weather cools off now so 'break up' has slowed up and will not be early as expected.

Later then! Miles

I am selling out of my second printing of the first book. Raak, my German printer I found through Helm has sent more books. The shipping cost is getting prohibitive. The cost of paper has gone up as well. There are now on demand printers in the USA, to compare prices with. I am still looking for ways to make selling art work more profitably. I have always known it is difficult to sell one-of-a-kind items. There can be more money in wholesaling to a gift shop, and letting them do the selling. The shop takes such a high markup, the only way to make money is to somehow beat the statistics. A unique product that cannot be easily or cheaply copied is one way. Another way is to have a gimmick, a secret way to create something others have not figured out. Summed up, a talent of some kind, a good business head. Rarely is a good business head and a good artist found in the same person.

Miles: Thanks for the quick response. I asked because I am buying a boat to push the houseboat to the Lake. I could find no one to do it for me so I plan to do it myself in the spring. I think my main problem will be gas, so I am thinking about stocking some along the River. That made me think of your place below the Toklat. Sorry to hear you lost it. I almost lost the JH Cabin in '96. It was very close. Only the helicopters with water buckets saved the cabin.

The cabin is now starting to sink on the South side. I have put house jacks under the two South corners to keep it level. I trap out there still, as I am able. My trap lines run all around the Lake and up the Creek above the Lake, and a bit along the Kantishna near the Lake. I hope you will not encourage anyone to trap that area or visit the cabin without my permission. I have left the cabin open so it can be used in any emergency. I am still flying my Supercub on floats in summer and skis in winter. Nancy is my favorite hunting/fishing partner at the Lake.

The Kantishna Kween (my houseboat) is moored in the lagoon near the mouth of the Chena. I have pushed it successfully up and down the Chena. In the spring, I plan to take her out in the Tanana and try pushing her with my new 21 foot SportJon boat. It has the 200 HP Optimax engine, which is said to use 5.5 gallons/hour.

I am still teaching firearms more than I would prefer because of the high demand. Thanks for the information.

Jerome

This email has been an ongoing conversation. I once had big dreams, and put a lot of time into the Hansen Lake area referred to. I had lived here way up the Kantishna River for a few years on my houseboat. Back in the days when dogs were my only transportation, and I got the mail out of Lake Minchumina. Jerome ended up with the area. He may have meant well, assume he meant well. We did not see eye to eye on the details.

He had said to me, "Well, the area has nothing to do with you. You have no claim to it. You made no improvements! It is I who put a new roof on the cabin and cut out an air strip." Jerome has money, and I do not. I put the time in. He put the money in. Time did not count, apparently. *Improvement?* I think with a frown. *How do you improve on nature?* Much like when the Natives had the land before white man. They had it for thousands of years. It looks the same now as it did when they arrived.

But civilization said, "No, the Native has no rights because he made no improvements." As Josh tells it, White man spends money to improve the land, then money to get it back to how it was.

Now Jerome would like me to help run his houseboat from Fairbanks to Hansen Lake. I do not want the responsibility of such an undertaking, stemming from the tentative relationship I feel we have. He may not be forgiving if I screw up and get his boat stuck someplace. I merely accept that I lost the trapline and all my work and dreams I put into the area. "Oh well." Not much I can do about it. But that does not mean I have to like it, be happy about it, want to partner up with the guy who 'ran me off,' or trust such a person. But anyhow, and sigh. I appreciate he'd want me to do it, and his feeling I am qualified. Certainly a big change from my early years. I hear from Jerome again.

> **Miles:** Your experience could be invaluable to me. I would like to discuss the trip in detail with you. May I come to Nenana and talk with you about it? If so, what days and time of day are good for you?
>
> Thanks for the picture. I miss the usual feather and/or drawing on your missives.
> **Jerome.**

He mentions the bird feathers I have enclosed in my letters since forever, for the past fifty years. *A legal problem!* Federal issues, involving the Lacy Act, which prohibits shipping wild bird feathers across state lines without a permit. Worse, if anyone thinks I sold them, this is a potential $250,000 fine and seven years in prison. It may not be possible to prove I did not sell them. The burden of prove is sometimes on the accused.

Those single feathers I'd enclose with letters meant something to a lot of people over the years. Now I toss them in the wood stove and burn them. Or still send them to trusted friends, being careful, risking going to jail. If a bunny hugger got such a feather and took the feather to the law, it could be both jail time and thousands in fines. I begin to believe there are sniffer dogs in the postal system, random checks on anything suspicious. Wildlife products, I'm told, need to be in clearly marked boxes. Not that anyone I know does that, but it's the law. No one I talk to really knows if such a law ever gets applied.

An email from Joy, who I helped raise as a child on the Kantishna River.

Hi Miles

Yes, things are quite different in my new life. I am enjoying being a wife and a mother. I did not ever enjoy doing engineering work. I was working full time as a surveying party chief/drafter, and I really enjoyed that. I got my LSIT (Land Survey Internship Certification).

Then our son was born. Now I do a little work out of the house (less than ten hours a week) mostly topo and map drafting, legal descriptions, research, etc. Computers and e-mail are nice, I can be a stay-at-home-mom and still stay up with my job, keep up on the computer programs at least. I miss the field work though.

We have completed our home, had to borrow money, now we have more to stress about, paying back our mortgage. But it is nice to have a college degree and no other debt. Our home is currently running off a Solar array, with generator back up and propane for water heater, oven, and dryer. We have a wind generator but have not installed it yet. So far our generator usually comes on when we run our well pump (our well is 700 feet deep, so the pump takes a lot of power). Otherwise, only on cloudy days, which are seldom now that summer is almost here.

It is very windy up here on the hill, can't wait to harvest some of that energy, and we will need it next winter. We have forty acres of rocks, sagebrush and juniper trees. We are currently trimming the trees near the house, so I ran the chainsaw all morning, trimming trees and cutting them into firewood. It always brings back good memories of cutting line for travis back in Fairbanks. **Love Joy**

The computer age is great, with everyone in touch by email. Fast, easy, while slow mail is getting obsolete as a form of communication. So many memories. Little three year old Joy out on the homestead. Helping her with home schooling. Teaching her how to snare rabbits. Building her the slide, the airplane made out of a cardboard box, with board for wings. She slid down the hill, hand spinning the propeller. Now she has a child older than she was when we met. She has made something of her life. She seems happy, well adjusted. No. We are not close. Possibly we could have been. Who knows? *I wish I had the same experiences with my own son!*

I saw Joy at the Tanana Fair last summer. Good to see her. I brought up memories. No. she did not recall.

"It was a long time ago, Miles! I was a baby then." Yes, of course. So vivid to me, though. For years our family saw hardly anyone else but each other. I was not married to Joy's mother. The real father stepped in later in life and took over. I helped during some hard years, and moved on. I did not go to Joy's wedding. Do not try to stop in to visit when in Fairbanks. I would not know what to say. It is enough I hear from her once a year or so, and know she is well and happy.

I reread the letter from Joy's sister, May, who wrote me this past winter. Joy never did like the remote wilds, and always wanted to play dress up and pretend she was in town. She does at least agree with self-sufficiency and off grid. More like I live now. May was a little older when we met, ten, so she remembers better. She has taken more to the lifestyle I helped raise her in.

Hey Miles,

Steven mentioned running into you and I was going to e-mail you, but you beat me to it. I have forty-three dogs and am training a fellow named Lynton McLean to run the Iditarod 2005. He will use the best sixteen. At least twenty-five of them could do it. So actually Steven does work at the Lodge full time. He was always fixing sno-gos while growing up so I say he can fix anything. So of course that is very necessary around here.

I had to chuckle about him looking like his dad. I've had that happen to me because I look like mom. Steven is a real nice guy. We are good friends and work well together and that is perfect. Since he is so nice, naturally he already has a girlfriend. I thought I'd just tell you so you didn't have to ask. I believe God has a plan for me. I am very happy now.

Buying the lodge was a big enough event for the moment. Ya', so I'm living my dream. Running dogs for a living. The folks that come out here are generally wonderful. I've liked all the guests so far. I am still juggling accounts and other office work.

I finally got the answer to the question you probably remember me wailing "Why do I have to do this math?" Answer = so I can run my own dog mushing business. I am still keeping in touch with Ramey and Cathy Brooks. They have a non-profit and want to do dog related programs with kids. Mom and I would like to have kids/teenagers come out here. 150 miles is a bit far to mush. So it has gotten put on the back burner. Perhaps once the Brooks are doing programs we could do an advanced program and include Lake Minchumina?

As you can see I am always daydreaming. I would like to share my answer to my above mentioned math problem with teenagers and inspire them as to what place book learning has. Kind of unfortunate news—Mom has decided to move back to Manley. She is disgusted that we can't do everything via solar. But we have to keep our standards up for guests. Only the rich can afford to fly here in the first place.

We saved lots of fuel this summer because of the nice solar battery system she had put in. Steven takes good care of it. To help you understand, I think she is having some of the same issues with me as she had with you. So we kind of realized mutually at least that its best she goes back to Manley. I had hoped she could live next door and host our guests for day programs. But she doesn't believe she will be making a difference in their lives. She's not excited about it so it won't work. She can't be at the lodge as she already nearly worked herself to death. She was right about most everything, but we got the feeling we couldn't please her.

Steven and her respect each other and get along well. I have to be thankful that she is willing to step aside and let us young folk try to make a go of it our way. All this snow is heaven sent. Friends are planning on helping break the trail out from Nenana-Minchumina The Iditarod musher Lynton and I need to mush in to Nenana right after Xmas. Ultimately, we need to have Lynton at the Copper Basin Jan.7th. We will spend most of Jan. on the road system.

The Toklat has not frozen yet. Hopefully it will by Xmas. All this warm fall weather is crazy! I heard that you had made it to your place. It is a farfetched alternative, but I was wondering if the Toklat doesn't freeze, could we go down your trapline and then cross the Kantishna below the Toklat and then get safely to Nenana? How is your trapline doing?

How far have you gotten in the past few years? We got permission to go beaver trapping on the Muddy. Hopefully we will make the time. I hope to get the lodge part running well enough so I can do at least some trapping again. Other friends want to Beaver trap too, when they come visit.

As far as daydreams go, what would you think if we wanted to work on your trapline trail from the Deadfish Lake end. Ultimately, I would like to make a direct trail to Manley. I would also like to do some trapping. I want to live the life I tell folks about. Sometimes I think it was a dream I ever trapped.

We mushed to the Osses last year. Seeing Deadfish, visiting the Turners, flying over your place the last two springs. I feel like I am connecting back to my roots. I'm not quite sure how I came to love the wilderness. My sister and Steven's sister liked it out here, but they have decided to live elsewhere. Becky lives near Phoenix and is happily married. I joke that if siblings had things in common like where they wanted to live then the four of us must have gotten switched at birth and Becky and Joy are siblings etc.

Anyways... I hope Mitch is doing well. I am sorry that so far it has never worked for me to get to know him. Perhaps he will be able to come visit and I will get to know him yet. This is a crazy world for everyone. But yet there is a plan and a path for true happiness.

Denali came out again.

I'd better sleep.

Hope to see you this winter-sometime.

Love, May

Like with her sister, Joy, I am glad she has found her dream and is happy, doing what she loves. I feel so proud of both of them for turning out so well as responsible adults. I take a little credit for it. May bought a lodge in the area she loved the most, where I helped raise her, doing the things we did. She'd like to take over the whole lifestyle, trapline and everything.

She is disappointed with the fork in the road I took. She sees my new style art with the casting, and work with power tools, and wishes I'd go back to the primitive by hand methods. I believe if I wanted to, I could work at the lodge and continue to live the old lifestyle. Karen, the mother has not changed much. She still lives how we lived on the Kantishna River. She is ten years older than I am! I can't say my change is all about getting too old!

May has found a way to live in the way she was raised and make a living. Good for her! There are aspects of the lifestyle that are very important to me, that give it the passion it requires. I have to remember Karen, May and Joy inherited a lot of money when Karen's father passed away. Enough to buy the Minchumina lodge. Without that outside money, using just subsistence earned money it would not have been possible. It's also possible the business cannot support itself. That's why the original owners sold it. Joining in that venture might be a hard road to travel. I do not wish to tell them that. Nor is it my place to discourage the dream they have. Helping out at the lodge would be a full time commitment I think would never end. There would be Karen to deal with, a major shareholder in the business. *This is not my destiny! May herself speaks of being guided by God, on a path.*

Getting paid to take people out who do not know what they are doing, who have unrealistic expectations, is not what I envision as a road to my happiness. I like to be on trails I am the only one who made, seeing what no one else has seen. Alone on a planet of my own making. Our neighbors, Tom and Lana, had a people trip dog business in the beginning.

"Miles, we decided we enjoy hauling freight a lot more!" They did not need to say more. They had the exclusive contract to haul mountain climbing gear to the base camp for those climbing Mt. McKinley. (Denali). This is an area restricting motorized transportation, so perfect for the dog hauling business they ran.

"If there are going to be others around, I may as well be in civilization."

Speaking of which! I need to write up my ring making class at the Student Living Center. Something about helping to get grants. Any chance I get, I want to promote art with the children. There has been the art train in the past. It is the same Student Living Center children I want to work with at 'art time,' after school in their dorm. *May spoke of a desire to inspire children. And I had once contemplated running a dog trip business, as she is running.*

I'm reminded of my own son. My father paid for him to go to a special private school. That had no art or music offered. What is there to say? I said nothing. Smiled and added my congratulations. The most important people in my life, making sure my son does not turn out like me is a powerful message.

I review the highlights of the ring class looking for backing.

Ring Making Class by Miles

The Nenana School dorm is very important to the community. The project has financially been a great struggle for us. We are concerned with what to do. We very much want to head in the direction of self sufficiency and taking care of ourselves and our kids, and the children of remote villages. Most of us simply do not know what to do. Most of us do not have a lot of money and most of us do not have the knowledge and skills to solve the complicated problems, economically or politically. Getting grants requires grant writers and skills the small community lacks. I want helping this Dorm project to be more than just talk. As a local artist, I volunteer to do an art project with the children. I donate my time, asking for the materials costs to be covered, and only because.

Most wanted to start from scratch and carve their ring. Some wanted to start with an existing pattern and adapt it. There were a lot of questions that showed insight and curiosity.

"This takes so long! How can anyone do this and make any money making rings?" I explained some of the short cuts, and various pieces of equipment a jeweler can use to turn this into an occupation.

They learned the different ways wax can be smoothed, with a file, sandpaper, or with a flame. A couple of students wanted to set a stone. The more talented were shown how to set supplied rubies and sapphires in a ring. A couple of students wanted to make and cast a necklace instead of a ring. That was accommodated. Most wrote their names in the wax, and made the project a personal, one-of-a-kind item. When copied in silver, the hope will be, this will be something to keep, show off, and remember the various positive activities they were able to be part of staying at the Nenana Dorm.

There are good people in the community to look up to. Some attend the Nenana

WIN group regularly. My friend Dale, the Magistrate, wrote up for a brochure what WIN is all about:

Nenana Wellness Coalition (WIN)

Some time ago, leaders in our community realized that many individuals and groups in the community wanted the same things for our community.

We wanted healthy, happy, well-balanced youth. We wanted strong families where parents and children work together, play together, pray together and stay together. But we also realized that our community itself was not working together. In fact, several groups in our community were applying for the same grants and inadvertently knocking ourselves out of the running. We saw a need to come together and talk and work with one another. We saw the need to keep each other informed and we saw the need to establish a coalition of the various groups in town so that we could harness our strengths and accomplish more together than we could accomplish working alone. As a result, we established the Nenana Wellness Coalition (also known as the Wellness in Nenana or WIN coalition).

The WIN coalition is an alliance of representatives from various organizations, government agencies, community groups and individuals that meet weekly to discuss, evaluate, coordinate, consolidate and help implement plans for improving the wellness and quality of life in Nenana, Alaska. The coalition consists of representatives of the following organizations and interested community members. The coalition has met virtually every week since May of 2002.

Dale is one of the big movers behind wanting a drag race track for Nenana, and has helped form the Nenana Sports Association. I am not highly interested, but will go along with what everyone else wants.

"Dale, when we lost the choice of being able to hold the drag races on our runway, I lost interest because the project requires a mile long strip we'd have to buy land for and put in. It's a million dollar project, at least! I can't picture that being spent here in Nenana." His definition of the purpose of the WIN group is not exactly how I'd define our purpose, but works, is certainly a main purpose. All who meet have a slightly different focus to bring to the group.

As representing the Chamber of Commerce, I focus on a good economy. Witty, a friend in the group focuses on mental health, since she is head of Mental Health and Addictions in the community. How to keep people sober, what to do with those who are not. That's tied closely to jobs, and our youth. Some church leaders are here to focus on the spiritual health of the community. Again, it all ties together.

"Yeah, right, Miles! But you still fly a pirate flag over your house, park in front of the fire hydrant, poach your moose each year!"

"Pobody's nerfect." I add. "And I say, "Liberty and justice for a few," at the end of the pledge of allegiance!"

"Yes! And that too, Miles!" So I'm not claiming to be a goodie two shoes. We try to make the best of who we are.

I'm a little down. Temporarily. Tripod weekend came and went. The community pulled off the Highways hosting 'OK.' In truth, the visiting group did not expect any more. They have been around the block and understand Nenana. They all mostly wanted to be here to enjoy a weekend away from wherever they are from to see the tripod go up on the ice and hooked to the clock. To say they had attended Tripod Weekend in Nenana. We feed them. Nothing great. We found places for them to stay. Without enthusiasm. The Wildlife officer came and spoke. We asked questions, got contact numbers. Brochures were handed out. It went 'OK.' I learned a little bit. Mostly the pat tourist answers found in basic tour guides. But everyone was happy. Nothing bad was said. This was not the great vision to others that I saw. If Nenana truly wants tourism this could be one of the greatest opportunities we could ever hope for in a decade. Everyone who runs tourism in the state is represented here at this event. Someone representing tourism in southeast Alaska said they got lots of tourists, but not enough of the kind of stories tourists want to hear. Interior Alaska has the trapping, gold miners, and other things to offer.

"If we could get some of you in Nenana to come down on the train now and then to talk to our tourists, we'd pay you and it could help direct interest to the interior and Nenana." No one else in Nenana is interested. Some of our artists could go down and set up a table where the ships unload and offer their crafts and stories. This was acceptable to the people in the industry down there. *What great exposure!* But no. There is no interest whatever.

I fit this in with the data base in my brain stuffed with bits and pieces of information. Like how the local artists cry the blues about "No money, no interest in my art, no tourists to sell to, nothing going on." In past years I felt for them! *Wow, bummer!*

"What can the Chamber of Commerce do to help?" Now I have about zero sympathy. "Then get off your butt and do something about it!" This is my irritated answer, "Do not tell me about it!" is my attitude now.

I read Karl Marx Communist Manifesto. An inspirational read. I now have a different view of = "Poor me, help me! We all need to be equal!"

At the tourism meeting, we handed out community brochures to all fifty guests who ran Chambers and Visitor Centers all over the state. This ensured our fliers would go up in those Visitor Centers so we can be known, and maybe become a stop for travelers. I'd think those in the tourist industry in my community would be grateful, glad we have a Chamber and this group. My own personal business gets known better due to these kinds of meetings. I'm always making sure I have a conversation with people from other communities, creating ties and exchanges of favors that bond us. I make sure everyone gets my business card. I made sure my name and shop got in the brochure. *As any business could if they made the effort.* Likewise, I am in a position to help out another business.

"Sure, I know the barge owner. I can make sure your card goes to the owner for when you need freight moved down to the villages. And I appreciate my card going to the knife makers in your community you spoke of." This is part of what these meetings are for, creating ties. A web of people, who know people, who can take care of something.

"Let me talk to him." Like that. I'm personal friends with the old lady who runs the Milepost, the best catalog about tourism in the state. I know who to call when I have a train question, an oil exploration question, someone who will remember me. I put all these contacts in my computer. Hundreds and more, "people who know people, who may know other people, who can make it happen." They want to know me because? "They may need a craft gift at Christmas time, a character to liven up their party, a fishing trip. I have the ear of the mayor, know a judge, and such things." *Or my connections and potential influence is somewhat exaggerated.*

I say again, "I have trouble feeling sorry for those who cannot make any money, who complain about the economy, how we cannot expect any better." *My business is doing great. I'd like to help you. But you know what? If you step aside and give up, I'll be there to step in, it's your loss.* So I feel bummed out a little bit. My accountant friend Bean is often cheerful, and reminds me of the bright side.

"Fifty people came to Nenana! Impressive! With a population of 300 people that is a sixth of our population! It was a big deal just to feed and house them." That is true. I know that already.

I think about other reasons I might be bummed by the event. "The whole process and interaction and dynamics of the community trying to make this happen was not as I expected, and a disappointment, Bean." He knows a little of it.

The local newspaper gal, Dawn, is an example. She is on the Chamber Board, attended the Highways meetings with me, and writes the news. I write for her now and then. Well, I used to write a lot more. All voluntary. To help her, help the community. She had said, "Poor me! Alas, I am trying to do good and there is just not enough money in this town to run a paper," sniffle, sniffle. It was partly to my advantage to be in the news. We had excerpts from my book in an ongoing story to follow. Dawn stopped carrying this story.

"I can't afford the paper to print it on, Miles."

Aside from that being a slap in the face to me—*my words not worth the paper it is printed on?* It seemed a strange thing to say. It puts me at odds with the paper, its purpose, Dawn's goals and view of what a paper is and such. I tell Bean, "I have gotten a lot of personal compliments on my writing and been told by many they get the paper for the sole reason of reading my story."

Dawn's answer to all this reasoning is, "Miles, ads are what makes me money, not articles!"

My mouth hangs open. "But Dawn! It all goes together. Businesses put ads in papers because people read the paper. They read the paper because of the stories. No one buys the paper to read the ads. Do you watch TV so you can see the commercials?" She did not want to hear about it. It's her paper, what do I know! Bean has no comment, but I tell him, "That's when I notice things I had not paid attention to. Dawn tells me she will be gone for three weeks, to Hawaii on vacation with her family. So what happened to, 'Woe is me I'm broke and can't afford to print the news?' Here I cannot afford a vacation. Here I have been donating articles most people get paid to write. Donated to help out a struggling newspaper vital to the community. And the money she saves from not paying her writers is what she uses to go on vacation with."

"Life is like that, Miles! It's not as we expect!" Bean often has stories from his life that are bits of wisdom. Almost Aesop fables. *And who will help me plant the wheat? Says Chicken Little.*

So along these lines, getting back on topic with Bean, "This Highways meeting in Nenana could have been big news, a story worthy of publicity for Nenana in a larger newspaper."

Dawn and I do not agree. But I feel strongly that if I was running a newspaper I'd have 'connections' to get my stories out. A headline like, 'Small Town Gets Big Visit' or 'Little Nenana Gets Huge Tourism Boost!' Followed by, 'Fifty Top Alaska Tourism People Meet in Nenana Over Tripod Weekend.' Quote a few tourist facts to keep up general interest-you know, how many busses went down the highway, total money made by the state in tourism last year, bla, bla. Somewhere in there, 'Nenana has potential.' Quote a few Higher Ups in tourism who said anything worthy of quoting. 'Nenana is an authentic Native village with a flavor of our state's historical past.' Have a nice picture.

No problem getting in the Fairbanks, even Anchorage news. 'Tourism looks good for the upcoming year.' You know, the usual crap people want to know, that sells papers. *Hey, at least it is something positive!* With luck, maybe even appearing in the bigger papers in Seattle, Chicago and New York. A quaint, small town story of interest. I'd contact my buddy, what's his name, Bob, with what's its paper, the Post or something or other, in that big city over there, south of us someplace. And he'd want the story because? 'The cute small town news brings a smile on the faces of people stuck in the rat race facing more huge problems than we have.'

I turn to Bean, "You know, a picture of the top fifty people who control tourism in a state bigger then rest of the United States! Not a suit or tie in the bunch-plaid shirt and jean people."

Bean chuckles. "Bigger than Texas, Miles, not as big as the whole rest of the U.S. of A."

"Well, close enough!" I add, "And that whole Art-train issue."

"How did that go, Miles? It seemed like a nice event."

"Yea, that's the problem, Bean, it was a nice event. It was an Earth shattering event of international proportions." We put on a bigger welcome than any other community in the state—places 100 times bigger than us. We got a train to stop in the wilderness for a community of 300 people. We had Indian kids from as far away as 1,000 miles who have never been to a museum in their life. "You should have seen their expressions, Bean!" Who took the historical pictures? A free salmon dinner that served 500 meals, almost twice our population. Native dancers in costume. Kids who learned a new dance for the occasion. Who wrote all this up and recorded it in the news media? Dawn did not even write it up for Nenana. Art-train itself would have used the story and pictures to promote their train tours. They would have used us as an example, all over the country. The poster community. We did all the work and pulled it off and the simple, easy part got left out. The follow up. It could have meant millions in advertising.

"It could have been the focus of grants."

"Like how—what do you mean grants Miles?"

"Dear Foundation: Find enclosed pictures of what Nenana accomplished for free from the motivation we show on our own. Imagine what we could do with a little help. Our Native dancers performed for the first time to outsiders. If we had money for costumes and travel funding, the culture of the Athabascan Indian could be appreciated." Or, "We are the hub for the Native school children. The student living center is necessary and centrally located and should be supported." *As opposed to the one proposed in Galena, Alaska farther away.*

"Well Miles, you are someone with vision. Not everyone can see ahead or grasp a bigger picture—or not in the same way you do."

I have written three grants and all three got approved. Nothing big. I'm not a professional grant writer. I do not even believe in depending on grants as healthy for the community. But sometimes I believe in a cause. I got five grand to the Cultural Center for exhibits, two grand to the library for building improvements, and a couple grand to the community for a public path along the river. Oh, and some funding to professionally record a tourism meeting with top speakers on various aspects of selling to tourists, made available to hear through the library on cassette.

"I found out from that lecture, why I do so well selling to the Germans, and so poorly selling to the Japanese!" I smile as Bean wonders what I learned. "The Germans, in general, focus on the product. It does not have to be in a nice package, bright and shiny, and could be offered in a junk yard. The Japanese tend to focus on packaging and presentation." I let that sink in. "Paperwork, who is in charge, being on time, and such things matter more to the Japanese. So these things have to be kept in mind when marketing."

ANOTHER TOURIST INQUIRY. Another summer has gone by, winter already!

Friday, November 18, 2004
Could you please send me your free vacation guide and also camping and outdoors activities.
Tks you.
Normand Malenfant
Canada G9P5J2

Hey Normand!
Nope. We got no free guides – not even guides you could buy. We are a community of 300 people. Our Chamber of Commerce is four people who volunteer. We have no office, no phone and no budget. What do we have? Oh—wolves, bears, trumpeter swans and a thousand lakes with no names. It's Heaven. We like to keep it that way. In some ways we don't care if anyone visits us or not. Well, we do, I guess, but we simply have no money to help you get here. No maps, guides, tourist information and such.
If you show up, some local will help you out—show you where to camp, take you out fishing, show you where all the birds are, fix your flat tire if you buy them a cup of coffee, lend you a canoe, give you a job if you're broke. Like that. We have a web site (did you arrive here from our web site?)This is my personal email address too, but I'm the head of our Chamber of Commerce. So I do not know how you found me. Our web is www.nenanahomepage.com, the best I can do for ya'. Hope you have a nice trip!
Miles

Another inquiry!

Hello!
We are in the planning of visiting Alaska within the next three years or so. We were wondering if you would be able to assist us in information for the following:
* View / Visit Wolves
* Visit Eskimos
* Sledding
* Wildlife
* Lodging

* Airline
* Helicopter rides to mountain
Thank you!
Warren Wick III

Hello Warren!

Sorry to have taken so long to reply. Several things are on my mind concerning your interests. (bla, bla, etc.) Now—what you want can be made to happen, but these days everyone I know is worried about being sued. No one I know can afford insurance. We all know the river and take our friends (bla, bla).

A commercial plane from Fairbanks to Nome is about $800. A private, escorted tour flight to just that one place would be, I bet, a cool three grand. None of the places you mention has a road to them (bla, bla) I therefore do not know how to respond. Your request is 'flabbergasting', I sigh, I smile, I throw my hands up, I shake my head. Honestly I do not know how to reply. If you are millionaires and want such a trip, probably one person could make it happen if you are healthy enough, if you are brave enough, if you are open minded enough. (bla, bla) I do guarantee it would be the adventure of your life, no matter what else you have done in your life. A world with more bears in it than people. Anyhow—things to do today, killed a moose and it needs butchering.

Miles—head of the Nenana Chamber of Commerce.

I sometimes wonder if it is worth replying. There are people who think I talk too much. A simple yes or no might suffice. Refer them to someone else. We do not get the high -end guides here, nor big money tourists. I do not know if even Fairbanks handles this kind of business. Hmmm. Well, as I said, I have a moose to butcher. It will be an all day job.

Mr. Martin,

Thank you so much for spending time with me on the phone, Talking with you was truly delightful. You would truly have to love the land to do what you all are doing. I give you credit for being so dedicated and concerned with your community...

I also am very dedicated to young people and truly believe that what we are doing for the Department of Labor is exceptional for the general public and our children as well. I have worked in the past with delinquent youth and have also taught school at the Junior and High School level so I was glad to hear that you are assisting with these programs for kids...

The database extension is www.onetcenter.org When you get to the main ONET Resource Center page, go to the top tool bar and click on US Department of Labor ETA. On the next page, click in the right margin Find It In DOL... On the next page, go to Find It By Audience and click on Kids/Youth. This page is full of educational games and learning tools for kids of all ages. There is another location for older children as well. I will let you know that one when I call

Have a great day!

Andrea Smith

Research Triangle Institute/US Department of Labor/ONET

OK. Sometimes people appreciate the time I spend. Or is there often a hidden agenda? I'm rarely certain in such social interactions.

Hello Andrea!

I copied your web address you sent and forwarded it to the various groups in Nenana who might be able to use the info—the library, the school, the court system and Mental Health. We may even discuss some of this at our next 'Wellness' meeting (how we can best put this database to use or get into it). Later then. **Miles**

A memo is created and emailed to the different organizations in Nenana.

The Chamber not only struggles to keep momentum, even just a quorum. It looks to me like the Nenana Chamber may dissolve. I can only "Ra, ra we need our Chamber" so much. The city is not paying for the home page web site as promised. Annette, who I work with has been paying the bill personally, for two years. She is getting tired of it.

Notice

There is a Community Pride and Village Safety meeting on Thursday the 22nd @ 6:30 pm at the Tribal Hall. This will be potluck style, so everyone please bring a dish or desert.

Okay, thank you. **Dawn**

Reply:

Yes, I agree we can't have a Chamber meeting at the same time, so we will have to figure out when a good time to meet is. My guess is Marylyn has the least flexible time frame. I will talk to her and see what works, then contact everyone else to see if we can come up with a good time. Later. **Miles**

It often seems a thankless job. So much work rescheduling, calling everyone, recalling everyone, working around everyone's busy plans. Then it's my fault we do not have a quorum, as another meeting is postponed. But. So far I have hope and keep at it. Weeks turn to months that turn into years. Gardening interests me. There is someone at the Fairbanks, University Extension Service interested in working with the community of Nenana. There has been an ongoing communication and activity. But much now goes through the WIN group, not the Chamber.

Hello Jay!

Sorry you couldn't make it to Nenana today—heard the lumber was not ready or no order or whatever? Maybe the boxes can be constructed elsewhere and brought over? Like at my place? More chance to get others involved if on the site though. You want this garden to involve the working together of kids and parents? I think you need to address 'Mental Health'—that is a strong organization here—and the Wellness in Nenana coalition.

If you were ever here on Tuesday at noon you could address the group. This might produce more results for your time than being at the garden spot hoping others show up. So hope it works out. Later then! **Miles**

Our community garden is doing well, with lots of interest last season. WIN gets interested. We learn how to put food by for hard times. We talk about nutrition, selling produce, saving our own seeds, exchanging information on results, and saving this for farming information in the future. *This is especially important in a cold climate with marginal growing conditions for many staple crops.* It is possible for us to end up over time, with plants adapted to our exact conditions. By working together we can save local seeds that produce. If times get hard in the future, food gets expensive, quality drops, or not available, locally grown produce can be a tradable asset. *I think through such ideas as a reason to stay involved.*

Miles, here is the tentative agenda. I have yet to hear back from Nita and will meet with Ralph on Monday at the Student Learning Center about the visit there. This is not set in stone so any suggestions you may have would be great. Anything I am missing?

Thanks for your help and we will be sure to give you some gas money for the boat ride. Take care and have a good weekend. She remembers meeting you last year when we were down. She seemed excited about what I sent her. Miles I was wondering how many does your boat seat? For planning the number of life vests we would need. Well, gonna go again. Thanks. **Jay**

Jay D. Moore
UAF Land Resources Agent
TCC Planning & Development

Saturday, January 22, 2005
Hello Annette!
Here is the work I have done for the brochure to be included in the send out to our

business people. The information is there, but as you see it needs to be cleaned up and organized better if you can do that. Or add any ideas or edit down some if needed. Anyhow I am leaving for my yearly trip outside to the big shows! Not back till mid-Feb so will not have much more time to do more on this.

I would like to email it out to all Board Members to think about for the next meeting when we look over our bylaws and mission (before our annual member dinner and nominations and any changes to come about) Later then! **Miles**

The Chamber is finally getting a brochure together. It's been a long time getting worked on, figuring out how to get it printed. A tourist brochure should follow, but for now, something.

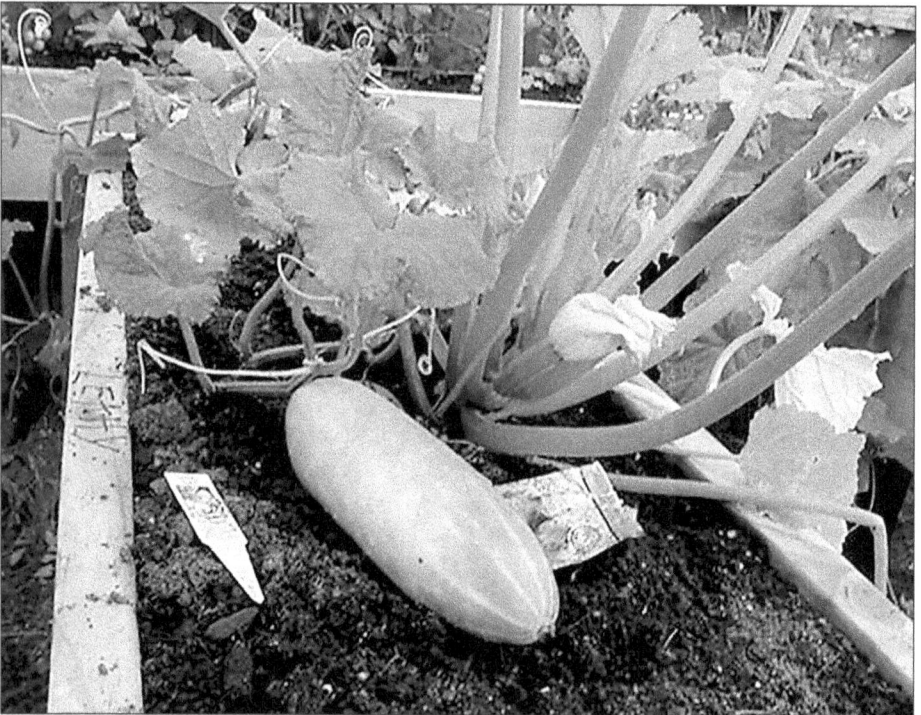

Cucumber from the community garden.

CHAPTER SEVEN

DISCOVERY TV

"Did you get some survey work this month like expected, Miles?" Will is wondering if I still get out surveying these days. It is June of 2006. Will asks about the forest fire in the news.

"Yea, Will! Nenana almost had to evacuate. The fire turned around due to wind. Fire trucks all over. City water depleted fighting the fire. 48,000 acres burned and still raging. The next while should be interesting." Seymour and I were out doing some homestead surveys in remote areas near Nenana. I tell Will how I enjoy getting to use my boat, "And get paid for it, Will!" We needed to get in some shallow water so Seymour bought me a jet unit for the outboard engine that allows us to run in two inches of water. "We went way up the Teck River, Will. Different up there!"

"See any bear?" People have heard there are more big bears further up the river then we usually see on the lower river.

"Huge tracks Will, dinner plate size. But we never saw the bear." I want to talk more about the boat. "My first serious experience with a jet on an outboard. Not much like that old jet Compeau boat you and I ran long ago!" Seymour and I camped out for a week, living in tents, eating by a campfire each night. I was not with Seymour the whole time. Part of the time I had work on my own, and part of the time another helper was with me who Seymour and I worked with before. "I suppose, Will, it is more like this guy was Seymour's main man. While I was a helper boat operator. The new guy is younger, learning to do actual survey work with the instrument." I was a little bummed out not being able to do the hard work like I used to, and now not being the main helper. Still, it's good work out in the wilds with clean air and making good money. We do a major chunk of seventeen homesteads. I go through 150 gallons of boat gas.

The Teck is a shallow, twisty river with gravel bottom. There are salmon in the fall. Grayling all year round. "Mostly in the side, more clear, creeks, though." Most creeks have no name, but one we stopped at is called Rabbit Creek. There were some log jams that almost blocked the river.

"Dang, Miles, how do you get there to survey if you have a log jam in the way!"

"Part of the job, what I get paid for, Will." We did not have to cut through this time. But once, the gap between logs was only three feet wide. Narrower than the boat. I was able to push one log aside using the boat. The engine never touched the log, so I can do a lot of maneuvering if the engine is safe. "If someone came up here to stake the land, I can get through, too!" But one spot on the river changed, and is not on the map. A whole new country is now the river. The part we need to get to is now all dry! We had to walk. Lucky it was only half a mile.

In July, I am in the middle of hot and heavy Discovery TV negotiations over wanting to do a TV show in Alaska, with me as one of the main players. I review my records, reminding myself where we are, how we got started. At first- not that much of a big deal, so did not keep records. So often these deals simply peter out, and are nothing but an inquiry that ends up no place! Ah, here it is, one of the first communications, almost a year ago. The beginnings of 'Reality TV.'

Hi Miles

Thanks for this latest note. This is all really useful stuff, in terms of the bigger picture of what's needed over the year to make a homestead—and this type of TV program—actually works.

Discovery is really keen on us filming with a family moving to Alaska to homestead, but perhaps we should wait until spring to start filming—and then lead up to winter, as you suggested.

I actually had one family come in over-night, they've got a forty acre off the grid plot with tumble-down cabin in the Kenai Peninsula—heading up there in Spring— aiming for full self sufficiency etc... Will keep you posted if we progress with them.

Do you have any VHS tapes of stuff you've done for TV which could be sent over to us?

Best regards, James

I forwarded Discovery some footage. I forget what. I have had commercials done, something from GEO, some local TV stuff done about me. I took the inquiry to mean they wanted to see if I could work in front of a camera. I've acquired four homesteads, and am the kind of story they are looking for.

On the phone James had said, "We want to catch the whole dream from the beginning to the end. You know, where the family gets fed up with the rat race. They inquire—learn, prepare, load up the station wagon, and head north to do it! We want to follow their first impressions, staking the land, building the cabin, and how their first year goes." It sounds good in theory. I estimate not even one family in 100 would get from the 'being discouraged with the rat race' all the way to 'successfully ending a first year on a homestead.' *It's also a truth I have discovered, if you are one to 'give up' on one life and be discouraged, then another lifestyle is not necessarily going to fix that. People who make it in the city can often make it anywhere, just as a wilderness person has a good chance of being a success in the city if given the chance.* It's not good odds if you are a film company depending on a finished product.

My thought of what would be workable I express,"Identify the critical stages you want to cover, then find different families that are in that stage—and tie it together with the story." I understand, not nearly as exciting to the viewers. One of my 'rules of life' is not to bet into another man's game. Meaning in this case, my level of enthusiasm is directly related to, if I am getting paid to care, or if I believe in the cause and the project. I do not believe the project as proposed will work, and I am not getting paid.

I'm told, "Until there is an official go ahead with the film, there is a limited budget and amount of time to invest."

OK. Well. I get talked into helping as a volunteer. I write an article for the local paper to help locate homesteaders and dreamers.

Nenana Discovery TV project
By Miles

A London based film company has contacted me with a possibility of Nenana area homesteaders being a part of a Discovery Show. (I assume international coverage.) This company found the community web site.

They are most interested in a family, and especially want someone who is not here yet and still in the rat race so the whole story can be told.

So if any of you have a friend or relative who is 'Outside' and planning to come to Alaska, Nenana or the Nenana area being mentioned on 'Discovery' is the best advertising we could have—more than anything we could afford to pay for. In the short term it might mean lodging, meals and business with film crews and related activities. In the long term, it speaks of our culture and puts us on the map. Etc., etc. Some homestead family could make some money in this.

Let Miles know!

I do not get any response or even any comments.

"It's just Miles with another of his sensational attention getters." OK. Whatever. I did what I was asked, gave it my best shot. No big deal to me. But still. I wonder if the Chamber of Commerce would have an interest in this project as a group that helps organize things. If this is a go ahead, there will be lodging needed, meals, services for the crew. I wonder then what any Chamber is for, ours in particular? I get inspired to write an article on the subject.

Why does the Chamber exist?
  by Miles

I smile. I do not get paid to write for the paper. It's all about volunteerism. I only give this a glance and move on, not worth reading. Those Chamber members who contribute $50 a year have a wish list. Yet how far do they think their $50 should take them? In their own business your $50 gives them about an hour of their time. If it's good for them, then what would you like me to do with the hour you bought?

The answer is often, "Come on, Miles! You of all people! The one known for showing up at community picnics for free meals. The one who sneaks through the fair gate under some pretext as a delivery guy so you don't have to buy a ticket, then sell your goods without a booth or business license. You're hardly a big time tax payer either, Miles. Who is calling the kettle black?" So maybe we all contribute in different ways, as suits what we can give, are good at, and have to offer. I hear, "The Chamber is too political, Miles. I do not like politics. Keep the politics out!"

There is nothing more political than wolves. Man seems to admire them. Nothing gets done in the pack without politics, the pecking order. This is all about who gets to eat tenderloin moose and who has to eat hoofs. Not getting involved or political means settling for liver. Nothing wrong with that, as someone has to eat liver, many are pleased if you volunteer, or do not want to get involved in what you eat. There's more tenderloin available for the go-getters.

I want to be the least political person you could imagine. I saw nothing, heard nothing, knew nothing. I spent a few years outside the city limits coming in to get my mail and minding my own business.

"You'd have to be nuts to live in town." I smiled and nodded at everyone. I didn't want to know your name, don't even tell me. So much is politics. A white man living an Indian subsistence lifestyle is one of the hottest political issues in the state. So is 'homesteading.' I became a symbol, and started marketing and selling that symbol, as a way of life. Turning it into money through art, raw materials, words. Everything is politics.

If you have three houseplants, two might conspire to send leaves out to block the third from growing. That's politics. It's a conspiracy. It's back stabbing. Is there really a conversation? "We two plants are sending out leaves faster than you are to get more light, you may well die, good luck." Hardly. Politics is getting an 'in' for getting firewood, or a parking spot in front of the local bar.

Discussing Reality TV in Nenana is politics. Who might make money, who might get credit. How might it affect the power structure? Speaking of politics and volunteerism. I have to finish up a library report; I've been on the Board five years now.

What's Happening at the Library?
By Miles Martin

"Better then the real news- better then the truth- you are about to read Miles Martin's version of reality!"

The Library has a new community book shelf. This is an area set aside for books recommended by organizations in the community. The tape series recorded by Kelvin, 'Tourism in Nenana' is worth listening to. This was a workshop put on by the University for the Chamber of Commerce on Marketing and Tourism in Alaska. (bla bla bla)

Oh! Yes, I forgot—the Easter Whoop—Dee—Do was a blast—I mean a stick! A stick in the mud? No! A stick in the piñata! The candy fell everywhere! Once the kids got on their sugar buzz we sent them home in a jiffy. It worked out perfect. We wondered why it was over so fast. Maybe the hot dogs at the ice rink? Nobody lost their basket—got hit with the stick, or stepped on a little kid. One kid had a balloon stolen! Or maybe it broke. The red one instead was OK though. The story reading sure was great! Now—a bunch of other stuff is going on, but it got edited out. The good stuff. I tell ya' folks, you need to be on some of these community boards to know the good stuff. Who reads the watered down version? But ya'! We have Library Board meetings every month and the good half of the stuff that happens, I can't tell ya' about. Sorry! Attend meetings and find out. **(smile)**

I attend city council meetings and there is a new hot topic at the moment. Well, an on and off again topic. The question of Nenana ever ending up in a borough, and what that might look like. When Alaska became a state, there was an agreement, that eventually every part of the state would be in a borough. A reasonable amount of time was unspecified and 'unorganized borough' was accepted, and might still be accepted. But also maybe not.[1]

Nenana to be in the Borough or Not
By Miles

The question of whether Nenana should become a borough has been debated over the years, and once again it is a topic of discussion. The Mayor agrees this is a subject that needs discussing, and a while back at a City Council meeting, he made up a task force to investigate the issue in an effort to gather facts. Alan Baker is head of this task force.

At the same time, the WIN coalition also brought up the subject as an issue affecting the health of the community. At the last City Council meeting, the efforts of WIN and the City Council were combined when Miles was asked to be on the task force.

The plan for now is to have the Borough Commissioner, Mr. Brochorst, come speak to us one day, and on another day have John Coghill speak to us (known to be against forming a borough). Mr. Brochorst has been here before to give us basic information and came across as ready to answer questions without bias—but another opinion is a good idea.

So, if you have strong opinions, you can bring them to Alan Baker or Miles Martin and your concerns can be brought to the City Council or incorporated into the questions to be asked at the public meeting. If you know of anyone who is very informed on the issue (either for or against) who might be a good speaker and can present facts, please bring that to our attention. Again, this is one of the issues to get to the bottom of.

And so ends a borough article I write.

REMOTE ALASKA and our more remote villages tend to enjoy, and take for granted many freedoms we have. It is nice to do things the way we want, and feel works in our area. Many of these freedoms are of concern to all village and off the grid people. Those off the grid have made life choices to 'fend for themselves' and not be dependent on government or civilized rules. Would being forced into a borough cause us to lose that which we value most? Would outsiders see how good we have it here, and want to force us to change, saying it's not right or fair or safe or 'whatever.' Such questions come up, as I talk around town with people. There is for sure gas and oil exploration with seismic work going on. The questions revolve around, what is being found, and if what we are told is truthful. We are told nothing has been found! Yet millions of dollars are getting spent again and again to add to the project.

Part of the role of the committee I am on is to be a go between for the citizens and various entities with a stake in the resources and interest in us being a borough or not. We can do record keeping, store correspondence, direct questions to the appropriate people and organizations, organize public meetings, lobby as a group to organizations, and our own City Council. I am part of this. I find an email from a Jim, who I know, representing Doyon, the Native Corporation in partnership with the exploration company. I glance at the gist of what he is saying without reading every word again.

Tuesday, September 20, 2006
Good to hear from you again Miles.
For future reference, we have a toll free telephone number at…
It clearly is the intention of the exploration group and the State of Alaska to minimize, if not avoid, any possible negative disruptions to the lives of local users of the country near Nenana.
Remember that the exploration group has to get permission from the State of Alaska for most of the things we do on State lands at Nenana. I suggest that you register your general concerns with them now.
#2 As for the exploration trails from last year, these are still public lands. The exploration group has no proprietary rights to them. I am generally aware that there was some misunderstanding at the beginning of the seismic program about local uses, but thought that those matters had been successfully resolved. If there are lingering issues, these people need to get in contact with the exploration group.
#3 We will continue to discuss the project with the Nenana community when and as plans develop. Doyon in particular has a big stake in making sure that local issues are addressed positively.
Regards,
Jim
James Mery
Senior Vice President

This information goes to the committee, and is discussed at public meetings or shared with concerned citizens.[2]There are the same disruptive people showing up as concerned citizens at every meeting. There is another group that refuses to attend, does not want information, and thinks borough talk is all a scare tactic, not worth hearing or knowing about. Public notices get put up, but it seems like some people simply want to be in the dark.

I hear from them, "We have heard it all before over the past twenty years! No one wants us in their borough, as we would only bring debt, there is nothing Nenana has to offer. There are no assets worth more than our debts! I called the Fairbanks Borough and was told, no, they do not want to annex us! I talked to my friend who runs the bulldozer across the river and he told me there is no gas there!"

I am not going to argue with such logic. I smile and am glad they trust what some secretary says on the phone, and what a local running a bulldozer says he knows. Those who want what they hope is more reliable information, continue to do work, meet, talk, write letters, and ask questions. I learned when living alone in the wilds, we will not get left alone and ignored by those running the world. *Life is a game, call it chess. We can settle for being a pawn, or work out way up the playing board with more effect and rights. We will not get what we want by burying our head in the sand.*

The communication from Jim is of concern. There is in fact conflict between local subsistence users of the land, and the exploration crew that is not being satisfactorily resolved for the locals. We feel certain the crews on the ground have instructions from above. Local trappers for example, are being harassed and stopped from getting to their trapping areas. The exploration people are treating us like they have exclusive rights to the land. If higher ups know this or not, getting put on record, having public discussions are harder to cover up or ignore and are more likely to be addressed, if there is a written record. Otherwise, people like Jim here can say, "I had no idea!"

As far as I know, local trappers just want to trap, not make problems or interfere in any way with the goals of the exploration crews. I know I pull over and wait when I see equipment coming down the trail. I try to go out early before crews are out. I go down old trails already explored, with no interest here for a long time, and no one covering this area. I'm the only local on this trail. I set a few traps off the trail, see where the crew goes, see if these new trails connect to anything of interest to me. I know so I understand access routes and how big game I hunt can be expected to travel.

The written agreement with the community is to provide side trails for us off the main roads run by equipment that takes the snow off trials we need. Locals understand this is an expensive demand for them, so we try to create our own side trails.

I talk to Dim, other trappers. They agree they want to stay out of the way, be no problem.

An official looking sign was put up on one of these trails I run, "Get out! Keep off!" Traps were taken. I can understand a potential issue. Liability for example. The gas crews do not want encounters that might end up as an accident involving civilians. Some good encounters were had as well. A lot of trees were bulldozed down by the road creating crews. Salvageable trees are neatly stacked at the side of the roads for locals to come get for firewood. I never had any negative encounters getting wood. It was politely requested, we use the roads most heavily on Sundays, the day the crews have off. I complied, though I would sometimes show up way early at 6:00 am before crews were on the roads. Other trappers had problems. I am unsure why. In my opinion, locals could be an asset in terms of us knowing who goes down the trails. We'd make better friends then enemies and cost less. Locals who feel wronged, are capable of doing great damage. So is it smart to piss us off? "If you want gas or oil, we do not care. We want to run the roads for firewood and furs."

I can see a big oil companies attitude about this. "You want to argue? We are used to arguments."

IT IS time to deal with the Discovery people again.

Hello Steve!
Glad the tapes arrived safe and to the correct address. I hope the tapes are useful in understanding what sorts of things you will maybe dealing with—and seeing what I have done and how I have lived. Yes, it will be interesting to hear what is going on with the Arizona family. Later then. **Miles**

I get a reply back,

We need to have tapes transferred to the UK format (PAL), so I will return them by recorded delivery or Fed Ex asap after that. One of our LA producers is meeting with the family moving from Arizona to the Kenai Peninsula today, so I'll keep you posted of any news on that possible story.
   Best regards,
   Steve

I get more correspondence. We have been talking on the phone and emailing back and forth.

Saturday, 17 September 2006
   Hi Miles,
   This is great—really appreciate the help, and thanks for putting across the issues and pros and cons so well here. I hope we can find people who fit the bill, and also hope we can help Nenana in any way possible—all publicity is good publicity, so they say!
   Please let me know what the response is—and I'll keep in touch too. Thanks again for taking the time and effort to pen this letter to the paper—much appreciated.
   Best regards,
   Steve

I review the email where he spells out better what he hopes to accomplish.

Sorry for any confusion with the e-mails. Here are some more details of the series. If you know of any families who may fit the bill it would be great to talk with them.

We're also looking for people to act as wilderness experts—coaching and mentoring our new homesteaders in the essential local survival skills. Would you be interested in this role?

Essentially, this series is tapping into the escapism we all feel when we look out of our office window—could I lead a fully self—sufficient life on a homestead in the country? And then filming with people who are being courageous enough to make that move, and do it for real. It's all about the improved quality of life, and the challenges we must go through to achieve that.

It will be a series of 3 x 1 hour programs on Discovery, with a different family featured each week—all will be leaving their life in the city to take on a new challenge and lifestyle in a remote part of the States. We are aiming to be filming from fall this year, and film on and off all the way until next summer, so we can get a sense of the challenges—and rewards—that each new season bring.

Each program will feature a local wilderness expert, who will be on hand to act as a mentor and guide to our featured families when they first move to their region.

We're looking for families who are making the move from the city to a homestead in the wilderness, and the greater the level of planned self-sufficiency, the better. So, ideally, we would like to film with families who are aiming to build their own cabin, or renovate up an old place, raise animals for slaughter, grow their own crops, fruit and veg etc., or hunt animals for meat. Our families don't need to be going off-the-grid, or really in the backwoods, but it would be a bonus if so.

The main factor is that our families need to be moving—or able to move—from later this year, as we'll be filming on and off until spring next year, to get a sense of the challenges that the different seasons hold.

If you haven't already, you can view all of our programs at www.ricochet.co.uk Many thanks for your time—I look forward to hearing from you.

Best regards, **Steve Christie-Miller**

Oh yes, here it is, an update about a family they are interested in, hmmm:

The family I mentioned earlier did actually first move up there in Oct 2004, then hunkered down for the winter—"just surviving" and then returned to Arizona to raise more money from jobs. They're back in March, but at least we know they've survived one winter, so they're fairly committed. The only thing they didn't get a chance to do was the spring/summer self-sufficiency—the crops, the animals, the long-term prep for winter etc…

We are hoping to get footage of our families 'previous' lives—the life in the city, to then contrast with their new lives on their homestead.

I'll keep in touch.

Steve

Another email below brings about changes.

Thanks for the heads up Miles. I have just got back from a 4 day break on the English South coast of Dorset. It was very relaxing with beautiful coastal walks along the cliffs, then stopping for beach picnics of cheese sandwiches, garnished with sand blown in your face by the cold driving wind as we drank warm beer from cans dressed in our winter hats and coats.

It's deeply comical, but you can't keep the English from the seaside on national holidays. Even in a storm you'll find beaches full of three generations turning blue as they all paddle in the choppy waves with rolled up trousers and one hand holding the sun hats from being blown clean off their heads.

Joe is the new Director. He is most likely making the film with you, as unfortunately I had to let Mark go when the last story fell through and there was no work for him. Joe will be calling to introduce himself over the next day or so.

Have a great week.
Steve

So ends this.

Hmmm, someone new on board. Re-introduce myself. A hundred hours of donated time and not on the payroll yet. After we have exchanged a few emails, I write the new guy Joe again.

Hello Joe!
Wondering how the project is going. I am home for about a week if you want to call to update me. I take off for more homestead surveying and this is the last job, should be about a week long. We had a huge forest fire near Nenana of 48,000 acres and within a mile of the village. Three homes burned, but four to five were saved. This is one of the hazards of a remote life.

I got some good pictures from the survey work. Some hunters killed a bear and a bald eagle was sitting on the gut pile. Saw a raven try to chase the eagle away. A grizzly bear walked near our tent camp and the footprint is larger than my foot. When I see interesting things I think of footage for the show! (Smile). So wondering if we have a family yet, and if it will be time soon for me to join in the fun. **Later! Miles**

I have not heard from Reality TV for a while. I assume they are taking care of the footage in the lower states, the beginning of the dream shots. It is now too late to get the fall—early winter shots. We approach the cold, dark months. It does not seem likely a film crew from England could come here and adjust to this climate to get the footage they want. I think they cannot comprehend dark forty below zero. Equipment just does not want to work unless you have had special training. I learned that in the past, just getting still pictures for the GEO story. *Oh well!* Winter on my mind now.

The grizzly encounter at the moose gut pile was interesting. As the grizzly ate, a raven and a bald eagle watched, and wanted some of his meal. As I watched, I could see the agitated birds, knowing they could not openly move in on a grizzly. I enjoy watching wildlife, so I settled down hidden to observe. I got a few pictures, but not good, I'm just in too thick a brush. The eagle bobs his head up and down making noises. The raven puffs up his feathers and squawks. The grizzly ignores them.

The raven leaves its perch, and harasses the grizzly, dive bombing him. When the raven gets the grizzly's attention, raven flies erratically just out of reach. Grizzly is mad and thinks he can catch this low flying, irritating maybe injured raven. Grizzly will teach raven a lesson, so lunges for raven. Grizzly takes a few more steps so he can reach up higher and get closer.

While this is going on, eagle quietly and swiftly swoops down unseen, and grabs some of the guts. Grizzly sees the theft at the last second out of the corner of his eye. Grizzly is infuriated! He roars and makes a mad dash at the retreating eagle, who has intestines in his beak, and getting away. I think the eagle could fly faster if it wanted to. I also think the eagle could have flown to a higher tree branch. Grizzly thinks he can catch this eagle if he moves faster and is clever. He is concentrating on the eagle now.

Raven shuts up and flies fast out of site behind grizzly. Raven grabs what he wants from the gut pile . Grizzly may have heard the theft. He turns to protect his gut pile, but it is too late, raven is able to take off with what he wants.

It looks to me like the raven and eagle worked together and conspired to both benefit from each others help. *Scientists will say it has never been recorded or proven, that animals interact between species to help themselves or each other.*

Sometimes I simply enjoy the impossible. Imagine if the film crew was here!

The grizzly makes a lot of noise 'grumbling,' as he buries the rest of his leftovers so no one else steals it. I consider digging it up after he leaves and burying it someplace else. I did this once before to a bear. *What fun!*

From my diary

Monday, October 02, 2006

Will stops by and we visit a while. We had not spent time together in quite a while. He reminds me we have known each other thirty-two years. Like in the old days, he is building me something. We are putting together a meat grinder. He has some parts, and I have other parts. I am trading an old antique rifle and belt sander for his motor and labor. We eat lunch at the Mondo.

His health is not great. He just got back from seeing doctors outside. Heart issues. He has a blocked artery in his heart, but somehow his body compensated and opened up another artery. He gets dizzy and blacks out, cannot move one leg sometimes. Doctors still not sure why. He looks old and slow. He's worried about his health. He might not be able to go back to work again.

Neither one of us could think of anyone from the early days in the '70's who is still alive. Prim, Jim, Cathy and the rest **are dead**.

"Miles, did you do the fair this year? You haven't talked about the fair in quite a while! I assume you still do it?"

"Sure, Will! Been doing the fair a lot of years now. Financially, I do better every year. I may have lost the thrill of it over the years. I'm not sure." I explain more what I mean. "Partly, I used to know everyone! Seems like I do not know as many people." I wonder if the group I know, about my age, friends have gotten older over the years, and are dropping out. In retirement homes, trying to make ends meet, on Social Security and such. I am not meeting the younger crowd as much. I'm unsure why. "Maybe, Will, the young are less interested in the kind of art I do—creative, one-of-a-kind, and the animal parts aspect. More environmentalists?"

"Could be, Miles. I used to see more guys wearing teeth and claws. You know, a bear claw necklace was cool in the old days. Indians wore them, trappers and all kinds of people." Will observes that being macho today is wearing a razor blade earring and chains. A tough guy is no longer someone who killed a bear defending fish camp. The tough guy is someone with an automatic pistol defending his turf. Not into taking care of his gun, nor reloading, nor pride in being accurate through regimented practice. It's all about picking a gun up and spraying the air with bullets. *Maybe.* "Hmmm," we wonder. Or just the economy?

"Will, I used to see a lot of village Natives come to the fair, homesteaders, outdoor types. I just do not see them anymore. Where do they go?" We do not know. The fees go higher to set up, while the services seem worse. Customers are more tight with the money, or maybe it is me who is changing. Not as easy or fun, more of an ordeal now. Physically exhausting.

"Yes, Miles! You used to sell all day and then walk five miles and dance all night, then walk five miles back to the fair, to do it again like it was nothing!" We smile. We were both young once!

"Yea, Will, half the time now, I need a nap about 2:00 pm! Ha!"

I tell Will the fair is still challenging. I enjoy figuring out how to make it work, what to sell, setting prices, what to make, doing deals. It's all a part of a lifestyle I still enjoy. I just do not get as excited as I used to.

"Oh, partly, Will, because the fair used to be my big social event when I lived remote! I'm in the village now, seeing people a lot, meetings, on boards, in commit-tees. No real need to go out of my way to socialize. That is not the big thrill of the fair to me anymore."

"And no great stories to tell the crowd, Miles! No new bear story!" I suppose. My stories are now out of the customers own lives, from the rat race. Meetings to go to. Customers want to be entertained with stories off another planet! Will has dinner with me.

"Dang, Miles, this is awful! Did you put this up yourself?"! I forget others are not used to my meals. The canning of the turnips did not go so well this season. *Too much vinegar and cloves and cinnamon.* "You didn't measure." *You didn't either.* I never throw anything away just because it came out bad. I consider it a duty to eat what I grow and put up. I should not waste. The planet is getting smaller, civilization grows. We cannot waste our precious resources. I am going to do something about it, not just talk. I feel grateful to have any food whatever, glad I am not starving. If it is not so great sometimes, 'Oh well.' I manage and press on, look forward to better next time, maybe. *All food is a gift!*

As with any gift I say, "Thank you, I am grateful!" Will already knows this. We have had this conversation before.

I told Will years ago how angry I was at Fish and Game's charge against me of wanton waste! I could be charged with a lot of things, but not being wasteful! I may or may not have taken that year's moose out of season, but I for sure did not waste any of it! This is a subject I can get on my high horse about, and go on and on working myself into a lather. Best to not push my button by asking. I forget others are not the same. Yes, I eat things that make me sick. Because it is my responsibility, 'duty' to take care of what I am responsible for, harvesting, killing things, any resource off the land.

"Karen was worse about not wasting, Will! Remember her? The gal I had with her children on the Kantishna? Anyhow, she still drags all the branches home from every tree she cuts, to burn responsibly in her wood stove. If we cut a trail, she bent branches out of the way. Trimmed branches. Did not want to cut any trees. It was hard to make any progress with trails by her methods."

"Well dang, Miles, how many jars of this crap do you have left to eat! Ha!" I feel offended, so we change the subject.

"You get to go moose hunting this season, Will?"

"I already emailed you! My brothers and I went out together and got two moose over by Delta, where we used to hang out, where your houseboat was built. In the Goodpaster River country." I forgot Will told me. Yes, he really likes that area a lot.

"I haven't been back there since forever, Will! I don't drive, and too shallow to boat back upstream that far without a good reason. I barely boat into Fairbanks anymore!" We exchange stories of when he and I took the houseboat down from Delta to Fairbanks. We both hunted with black powder in those days.

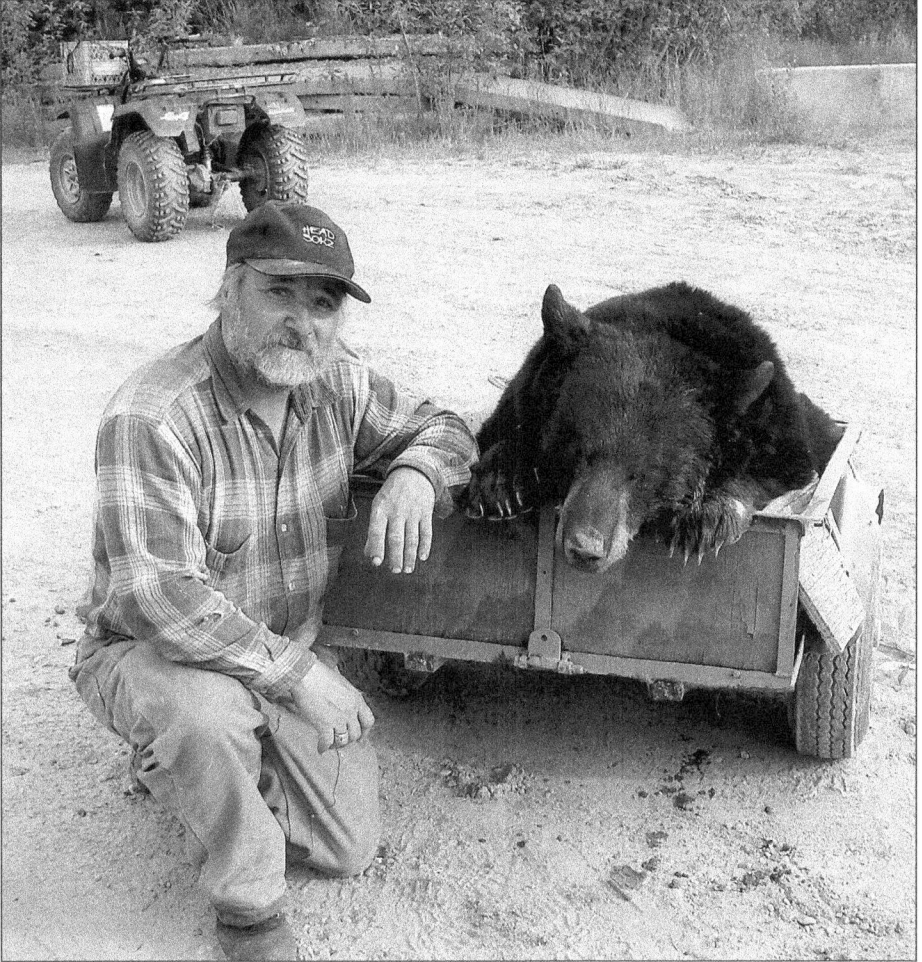

Black Bear I shot on Kantishna River. This one bit into gas tanks and I lost 50 gallons so had to float downstream to get more gas!

CHAPTER EIGHT

TWO BIG FAIRS, ART MONEY, A VERY DISSATISFIED CUSTOMER

F rom my diary on Valentine's Day:

Tuesday, February 14, 2006

Tucson show

Had good Tucson show this year! For the first time may be headed home with more money than I arrived with, as well as having bought all my materials for the year. Also for the first time, shopped for someone else (England Fossil Farm) and took tusks on consignment to the tune of $4,000. Both these events are what I had in mind for a future goal.

The old Vagabond Hotel got shut down. The fossil people get divided up to several other parts of the show around Tucson. I choose the new Ramada on I-10. I am not happy; it is in a cement world. I am in a parking lot with no grass. The good news is, the whole show is along an old wash with walking path. It is easy for customers to see us, pull in, and park. It's a little bit of a high—end show, with a very high percent of serious fossil buyers. There is less of the family locals who are just out to look, window shop, or with a $5 budget for the day. Eaa is still set up at the old Four Points Hotel farther out where we met years ago. He never expanded, but still shares a single outdoor table by the pool for $100.

I stay with Mom. She gets older, slower, and I can see the changes each year. I sigh at time passing. It is still good to spend the time we have together. Her boyfriend Les is aging faster, and has Alzheimer's now. Still getting around and driving, but should not be!

"Remember the cab driver, John, Mom?" She smiles.

I had been nervous my first trip to Tucson. I did not know how to get my goods to the show. The cab driver gave me a place to stay for a night with him, for free. He lent me a dolly to move stuff around, saying, "Just call me when you are done with it." Amazingly trusting, and you'd think a cab driver would know better! Just another example of the kindness of people if you allow it to happen and are trusting yourself.

Mom asks about my love life, and if I met any women. There could be something going on. I have to review how it all started and what it might mean. I record how it happened…

I met Lye Lye at the Nenana Culture Center in September. She had picked up my book as a tourist. I happened to have walked in and seen this. I approach her, and inform her this is my book. She asks some questions. I spend ten minutes talking to her and I leave. I forgot about it, just another tourist I talked to out of many.

She emails me (address is in the book). She basically wants a wilderness experience. I get such inquiries often, as a response to my book. Could I take her with me on one of my adventures? I said, "Not really." *I'm not licensed.* She asked if I knew of a remote cabin she could use for her experience. I told her yes, I have a remote cabin and she could use it. But that I'm busy, and may not be able to give her any time.

She is all excited. Keeps asking questions, wanting advice, etc. I reply, but keep saying I am busy. I really do not have time to be a personal guide or mentor, nor give private free lessons on survival. *Maybe if I had time.*

I did agree I could probably take her out to the cabin. I assumed she'd pay me. (As she did not come across as a user.) One trip in, one trip out, I assumed. *Ya', ya', whatever, go away leave me alone, I'm busy!* It is not what I wanted, and do not know how I ended up agreeing. *Just trying to be nice.* The original plan was to allow her to use my cabin, and she charters a plane in and out that I have nothing to do with, bringing in her own supplies.

She writes

"I know I have a lot to learn and I am looking forward to that. If there are any other things that I'll need, please advise me. Thanks.
    Sincerely,
    Lye Lye"

She told me how she had climbed mountains, is an outdoor person with much experience. She just wanted to round that out with a winter experience. This sounded reasonable. She asked what to do—it is late in the season and she loves Alaska, and knows she wants to do this. I suggested she come here, and at least be in Alaska! Maybe she can get to the woods this winter. But if not, for sure she can experience the cold, learn some skills, be available if opportunity knocks. For sure she can venture out for a day at a time, see moose, see the northern lights. She might end up at my homestead cabin if all goes well, but maybe not. I suggested she leave an 'out' to have enough money to go someplace else—back home or a 'plan B.' This advice is based on my own life and experience. How it was for me. Wherever I go, there is work, opportunity of some kind.

She said she wanted to be no trouble, and could stay in a tent in my yard. She must be pretty tough if she anticipated winter tent life in Alaska. I assumed she might stay at the Rough Woods Inn, or rent someplace—mostly because I told her my place is small and dirty. I suspected she would not be happy to stay here.

Lye Lye told me what she was buying in preparation.

She writes

"I do not have snowshoes, but I can learn to make one out of wood if you advise me how. I have some fleece clothing's and a few ski-type coats, winter boots and woolen socks, scarves and mittens. Do I need a parka?

I'll bring my own food—50lbs potatoes, 50lbs flour, 50lbs spaghetti, 50lbs rice, 50lbs dried beans, 50lbs sugar, salt and spices, 1 tin cocoa powder, 20lb apples, 100 fresh eggs, cheeses, 5 doz. bagels, a large box of milk powder, 100 tea bags, 5 doz canned tuna. Are these foods enough to last me thru the winter? I've a metal plate (for use as a hot plate) that is placed over a fire ring. My cooking utensils are a 6" frying pan, a 1-litre pot and a 1-litre kettle, all lightweight and the handles are foldable.

As for lighting, I'll get a lamp. Also, I've a few LED torchlights that do not require the use of batteries. With a few sheets of aluminum foil (for reflecting purposes), I can enhance the brightness.

Now this list, these questions, I find slightly irritating in that it makes a lot of assumptions on my part. It is like asking a lawyer for free legal advice, or a doctor for medical advice, or a mechanic how to fix your own car. It implies a level of liability and responsibility. If I give poor advice, and my advice costs her life, or extreme discomfort, I will feel bad and be liable. If I spend time to think about it, go over this list with her, become an advisor—this is normally worth a whole lot of money. People pay thousands of dollars for expert guidance in the woods for a private outfitter, guide, mentor, guardian, and personal escort. It requires a license, insurance, equipment, and cost $500 a day to a client as a result of all the costs. An entire winter? As a business proposition it might be worth 10 grand. There is talk of some form of payment.

She writes

"How much does a snowmachine costs? If it isn't too expensive, we can split the costs (half-half)and get a new one."

I spoke of costs, but nothing concrete. I write:

"I have much of what you need, but you may need to buy it from me as used. Lanterns, extra clothes, snowshoes. I may have to fix up the big sled (now stored in the woods). We may even make a trip out and back. After looking and coming back, you may know better what it is you need or want. The cost can change depending on the trips and needs. I usually expect $100 a day plus my out of pocket costs."

I thus assumed there might be some money through 'rental' of various things. I was sure it would be nothing like the 10 grand possible. Sounds like she has money if she considers buying a new snow machine and such.

I glance at the list of what she is getting, where she gets it. Some goods I see are needed, and much I see is a waste of money and weight. *I should tell her what?* I pretty much summed it up by saying stop.

"Stop buying. All you need can be got right here locally, and you and I can spend a day in town getting all you need. In this way I can look over the supplies and make sure it will work and not be a waste of money." *How did I get roped even further in?* Partly out of concern for her spending money on useless items, but partly the selfish reasons. If she spends her money on junk, there will be less of her money for me. Why not be efficient, get the right stuff for less, and pass some of that savings on to me, and we both win? Partly I see her spending many hours shopping, wondering, making lists. I feel I could accomplish in a few hours what is taking her 100 hours. My view on 'help' in general is, offering something that is easy for me, but hard for you, that you will appreciate.

There was not an understanding on her part of what this life costs. She writes:

"For any other travels whereby we will be traveling together, we will share the traveling expenses, 50-50, is that ok with you? When you travel to the cabin where I'll be staying, I'll also split the cost of gas, 50-50 with you, ok?"

I tried to explain that gas is a small cost of a trip. It cost me $10 an hour to travel in the wilds. This single fact is why I really am not interested in going in business. I have met no one who believes me, or understands this one single fact. "$10 an hour, my cost," it sounds impossible, highly exaggerated. As a result, anyone I tell this to snorts and feels like I plan to rip them off. In truth that is minimum cost. It goes only up from there.

Breaking costs down, I explain to my mother when she asks, "Let's discuss some facts and numbers. Gas is less than ten miles to the gallon." The other costs? The snow machine cost $7,000, and in 5,000 miles I need a new one. This is the average time. That's normal. Many mechanics and dealers tell me this is what the machine is designed for. So that's a dollar a mile depreciation. During that 5,000 miles, past experience shows I can expect a $1,500 engine replacement—or other major costs. I needed five belts at $45 each, three sets of ski skins at $65 each. I needed 10 spark plugs at $2.50 each. There was shop time for fixing—total $500. I needed fiberglass to fix the cowling. I lost more than one thermos. I lost a rifle. I go through rope. I have a sled I pull. I need a fan belt. I needed a fan—$300. This is off the top of my head. Over a 25 year period I add up the costs, and divide it by the miles I travel. It's roughly $10 an hour or $2 a mile. Boat is about the same deal.

So the fifty mile trip in and back out is about $200 'my cost.' At $200 I make nothing. Who would believe that? It is common for people to offer."Let us split the fuel costs." Thinking $20 is 'fair.' Right from the get-go, we are not singing from the same sheet of music. This is the main reason I do not want to help people with their wilderness experience.

Plus, 'split the costs' implies I am doing this for fun—enjoy taking someone out, or we are 'friends,' like we are sharing something. No. Enjoyment is me going out alone. My time, my way, doing what I want, how I want, in the peace and quiet of the wilds. I eat what I want, when I want. I stop to warm up when I get cold, not when someone else gets cold. I take a break to take a picture where and when I want. Sharing with a loved one, or dear friend sounds like an OK experience, but not one I have little experience with. Others have nothing to contribute to either the joy, or safety of my experience. Mostly the need is on their part, not mine.

The wilds are harsh on equipment. The rich can go out with new equipment sort of reliably. The 'weekend warriors.' It's a false sense of reality. They have a new $10,000 piece of equipment, not the well used $7,000 one as I have. If theirs makes a noise—if it even gets a scratch—it is brought to the shop. Experts with tools change the plugs, go over the nuts and bolts, replace worn parts. It's much more safe. But of course, costs twice as much all around. Weekend warriors put the 5,000 miles on a machine in ten to fifteen years. The machine is replaced. I could, in theory, put that many miles on a machine in a single year. Most weekend warriors have no reason to keep records, face what their toy costs. If it's $20 an hour, so what? It's three hours a week. I suspect these folks are the ones tourists and folks like Lye Lye talk to, who are in civilization, and glad to offer advice. It makes it all the harder to clue in people who want to seriously consider this as a way of life.

So I see Lye Lye in this light. A dreamer who wants a wilderness vacation 'cheap.' A champagne dream on a beer budget. There is some truth to talk concerning wilderness people about how cheap it is. In that, you often don't pay with money, you pay with sweat and hardships. Either way, it is not free. How will this woman ever know? It seems obvious, not with my words. She will have to see, and figure it out first hand. My thought would be to have another conversation after she gains a little knowledge. I assume a chuckle and she admits, "I guess I do not know much, huh?" With a willingness to pay someone else to make it happen.

Concerning "Maybe having to stay in my house till we go out," she writes:

"Thank you for allowing me to stay at your place for a week. I'll help out with housekeeping and also any odd jobs to compensate for the stay. I can get my own groceries for that week too."

I sigh. I see all this enthusiasm from this Lye Lye woman. I assume if she is a nice person, she will come to understand at some point, what she is getting into, and make it right financially. I see well enough, she is not listening. There is no point in me telling it like it is. It's not sinking in. She will take one look outdoors, and see how silly it is to think of staying in a tent (for example). She will go out for half an hour in the cold dressed as she thinks she needs to be, and suddenly comprehend she needs more than earmuffs. More than all the words I can tell her.

I say, "Hold that thought, just get here and deal with it one step at a time." I did not want her to get all this 'crap,' get here and be out of money to get what she needs. Ideally, she should arrive with nothing. But no. I'm sure she does not have a clue why I would say that.

My belief is, any decent honest person may think the costs might be a few hundred dollars. But upon being introduced to reality laugh and say, "How silly of me, sorry, I can see it is costing thousands of dollars, not hundreds of dollars and I need to be fair with you, so let's work something out." This is what I assume will happen.

She writes:

Hello Miles,

I look forward to observing freeze up of the river. I saw in a video movie that during breakup, the ice creates a tingling kind of sound. Will there be some kind of avalanche during breakup? How exciting to witness the real scenes!

I understand.[1] *If I dream of the city, I dream of museums, good foods, the wonders of the bright lights, live music to dance to. How much do I really think about a job, and how it all gets paid for? I do not try to think about getting rolled, being hit by a car, insurance, etc., etc. Yuk! I learn all that along the way, I guess. Such is life.*

"She arrives and is ready to go out, mom!" All eager! She had quit her job. Here for good! No turning back, and no way out if this failed. I told Lye Lye the river had not frozen yet as expected, so we cannot cross yet. It might be two weeks or more. I explain how it was to mom—how this girl and I met.

I barely remember meeting her when she got my book. I do not know what she looks like. She is less than 100 pounds, Asian, fifty years old, but could pass for thirty. As I get to know her, I see she cannot lift more than thirty pounds. She hates engines, gas, and mechanical tools of all kinds. Which is common among those who wish to return to nature. She has no experience with a bow saw. She has a light hat and earmuffs, and thinks this is enough.

I tell mom,"I had told her if I did not think she was prepared, I would refuse to take her out and be responsible." That was the agreement. I had suggested she have the backup plan, a way to go back home for example, saying, 'Oh well!' and not holding me responsible.

I take her around Nenana on the snow machine. We are out half an hour, and she freezes, is seriously cold. I let her know the trip to the homestead is six to eight hours. I expect her to think, *Wow! If I cannot stay warm for even one hour, how will I last eight hours! I need to adjust first!* No, she is asking other questions. She is worried if the door to the remote cabin has an inside lock on it, "In case the bears or wolves try to get in." I have reason to pause and wonder how things might go for her. Wildlife breaking in would be the least of her worries.

We gather wood. Lye Lye picks sticks up off the ground the diameter of my fingers. This, she feels, is what she needs to heat the house for the night. "All by hand, like our ancestors!" She says. It is soon obvious to me she cannot start the saw, generator, snow machine, and never will be able to. She thinks the saw I am using to cut wood is electric. I doubt she knows what a spark plug is. No way can she sharpen the chain. She will not touch anything that has gas on it. She wears gloves for that and closes her eyes. I myself may have been incredibly ignorant about the lifestyle when I first arrived.

Yet I never said, "No, I will not, cannot do this part" I said "I will do it no matter what, even if I am scared, or hate it, or think it might hurt me. It must be done if I hope to live."

She shows me the tools she got, and offers a pair of tin snips almost three feet long to cut firewood with. There is talk of how the tools do the work she needs done. I think, *No, the tool does not do the work for us! We do the work, and the tool is the means. It is necessary to know what tool, how to use it, and how to take care of it."* I image her thinking, *'Tools, I need tools, OK'* and grabbing 'tools' at random off the shelf saying, "I now have the tools. I am set." It reminds me of a man who might decide to be a cook, so he goes to the store and buys 'stuff' related to cooking. A mixer without a bowl. A bottle of vanilla extract and a can of chili powder. Then feels qualified to be a chef. But forgets to buy a pot. *While I have always said, 'Let the tool do the work' I now realize no, the tool does not do any work. We do. The tool is useless without a skilled user.*

Lye Lye cannot light a fire in my woodstove, even in two hours. She tells me, "Well, I know how! You get small stuff, make a pyramid, and layer it…"

I say, "OK, so do it." She cannot find the right sort of material around to do it. She read about building fires.

"How hard can it be?" She uses newspaper and green logs. She tells me: "Yes, but out in the woods, on my own, I'll figure it all out. I have no need to figure it out now, this is town."

I reply, "Well, just humor me, show me you can do it, even if you know you can. I need to know. So pretend you are alone in the woods, and need to get a fire going in the cabin."

I see her reading a book. No fire is going. I ask and she says, "Oh, I forgot. I got side tracked." I have to decide what might happen if I drop her off in the wilds in the dead of winter as requested. Will she, as she believes, suddenly sober up, get with it, and be on a fast learning curve? Or, will she freak out and die? From what I know of her, my opinion is, she will have about half an hour to get a fire going. After that, she will be in panic mode and will die. I will, of course, build her first fire and perhaps make sure she has a week of wood. So she might live two weeks.

I'm now told that it does not matter if Lye Lye writes a statement saying I am not liable or responsible. Sort of like if you are the driver you are responsible for the passenger having a seat belt on. There are no exceptions. If I have knowledge she does not have, and take her out, and she dies, or gets hurt, it is my responsibility. Hmm. Especially if I have accepted money and been hired. Not good that I am not licensed as a guide or landlord. Normally, no one would care. Society will care if this woman dies. I may be cold hearted, but believe we a have the right to die. We have the right to make serious mistakes if we chose to. I do not feel anyone owes anyone else a way out, nor should interfere with another's rights. I may feel strongly about this because I was told almost exactly the same thing! I could not find pilot to fly me into the wilds. The one who did fly, told his wife he expected to never see me alive again. He was dropping off someone who wanted to die. That was the 1970's. I wonder today if a pilot would be arrested for negligence or murder.

I do not mind helping someone out, but now I am risking a lifetime in prison if she can't cut it. It is up to the individual to weigh the costs, balance the rewards, and decide the risk.

She'd learn more in her first week, then in the past twenty years of studying and reading about it. She might die, but 'probably not.' She is obsessed. She will not let this go till she 'knows,' and nothing else is, or will ever be, on her mind. It is what she dreams about, lives for, and talks about. Nothing else matters. If she gets talked out of this, she will be like this the rest of her life. Wondering. Being resentful that others deprived her of an experience she wanted and demanded. She will forever think she missed out on seeing northern lights and hearing howling wolves out in the Great Alone. She can never be at rest, or feel good about herself till she has her answers.

What right do I or you or anyone have to deny her this? Who are any of us to judge? I have an opinion, and it is worth what? I might be wrong. After all, wasn't the world wrong about me? Weren't bets placed on how many days I would survive? Did I know much more than Lye Lye when I took off? I sigh. Some locals tell me, "But Miles, you are a man, she is a woman!" Also, I had some minor outdoor experience. I had been camping with my Dad. I had fired a .22 and BB gun, and knew a tiny bit about guns. I was willing to pick up a saw.

Lye Lye says, "But it does not matter as it is all in the head and willpower. I have motivation, and I will figure it out without physical strength!" Sounds logical. Partly true. But totally? If she cuts a tree down then can not move it, what then? What if she can't roll it over to cut the limbs off, or lift it out of the snow to section it? In truth, this is somewhat a physical life. Those who live it tend to be muscular. Women can usually lift two buckets of water, at five gallons each, and haul them from the creek to the cabin. It is a bush test we joke about. We call them "a good two bucket woman," and it's a compliment—an indicator you passed a test, so you might make it. That's a total of sixty pounds, a minimum requirement to be 'one of us.'

"So a month has gone by, Mom!"

"Goodness!"

I have not got Lye Lye out to the homestead. "There is her version why, and my version why." I explain to my mother. (Do I smile here?)

The Lye Lye version as she relates to me verbally is, "You do not really want to take me out! If so you should just say so. You have mislead me and now I understand why no woman will live with you. You are all talk. You are deceitful and not trustworthy." She is now not speaking to me as we avoid each other in the house. I do not have a clue what is going on with her plans. I do not know if she has contacted someone else to take her to my homestead for her wilderness experiences, and if so, when he will arrive and she will be gone. She has been making 'secret' phone calls. She may have plans to find some other place to stay, and move out, or stay someplace else for her experience other than my homestead. She has hinted at alternate plans, but I think she has found out what a pilot will charge.

I have the snow machine and sled ready. The river sort of froze. In theory, we could be headed out to the homestead this morning. But 'only if' and 'in theory' I sigh. I see much misunderstanding between her and me. Now think it cannot be resolved.

First, I have no intention of going out on a dangerous, risky trip with someone I am not on speaking terms with. With someone who does not trust me, and feels I am a liar, a deceiver and incompetent or whatever. If we get in trouble, I need someone who will work with me, not be my enemy.

As bad luck would have it, the river froze a month later than usual (global warming?) I have no control over the weather. There is simply no way to get there from here without crossing the frozen river. Everyone who wants across is waiting. I do understand many civilized people cannot comprehend being told by God you cannot do something. There is little snow. Again, not normal. Usually there is more snow. Again, I have no control over that. There was no way to predict.

Next, this is not my trip, but hers. I have no real reason to rush out to the homestead before it is safe. I made a trip once I knew I 'could,' but knew it was not good conditions. It was, in fact, the same exact situation with my ex, long ago. We were out, and she wanted to get to civilization. I told her waiting another month would be a lot better. She freaked out on me. Demanded I take her out now. I told her it was possible, but the trip would be hard. I told her she would probably not die. The trip was exactly as I described. She never agreed I was right. We walked in front of the sled dogs the last ten miles. Not on speaking terms. A forced march few civilized people can comprehend. Almost routine when you live a wilderness life.

With Lye Lye, I decided to go alone, due to the dangers, and the fact it appeared Lye Lye is more green then I understood. The longer I know her, the less comfortable I feel about this whole venture, instead of more comfortable. I recall saying before she got here, she may not get out at all, that it depended on a few things. I recall saying I'd have to check her out a week or so to determine if she can make it alone out there. I think Lye Lye was not hearing that part. I think she was simply excited by the 'yes,' and heard nothing else. I do not 'blame' her for that, a natural thing. But causing 'problems' at this point. She assumed it was a done deal. We were doing this no matter what. That she is qualified, not a problem, and assumed I'd agree.

She suggested I cut all her wood for her. I am not being paid. Wood is worth $200 a cord. I do not cut my own wood for more than a week at a time. Why do it free for someone else? I'm resentful to be put on the spot, obligated. She suggested I bring her in from the wilds so she can see the Iditarod dog sled race. I myself cannot afford to see the race. On whose dime I wonder? I could go on and on. In all honesty, I like to think Lye Lye simply does not understand the trip. Thinks it is simple, easy, no big deal, and not at all costly. That somehow I'm making it all up. I get the impression she considers my talk the usual guy macho stuff.

"I can do it, but you can't." She honestly feels paying half my gas is plenty fair. She gave me $60 and feels this is enough for several trips. I think she feels this way because in civilization fifty gallons of gas would take her a long way!

She says, "If there is brush, let us stop and cut it all. If there are dips in the trial, let us stop and use the snow shovel to fill them in!" I hear such things, and more and more see how she might not survive. Yes, it is easy enough for me to do. I forget. I simply forget how little others know. I see more and more this is like taking a five year old out. I did not know that when we wrote.

I tell my mother all this.

"Goodness, Miles, you and your adventures! Were you sleeping with her?"

I sigh. I begin, "Well" and pause. "Well, it has been three nights in our small cabin with me sleeping on the floor. She takes a shower. She comes out to the wood stove to get warm with a towel around her. I'm there. She 'accidentally' drops the towel and then suddenly feels cold. Throws her arms around me to keep warm." And that was that. I frown. "Did you ever do that to a guy, mom?"

"Oh, a woman never tells such things!"

"It's not nice mom."

"Whoever said the world is a nice place, Miles? So what happened, where is this woman now?"

"Lye Lye and I are at a point of not speaking to each other in the same house." I explain how it was. It has been over a month she has been eating my food, using my hot water, my computer and printer, rearranging a few things—and not paying anything while insulting me. It seems to me I should be the one who is angry.

Lye Lye wishes for the full meal deal—the total wilderness experience. Yet still likes her daily shower, spending two hours putting on creams and getting ready for bed in a warm environment. She finds sand in her bed unacceptable, and wants lots of heat in the house. She could not get a fire going in two hours and 'forgot,' sat there reading, quite happy to let the oil stove kick in and keep her warm—while at the same time hating the oil industry and oil pollution.

I took a trip to the homestead I would not have made on my own. I did this for her. To bust open the trial, ensure we could get there. I hauled some things of mine as well as a few things for her, just so it would not be an empty trip. But in truth, these items of mine could wait a year! I'd have waited for more snow. The trip was needlessly hard on my snow machine. As a result I broke the undercarriage. I need a new part costing $200. I did irreparable damage to the track. The track is not safe now, and cost $1,500 to replace. The broken part dug into the track and tore it up. The lack of this shock absorber puts a strain on the drive line. After talking to two experts, I can expect fifty miles before the machine totally fails.

The new snow machine, to replace it, is $8,000. There is no talk from Lye Lye now about sharing costs 50/50. This is what I mean when I quote costs, as 'conservative.' Actual costs can get unimaginably astronomical. I have had what should have been routine trips cost thousands of dollars because a $5 part breaks. Many dreamers tell me, "But I am careful and will make sure this does not happen to me!" In truth, those who do not have knowledge can expect to pay the high end of the costs.

Lye Lye says, "You broke it, not me!" There is no winning an argument with a woman. There is only one right answer: 'Yes, Dear.' Mom smiles and agrees. Now I do not have a snow machine to take her out. Still. She seems not totally evil. She simply is incredibly naive. She tries to be nice to me. Does a few things that she can around the house. Likes to be with me. She likes to be with me wherever I go, and wants to learn. I can hardly get rid of her without being mean.

I call her "Little Duck," as she follows me around like a duck. She calls me Papa Duck. No, she does not have to go to the homestead. She can just stay here with me. She likes me. I'm adaptable, I suppose. But she cannot run the house by herself while I come to Tucson! She has an offer to house sit for someone else while I am gone. Someone with a furnace, with an easy to take care of home, more like what she is used to. She may be able to just stay there and further her plans, without me. She has been asking around for available cabins easier to get to than mine, where she might move in, for free. A few guys are eagerly trying to help her out. Envious of my situation. She is quite good looking. Men like to help her out.

After a pause, I tell mom, "You know, mom, I notice there are shelters for battered women. There are no shelters for battered men!" We both laugh. Lye Lye knows how to make the locals jealous, me as well. This city slicker moving in on us country bumpkins. Yet I see her sometimes, see her loneliness and pain. Feel sorry for her, even. I sigh, and see this as lessons in forgiveness and understanding. Since she is not really getting what she wants. It only looks like it on the surface. She spends two hours a day putting on creams and make up. Not a lot of makeup, but making sure she looks nice. It's all about looking nice.

"That's how I keep my skin looking thirty years younger!" she tells me it's these creams and lotions "And not touching gasoline, Miles!" Yes. Well. *Someone has to touch it. There is no use insulting that which you benefit from.*

She has this place to house sit, getting paid something, that might turn into permanent. All her things are gone. She is out of the house. The local guys are laughing, "Too hot to handle huh, Miles, let me help!" She is terrified of the dark. Sometimes hints of things in her life. It is hard to know the truth of where she is from, how she has lived, what her income has been, where her people are, why she is here. I and other locals agree her ID looks fake. She had to show it to get a library card for example. She has tattooed eyebrows that are not hers. Hers were surgically removed.

"Is this part of a culture, or part of a deliberate disguise, mom?" Mom does not know much about other people around the world. Lye Lye likes the curtains down, and likes to cover up, and looks around in crowds like she is afraid. Is she on the run from something or someone? Her stories do not add up to a believable reality. *Somewhat like Moon?* She does not know how to do simple things like change a roll of toilet paper on a spool. Has someone done that for her all her life? It is hard to believe. Was she in a mental institution?

She goes off the deep end now and then, screams, does not know where she is. Sometimes she can't be alone or she will kill herself. So she follows me and I can't leave her alone because she is unstable. I have to watch what mood she is in. Is she

221

whacked out on drugs? I have not seen any. How would she be buying them? Has she been taken care of in jail? Is she from a wealthy family? She is always on the phone with her bank doing transfers. Running a business even. Never lets me overhear. Very secretive. So much to ponder. Mom has been entertained.

"You do not have much luck with women, do you, Miles!"

When I get home from Tucson I am only a little glad to come home to an empty house with no one in it. Lots of emails to get to. One I want to see first is a reply from the Reality TV people!

Hi Miles,

How are you..? It just occurred to me that the last time we spoke was way back in July and I just wondered how everything was going. In the last email you sent me you had been out surveying new homesteads—anything interesting come your way? I guess you're preparing for the long winter—how's the weather this time of year, getting colder by the minute I bet!

As for our little Off the Grid project, well what can I say, sadly we didn't get our Alaska story and we ended up just filming the one episode in Montana. We have nearly finished it with just a final winter trip to go. We are all so bummed that we didn't get to work with you on this project, it would've been so much fun. That's not to say that we won't get to work together and I know that we had spoken briefly about a different homesteading project with you in mind.

I don't know if I told you but I am now based out here in the States working in our LA office which makes communicating with Alaska so much easier. Anyway it would be great to catch up properly and fill you in on what's going on. Email me your number and a good time to call or feel free to call me on the number below.

By the way Chris and James say a big 'hello' from London—we all miss your pictures :)

All the best and **I hope you are well**

Katie Sole

Segment Producer

Ricochet Television

323-(blank) -4680 ext 1051

ksole@(blank)

It looks like two issues came up—money, and finding the couple who would make it to Alaska through a winter. It sounds like another plan we spoke of might work out, so I may hear from them again. Josh wants to know how my trip went.

"Good to see you, Mr. Maw-Tin." Always formally said as if, "Kind Sir" said with an English bow. "How is life going for the man with the golden pen?" He has a twinkle in his eyes, letting me know he wants to hear the latest with Lye Lye, or he has some gossip to pass along. I mention the TV show first. Josh was excited there might be some of us locals involved in such a project. I had said it would be natural for a famous Athabaskan dog musher, winner of the Iditarod dog race, somehow getting into an episode or two. Josh is, in fact, quite the character! Being Native American would fit in with the public's notion of what remote Alaska is about.

"Well, Josh, I think I said it is not worth getting excited about till there is a deal of some kind. We have heard it before, promises, needing information, and suddenly it is not cost effective, or something simply falls through for reasons we may not get told."

"You put a lot of hours into helping them, didn't you, Miles? You are such a sucker for helping people out, Miles."

"Thanks, Josh! Just what I need right now."

"Speaking of needs, Miles, I hear Lye Lye wants to come back to you."

"You mean Josh, she realizes which side of the toast gets greased with butter?"

"That's between you and her, Miles. You two work out where the butter goes." Speaking of sticks of butter, yes, I got a note saying Little Duck misses Papa Duck. How she is ready to behave now. Sorry she was so distrustful. Well, I believe that, up to a point. I mean I believe she wants to go live alone in the wilds for the very reason she does not like playing games, using people, depending on others. I'm guessing it is not all that rewarding for her. It's not love, respect, or trust. I also think she cannot change, or will not, and this is all she knows. Meaning, even in the wilds she will apply her creams and want to look thirty.

When she shows up on the doorstep crying, looking helpless, with nowhere to go, I have to sigh, and wave her in. It is not my nature to kick her or anyone out with nowhere to go into the cold, cruel, world. I will take care of her as best I can. No. I do not want to have sex. I would want us to be friends first, and get along well enough to be intimate. Or, I am too scared to be made helpless by hormones, and maybe believe what she says. Thus being more part of the problem than part of any solution.

"Sometimes, Lye Lye, things happen for a reason." *Some good may come of this.* I can, for example, teach her what she needs to know to be free. I have the knowledge, and she seems a willing, enthusiastic learner. Maybe I will not just be another sucker. If I help her just for the sake of being kind. It may cause her to think and ponder the ways of the world. And what, might I get out of it? Well, how to get along with others?

Spring comes and Little Duck and I are still together. Life is a little better. I know what scares her, and learn to avoid those situations so she does not go off the deep end. I learn her strengths, so she can feel some accomplishment and help me out. She loves the garden. She is excited to learn to grow things. She digs and cleans the greenhouse, pulls weeds, waters every day. I can't go to the post office alone. She rides behind me on the four wheeler. Partly she wants to be with me. Partly she does not trust me or anyone. Little Duck gets jealous if I even wave at another woman. If I even get in a line at the store with a female checker, she wants to know why I did not choose the line with the man at the register.

"Miles! You show your art to all the women! You got into this jewelry business just so you could be around women, didn't you!" I put my arm around her.

"Sure. Women are prettier than men." No, I am not going to lie. I am in hopes that in time she can feel I am not chasing after anyone. Yet the more she likes me, the more jealous she gets. That must be awful, to want someone, and think they are going to leave you. I'm sure it happens with her all the time. Much is simply up to her. She can stay, and if so, I will take care of her. Or she can go, and if so, I will wish her well. She is beginning to learn some skills she will need to survive in the wilds. She still cannot build a fire.

"This is pretty important Little Duck. You should read, 'To Build a Fire' by Jack London, and you will understand." I do not know why building a fire is such a topic to her that she refuses to learn or even try. The garden is in, and we go out in the boat. Lye Lye loves the river. She is thrilled to catch her first fish. She loves camping out in a tent. She is happiest when there is only her and I and no other women around, like out alone in the wilds. She is in fact calm, secure, at ease. *A little like me.* In that, I am happiest and most secure alone in the wilds. About all my issues—problems have to do with civilization.

It was true of Karen as well. I concluded, watching Karen, that all the problems stemmed from childhood experiences that got programmed into her. All these fears and pain are associated with specific triggers. Sounds, smells, certain words, or looks, or situations, send her into a panic survival mode, or like reliving the original event. Once Karen went off the deep end on me and was screaming, foaming at the mouth, eyes rolling up in her head, yelling at me, someone else's name! How could I possibly get mad in return? She did not even know who I was.

I ask later who this 'Dave' person is and she looks at me puzzled and does not have a clue. She has no recollection of screaming this name. Was it a relative? Some event from long ago she wiped from her memory and never came to terms with? I assume. In the very big picture I did not enjoy taking punishment in someone else's place for things I did not do. The situation never got better. Even, the more confident she got, the more she acted out. I'm not sure my putting up with it helped.

Well. I suppose I, as well, have issues based on long ago. That have to do with why I can't use a phone, or drive. Why I avoid certain situations, normal to most people. There must be a reason I cannot recall names dates times and hate instructions. I'm realizing watching Lye Lye, in the wilds all the triggers are gone. There is nothing in the wild associated with the trauma, so I can feel 'safe.' I know what is going on when I watch Lye Lye come unraveled at the seams.

Yes. I had a sled dog, too, the same way, now that I think on it! So very odd that an animal can have a mental problem…I had this young black lab go ballistic on me for no apparent reason. "Geez puppy—what is wrong?" Barking, twisting, and crying, as if she were being beat to death. Over nothing in this world. I had done nothing. I was not mad. I was not reprimanding her for anything. My instinct was to yell at her to shut up! But I knew it would only feed her frenzy. So I did the opposite.

With infinitely kind, soft words, I spoke gently, slowly, kindly. Bent down and looked her in the eyes, trying to have a calming effect. "Everything is fine. Look around. Nothing is about to eat you. Are you OK? I am worried. Why are you so upset?" I scratched her gently behind the ears, looked with love into the depth of her confused eyes. She stops screaming, but is trembling uncontrollably. She 'snaps out of it.' Suddenly, I see the lights come on in her brain. Her eyes are like one recovering from an epileptic fit. Puppy looks around, as if she does not recognize where she is, why she is here, how she got here. She focuses on my eyes. Gives a little last shiver, whimpers and snuggles up against me, all calm now. I'm sure she was someplace else in her head, having a bad dream, but not asleep. It all took place in a handful of seconds. "Where were you Puppy? Huh?" Someplace horrible.

And just so, is Lye Lye and others I have met. *Am I a magnet for such people?* Is this common, normal, and everyone is like this? Simply hides it from public knowledge? Who will help Lye Lye if I do not? Perhaps God sent her to me, because I can deal with it. So maybe she reads my book and 'understands.' Knows somehow that my life would be good for her. The demon does not know how to find her in the wilderness. Even if there is no bed you can hide under in civilization. Even if it is me that can be a trigger to her pain. Still. I can teach her how to be safe, live alone in the wilds. Her pain just hurts me so much. I am brought to my knees. Even if it takes from me. I have lots of strength. Maybe God gave this to me for a reason?

It is not like I totally feel sorry for Little Duck. Any more then I indulge in self pity. I am unsure if Little Duck views all this the same way. I may well be simply being used. If so, it will be her loss more than mine. Her view might well be, it is she who is doing me a great service with her presence in my life. Which is possible. But in my opinion, it takes years to build up trust, honesty, and love. No one is going to win that in a year or even two. We can simply begin a journey down the path and see where it goes.

Seymour the survey boss does not think much of Lye Lye. "Miles! We went out on a job for a few days. She was supposed to stay home and take care of the garden and home front. You get home and she is gone. You do not know where. There is no note, and half the plants are dead. This is not lessons in how to be kind and get along, Miles. It is called being used and being untrustworthy!" Yes. I agree. Lye Lye calls one day from the airport and wants me to come pick her up. As if nothing had happened. I go to the airport in the old truck and she has a suitcase with her.

"I was just out on a camping trip with some girlfriends. I told you I might go, remember?" I stare at her. She has no camping gear. She is clean. Dressed for the city. She'd just had a shower. Her suitcase is a town suitcase with no wilderness on it. There is pretty much no way she was out camping. And what does the airport, and picking her up here, have to do with camping with friends locally? She flew somewhere. Where did she even get the money? To do what? And why not leave a note, and why choose a time I am gone, and neglect the garden. We depend on the garden for our food as a major priority, much higher than a camping trip.

I trust my friend Seymour. He knows me. We have known each other many years now. He kept it short and simple. "You can say anything you want to defend her, Miles, but the bottom line is, a good woman does not do that." If I am making up excuses, that is not a good thing. If Lye Lye is not a good woman, maybe I do not deserve any better. It is said we get what we deserve. It is said everything happens for a reason. If I deserved better, wouldn't God put the right woman in my path? Isn't that what makes sense? Like with Karen, I thought I might help, but in the end, things seemed to only get worse. Possibly in an entire lifetime, I could have been of help. I thought at the time it would not be me. Maybe someone else could be that right person.

Meaning, I see the path Karen is on now, and the path I am on now, and it would be hard to combine our ways. She still lives in a sod hut with a lantern that does not work half the time. She still drags branches home to burn in a rusty wood stove. At seventy years old, she still has no preparations made for the future, retirement, old age, or what to do when her health fails. She does not like or want any of what I have. She does not want life to get any easier. She got mad when I built her a chair. She will spend her life sitting on a tree stump. That was, well a stage in my life when young. A stepping stone for the rest of my life. Lessons. I cannot imagine my life without my art work, or my books. I have a path, a destiny. I hoped she'd find a guy stuck in the Stone Age.

I am reminded of a poem I wrote long ago,

"I take my life
like I take my coffee.
Straight, strong and hot,
right from the pot!"

It is just a poem. It sounds good. It's a line that could be out of a movie, said by an actor. In reality, I like Mexican vanilla in my coffee, as well as sweetener, chocolate and milk.

If Lye Lye will not learn how to make a fire, how could she survive alone in the wilds? What am I wasting my time teaching her all the other things for? If we are planning a life together, how can that be when she takes off like this and does not tell me the truth? Yet 'reason' is not a major factor with women, my friends tell me. There is little that is reasonable about a relationship.

I ask, "Then why get into a relationship if it's not reasonable?"

"Who said anything about choice, Miles?" I end the conversation that goes like this so often, and absent-mindedly go home and check my emails. This is from Seymour's wife,

Miles,

I received your email last Thursday, but was too busy to answer it until now. I will give the message to Seymour when he returns home. I did send you a reply after your fair email, so sorry if you thought I hadn't answered.

We did do the job for URS at Clear that I called you about, but they needed it done during the fair, so Seymour and Oliver did the work.

Seymour is going moose hunting with his brother Brian and his son Andrew at the beginning of the season. We don't have any big survey jobs this fall—just a couple very short jobs that Andrew or I will do with Seymour.

Hope your fall goes well.

Elsie

It looks like survey work is over for the season. Only one or two short jobs all summer. I reply:

Hello, Seymour and Elsie!

Sounds like summer is going well for you two. Hope you get your moose, Seymour! Well, Lye Lye is not with me now. When I mentioned the fair, she did not want to do that, and did not want to be alone at home. She said she met someone else who is in the wilds so she can live the life she came up here for. I took her to a storage unit in Fairbanks where she has things stored, and whoever she is to be with will meet her there. I dropped her off when I came in with my fair goods. No hard feelings between us.

I got a letter from a guy I heard of way up north, Hog River Gary. He wrote and told me Lye Lye had contacted him and suggested she move in with him. He is married and thought it very inappropriate and odd, so wanted to let me know what my woman is up to. Implying I need to keep a leash on her, or at least be aware she is trying to leave! Lye Lye said No! She was merely inquiring about any job he might be able to offer, strictly business. Gary must have misunderstood.

Anyhow, yes the fair went well. Good weather, lots of friends around, made some money.

I ramble on about survey work and get this sent off. The internet business grows slowly. I figure out how to run it better. Being fast at taking and editing pictures has helped.

Thursday, August 31, 2007

Letter from a customer who buys my book, Bill Pebble:

Dear Miles

Picked up the books, you forgot the five cards for postage $5 sent. Will credit that to something, later.

Miles there is something troubling me I want you to consider. Your book projects a wilderness hero honoring the simple life and oneness with nature. You have been basking in that sunlight since publishing the book and having your public honor you!

Now it appears you are turning yourself into someone consumed with selling reproduction art, time on web orders, packing, shipping all the 'monetary' facets that are turning you into another Miles, not the idealist philosopher in your book.

To tell me over the phone you had rather invest $2,000 in supplies so you can make $10,000 rather than invest the $2,000 in publishing your second book is a lot of poop.

Let's face it, some of your art things will be appreciated for a long time, some thrown into a drawer and forgotten, some lost!

If you are the man of your book (remember I bought 25 copies to send to friends) then you will get your priorities in order, set aside a block of time, get away from your present situation and get the second book finished and **published now!**

I point out a few things from my perspective, in a reply:

Sorry I forgot the post cards. They were meant to be a gift, something free, not something I am required to send, or that you paid for, and can demand. The postage covered the shipping of the book.

I do not see myself as a hero. I am trying to write honestly, about a lifestyle many wish to know the truth about. Part of this, is the truth about an individual. What that truth is, is up to the reader. The life may or may not be 'simple' likewise basking in sunlight, being honored by society is, I think, a misconception. Maybe some honor what I stand for. I feel I am also among 'the unprotected,' minority without the rights of others. Asked to move along by the police.

And 'getting my priorities together' is up to me, to decide what those priorities are. The book is, among other things, about personal freedom. There is a certain reality called 'bills to pay.' Paying my bills allows me to eat, have a home to work in, and dress myself. My art business pays these bills. While I can dream and hope for book sales, and keep moving in that direction, there is a truth to accept. The art is what makes the bigger profits, that buy me time to work on the books. I am excited by this, because so few artists can make any profit at all. I am excited for the books because many dream of writing! Yet never find the time, can never buy the time it takes to finish such a dream. I am not discouraged. I will have to save, and wait, to get book two printed. The books are also about perseverance, patience. I do understand not everyone will read my books and get the same things out of it. Some may even see a truth about me revealed I am not aware of! Most important is not that I look good! I'd be pleased to tell a story about a very messed up person, and tell it well.

MANY VENDORS TELL me the bigger Palmer State Fair is an event to consider selling at. There are many ways to skin the cat. One way to sell art is to do a lot of shows. Some friends are out working hard every weekend at some event or other. Sometimes I think staying home and working the web site is a good solution. I will go take a look at the Palmer fair just to see what it is about. Written in my diary:

Thursday, August 31, 2007
Palmer Fair

An incident at the Palmer fair. I am getting older. I get tired. I'm eating junk food, not sleeping great, hauling a heavy bag in the sun and it is long hours. I decide I want to lay in the grass in the sun a bit and relax, set down my bag, rest my weary bones. I recognize I am getting cranky and not alert. This is not a good thing when trying to conduct business, and is contrary to the atmosphere of a fair. I pick a tree in the grass. Kind of off the beaten path and lay down.

I wake up to security saying, "Hey get up, no sleeping on the fairgrounds, move along." One of the security guys knows me, now recognizes me, and apologizes, but saying, "It doesn't look good." I was unsure what that meant. I have learned enough, however not to argue or speak of my rights. It is much better to cooperate- apologize and do as told, saying it will not happen again. Yet the incident puzzles me. While walking around there are plenty of people lying in the grass. Teens laying in each other's arms asleep, and children taking naps in the grass. So what was it that was different about me? Had someone complained? I was not aware of being in the way, being a distraction, looking like a bum, or a dangerous person.

In my own mind and my opinion? I was an anomaly. I look different. I do not dress as most. Beaded hat with a feather in it, looks like a dirty old man, maybe. Teens making out in the grass, little kids, that's all 'normal' I'm out of place. Still, it adds to a sense of not being welcome. Not being under the umbrella of protection offered citizens. In my mind, what is wrong with an elder who needs to take a rest and finds a quiet place? Did I look like a drunk? All I know is I could not do what others were doing, and do not know why.

It seems to me the bigger fair is not right for me. There are more rules and more stress. As I tell my buddy Crafty, who loves this fair, "Crafty, there is no specific craft section like there is at the smaller Tanana Fair. I'd be set up among the junk food vendors and children's rides." I notice the fees are twice as much to set up, but I do not see twice the traffic going by any single booth.

"Miles, there are three times as many customers at this fair!"

"Maybe, but there might be five times as many vendors." And think as well, "Not as many going by any one spot." I do not see the group who shows up to collect art at a craft section like at the Tanana Fair. I go back in my diary to review how this went for me this season:

Diary Tanana Fair

The Anderson Blue Grass Festival was an indicator to me that my latest direction in art has been the right decision. I made $1,000 in three days with only two small tables set out. But more, I made twice what other vendors made who had more space than I had. So I was more optimistic than usual for the fair.

I expanded my booth five more feet back this year and opened the back so light came through. This allowed me to set out trays without having to stack any. Lynn, of course demanded I pay another $140. By the time she came around to ask for the extra I had no problem paying it. Opening Friday seemed only normal income, and even Saturday. I did better Sunday than any other Sunday I've ever done. My week days were exceptional with over $1,000 days sometimes, when I might expect half that. My neighbor was getting $200 to $300 a day. Supposedly attendance is down, and most vendors say sales are down. So when mine doubles, this means something.

For the first time I hire a full time helper. Sort of a problem slow person, but I do not pay her much. This teen does not need the money badly, as she is on public assistance as unable to take care of herself. She cleans, sorts, and gives me time to take breaks. I do not allow her to sell, nor does she know how to make change, but she can tell people I will be right back, and stop theft.

Quite a few sellers come to me with items I need—knowing I will be here. I got my year's supply of small fossil teeth. Tusk came by. I got a mammoth tusk which I sold, some mammoth bone, knife scales, and scraps of all sorts. I got some orders as well, like restoration of a tusk. I ran out of business cards, having given over 200 away to important customers. I did my usual trade for pottery with Birch Grove.

I brought a case of my books, fifty books. I only have a few left. One customer bought ten! Lazy M next to me did not show up this year. A vendor who is not handcraft is temporarily in the space. The space might be up for grabs. I will consider having two spaces next year! Probably not though, because two tents and tables needed would not all fit in the truck. I might be well enough off just going with the five foot expansion again. It is just a 'new level' even to be in the position to consider it! Very few hand crafters can fill even one booth, so it is a big deal to have inventory for two!

Yes, I see I enjoy playing with numbers, as my customer, Bill, so rudely pointed out.

"Just another capitalist, talking money!" Well, it is the life I was born into.

More and more I think I really like just being home, taking off now and then for an adventure, with some routine to come back to. In my lifestyle, I just pick out a nice grassy spot along the river, pull over and go to sleep. Or sleep on the front deck in the sun where there is a slight breeze and no bugs. But anyhow, choices to think about.

One of the places I pull in to take a nap in the sun on a long trip.

I took this picture of caribou on a trip to Nome selling my art and seeing the end of the Iditarod race.

CHAPTER NINE

A BOAT RESCUE, MORE MAMMOTH HUNTING, A TRIP TO NOME

F all is here. I get out on the river for moose hunting season. I write in my diary:

Thursday, September 07, 2007

A boat rescue Miles Martin

I had planned on going to the Kantishna homestead for a few days of the old life—haul a load in, maybe look for a moose and get a few things done. Maybe work on my book on the laptop in the quiet there. My life has changed. I need to plan 'get-a-ways' more. This is the time slot that might work if any time would. It is a small window of opportunity. I load up and take off.

About twenty miles downstream, someone flags me down. Boat problems. I guessed who it was. There were some hunters hanging around Nenana saying they were waiting for an overdue boat that was to pick them up. They wanted to hire a boat to go look for the overdue boat that is to take them hunting. I was not very interested when Josh told me about it, because this sounded like they wanted hunting guide service. This would be illegal. It did not sound like they wanted to pay much. I'd also been told it was way upriver. It is not good to go on a long trip at the drop of a hat without preparation, with people I do not know. I did not want to get involved. Seeing the group, I slowed to see if it was an emergency.

Eagle was in charge—so to speak. The hunters were staying with her. I pull up on my four wheeler as she is looking in the phone book with cell phone in hand, I'd guess trying to find a boater. The hunters were gathered around her. She never looked up.

"We don't need your help. Miles"

I said "OK", got on my four wheeler and left.

So here is the problem in front of me on the river. The boater I'd heard about. The

233

old guy in a broken down boat tells me his troubles. He hauled seven hunters 100 miles upstream, left them and came back for the others, and broke down—four days ago. The upriver hunters expected him back later that same day or the next day. There has been no communication. The hunters left upriver have no supplies. Two more had been dropped off on an island with no supplies, because the guide had been overloaded. The clients are supposed to be on an island he points out to me, just ten miles from Nenana. He hopes someone has picked them up.

The guide's boat is huge, and weighs 6,000 pounds empty, with a 450 horse engine. He has run up on a sand bar and done something so the boat will not run right now. He has had no sleep for four days, is out of food, wet, hypothermic, dehydrated and worried. His health is not good—he has lung cancer, and other health issues. A rescue helicopter had stopped by yesterday, but he had said he was OK—his engine was running again. But it had lasted only a few miles. No other boats have come by.

He wants a ride back to Nenana. This might cost me my trip—the only slot of time I have. I need to help this guy out as he might not even live another day here. I might be able to bring him back and still have time to return for my own trip. I unload my main supplies on the sandbar to lighten up to get him back. We take off. Another search party was headed out, so we have to get word out he is safe. I drop him off at the 10th Street Nenana boat landing where his truck is. His truck has been broken into along with eight others. His dry clothes have been stolen, he almost breaks down crying.

"We have to find someone to haul my boat back, and get supplies to my hunters." *What's this 'we' stuff?* I do not share this problem.

"Yes, I understand, the other group is safe here staying with Eagle." It is hard to understand, as this old man is acting confused.

His other hunters are staying with Eagle, in her Railroad Museum. I go chat with them briefly to find out better what is going on. The trooper is located to call off the search for this old man, Walter. I see Rachael, the trooper, interviewing the hunters, and a little bit with Walter. I give a statement. We are told Walter broke down, needed food and rest, so he could not now deal with any of his problems. The hunters with Eagle are very upset. They tell me they paid Walter $26,000 or $2,000 each. Walter told them he had spent all their money and could not refund any of it if he could not get them out hunting. The hunters are ready to sue him. Walter had told me he got money and gave them a deal, but the deal was so good it would cost him money out of his pocket, so this is a real mess for him. It was hard to truly feel sorry for him though. He had planned on doing a cheap job. No camp cook, no helpers, no boat operators, no spare back up boat.

Walter expected to get twelve hunters and all their gear 150 miles into the wilderness, reliably, with no help, so he could make more profit. He has supposedly (he told me) made five successful round trips already, all back to back, which is a lot to

234

expect. This is a lot of miles and work. Walter said he had also made trips ahead of the hunters to find good moose areas. He said he burned fifteen gallons of gas an hour, and it cost him $600 a round trip, traveling at forty-five miles an hour. I feel thirty mph is too fast for the conditions. Walter said he could do sixty miles an hour and burn up to thirty gallons an hour fuel. My thought was, this is not a small operation! By the time it was all figured out it was 1:00 pm and too late for me to head back downriver. It turns out no one I know can tow a big boat like this. Walter wants to rent my boat or hire me, but my sixty horse motor cannot haul his tons of supplies and people. He also tells me he has no money. I have a moral dilemma. We are all obligated to help our fellow man in a rescue to save lives.

I told one of the hunters this whole operation looks like a cluster f*&k. The hunter agreed (sorry for the language folks). One hunter seemed in charge. He sounded like he was from a ranch outside, but said he is from Wasilla, Alaska, and these hunters were all his friends. My Iditarod friend Josh, who was with me, was sure he was from 'Outside.' He had a very strong accent, and dressed like a cowboy. I forget his name, but was the one to talk to the trooper, and who the others turned to. My guess is they are all from outside the state, but do not have non-resident hunting licenses, which are expensive, and had purchased cheap permits by lying about where they live. Some of this fiasco group is safe. They are the ones who need to come up with a solution to fetch their buddies. I'm not doing it free as a rescue, when I cannot carry everyone anyhow.

Eagle had not wanted me involved days ago, because she is searching for a way she can dip into the money pie. People's lives are at stake.

"Call 911! It's an emergency rescue at this point!" No one will make any money, Eagle is stalling the rescue. The guide cannot pay, the hunters left behind do not want the truth of being non-residents to come to light. Meanwhile, we have as many as twelve people out in the wilderness without supplies for a week.

I head out early the next day on a beautiful fall warm morning for my own trip. I stop to pick up the load I left behind at the broke down boat and notice the boat has been hauled off. I had heard it got towed and assumed Paul Essau had stopped on his way back from Minto, and wondered how long it took to tow it. I have my moose rifle with me and hope I will get a moose while doing this freight haul.

Up the Kantishna near Tom Slough I see a camp, and assume it is the camp of hunters Walter left. They just wave and seem OK. I do not stop. They have been in touch by cell phone I think, some plan must be in the wind. I had been told the phone was not working and low on batteries. I get to my homestead in six hours, about 3:00 pm. I find my hidden canoe, and canoe up the creek to my cabin, get a fire going in the stove and start hauling freight from boat to cabin using the canoe. On the third trip I shoot a bull moose not far from my cabin. I spend till late in the evening gutting and butchering.

The next day is spent dealing with moose meat, and hauling it to the boat on the river. I cover it well, away from the heat and flies. I spend the rest of the day building a storage shed by the cabin. The third day I head home, on Sunday, September 10th. About six miles down in Tom's Slough I see the boat, 'Wild Thing', tied up at a camp, and see two guys awake. I pull in to visit, and maybe share some moose meat. Walter greets me, and tells me how he got here. Last time I saw him, he had been a physical and mental mess, so it is good to see him with his strength back. Walter tells me he hired Crowley Barge Line in Nenana to tow his boat for $1,000. The boat was trailered to Fairbanks and fixed. It was brought back to Nenana and here he is!

Walter tells me there is still a problem with his boat. The engine is overheating, and he thinks it is a radiator cap problem. Yet he does not know for sure. This sounds like an odd problem to not find out about in Fairbanks or not be able to solve. *A leaking radiator that would stop the boat would be spraying liquid all over?* So the story seems odd to me. He has hunters camped upstream, and plans to use this big boat to go back and forth between camps. He is not interested in any moose meat to share with his hunters so they can see what moose taste like if they do not get one. I'm served coffee, and we exchange hunting stories. I do not agree there is a tiny radiator cap problem with his boat. I'm guessing the engine is overheating, and the radiator water is boiling. I suspect the reason is the boat cooling system sucked up gobs of sand which has plugged the internal cooling pipes, maybe inside the engine. Or if the engine is overheating, this is not a small problem; he may need a new engine.

There are now twelve hunters he is in charge of, who depend on him. I'm concerned for him, and inform him I have a canoe upstream he can use, but he is not interested. I wonder if he needs a spare motor or small boat with motor as a runabout. He is not interested. This looks like another problem waiting to happen. One of his hunters has sore or broken ribs. The hunter told me Walter hit a sandbar and threw him into something that broke his rib. The hunter does not want a trip out for medical attention. Walter shows me his rifle. I forget the caliber, but commented it is just like mine, a Ruger stainless steel with synthetic stock, just a different caliber. I recall a big caliber like .338, as he tells me he hopes to get a grizzly bear.

Walter has shown a video on hunting to his clients, and tells me he is staying with them right here till hunting season is over. They are camped on a meadow and 'hunting.' We discuss hunting methods on how to deal with this meadow (walk around it or just sit and be quiet). Another group of his hunters are within sight across the river, with another group further upstream someplace. Walter tells me he will be going between all the camps helping them get a moose. He tells me he has been a transporter out of Wasilla, Alaska for eleven years and his area has been the Novi and Nowitna off the Yukon. But there are new laws now about having to separate the antlers, so he will not go there anymore. This indicates this is trophy hunting with no or little interest in meat. Walter tells me he is selling his boat. This is his last season.

For this reason, I decide it is not worth turning him in as long as he never comes back! He is guiding without a license, being only a transporter, and filling the area with hunters, over hunting the area. Not adequately supplied.

I wave goodbye and continue on my trip. At Tolovana Road House, I hear Dough and Becky who own it, have seen 'Walter, the illegal guide' zoom by, going too fast for conditions, and overloaded. They tell me he had stopped at Fish and Game's camp near the mouth of the Kantishna and was given thirty gallons of gas and food. A young woman at that camp confirmed they had helped someone. I have an easy, fun trip home to Nenana.

On Sept 15th, I hear Walter has broken down and or is stuck again, and has been flying his hunters out. Someone at Coghill Store passes this on to me. I guess Walter was looking for help of some kind again. I mention the various issues to our Mayor, who tells me he has seen Water off and on all summer. The mayor also says he knows for a fact Walter knew the hunters were hauling in a lot of booze. Walter had told me he was 'shocked' and 'upset' and had told them not to bring any booze, after I told him what I think of guys drinking, with guns in their hands. The mayor tells me he thinks Walter was around last year as well. This is not the same story Walter told me, and has me thinking Walter has moved his guide area to here for good, and might well be back. This mention of 'planes' had me thinking it is possible Walter has been using spotter planes, and has plane back up and is why he was not interested in a spare boat or motor and did not hire anyone because he knew he was up to illegal activity. The realization that Walter might have been misleading me and might be back prompted me to call Gary, my 'go to' guy at Fish and Game the past fifteen years.

Gary had previously told me he thought there was a serious moose hunting issue going on up the Kantishna River, my stomping grounds and trapline area for almost twenty years, thus of great concern to me. I had no knowledge of problems, but Gary asked me to let him know if I heard anything. This conversation had only been a couple of months ago. I still have his card. Normally, Nenana residents might not be inclined to help out, due to past issues in the community with Fish and Game, and Federal Fish and Wildlife, but Gary seems OK, maybe willing to work with us. For this reason, I emailed him for the first time Sept 16th

But on September 19th I talk to Josh's dog handler who lives at the boat landing. He tells me 'yes, Walter came in the other day with his boat and hunters, and is gone now, all finished.' I contact Gary and pass this information along, and give him the GPS coordinates near the camp where I visited Walter. These coordinates were actually for the camp across the river, but stored in my GPS because it is a landmark, the slough my friends Tom and Lana live on. We are both original homesteaders from the first land opening on the Kantishna, back in 1988, and has been home for us all these years. This is about six miles downstream from my own homestead, where I successfully got my moose.

I am, in general, tolerant of behavior, not seriously hurting the environment. I myself have had 'issues' with game laws, so who am I to throw stones? Yet, if this activity is flagrant abuse, big time, serious, and hurts the name of friends who are honest, good guides, hurts the reputation of Alaska and my area, and depletes the moose population by over harvest and salvage of antlers only, no meat salvage, then **I want to help stop this.**

I get another email from a woman I met in Seattle doing the trade show. She was set up not far from me. We got to talking, get along. A very nice looking woman, who used to be a well paid model and actress. She had said she was one of the girls who got painted in a James Bond movie, 'Gold Finger.'

Hey Miles, It's Friday morning and I'm home today taking care of art business, Getting supplies, Printing Art for framing, Returning phone calls, feeding cats and having morning coffee. There's nothing like that first cup! My days at Pike Market are nice, but very tiring. I get up at 5:00 am leave my house at 7:00 am then commute for one-and-a-half hours into Seattle, morning traffic is horrendous. We have a Roster, so being a newcomer, I'm number 229 I get one of the Booths that are left after the other Vendors have chosen, but this is still OK. We set up in about a four ft space, sometimes more and sell till at least 4:00 pm then commute home for another one-and-a—half hours. I should do three days a week, but usually do two. It's a much easier market to do than either a Farmers, where you have to set up a full ten x ten tent, or an Art show. The money is so-so, best day $290.00 worst day $47.00 but it doesn't cost a lot to do, and the people you meet are from all over the world.

I can't believe you are making the kind of money you are on your website! Can you tell me again how you get the Spiders to notice your site. Also, who is your server, who lets you set up several sites and link them together? My server didn't seem to understand this.

I'm getting more design work now, Ads, CD covers. I think that this is my favorite kind of work, I can sit at home at the computer and make attractive designs and pictures. Definitely fun. I'm about to upgrade my computer so I can also design, brochures and Websites, I've had some requests.

'The Perfect Partner'? I gave up on that dream quite some time ago. Romance is one thing, but the reality of living with someone else is quite another. Not at all romantic. Remember what I said 'After the Passion, The Laundry!' Marriage is a business contract, In the olden days, people understood this, but the romantic notions I had when I was young were so unrealistic that I was very disappointed in the reality of married Life. Plus, I think I guard my freedom very fiercely, that comes from years in boarding school, when other unloving people had total control of my Life. I'm sure you understand!

The modeling years? No, Miles, no union, no retirement. You're freelance and nineteen years old, what did I know about finances! My husband and I had lots of trips to Europe and expensive dinners, all courtesy of me, so no savings either. For me, it was like being a dancer. A good model is an artist, she knows how to make beautiful pictures for the photographer to photograph. I never missed it when I stopped. Photography was much more satisfying.

Do you have any more pictures of your Huskies, Would love to see them and know their names. Also, some more of your house.

Anyway, must get on with my day Your Friend **Susan R.**

Susan was kind enough to store two tables at her house so when I come back, I have tables for the Seattle show, and will not have to buy new ones. Tables are rented, but it is about the price of buying them. She had wanted to take me home with her for the weekend. Other vendors noticed her looking at me and told me she wanted my body! She seems a kind, giving woman. Very tall, needs no makeup, needs no fancy clothes to be beautiful. Prefers to live simple, dress plain, work hard, earn her own way. I admire these things, plus being an artist! Lye Lye has gone, come back, gone again, I think for good, or so it appears. At least I hear rumors she is living with someone I know on the river.

I write back to Susan:

Hello Susan!

Nice to hear from you. Yes, I enjoy hearing about business and talking about it. Guess it occupies much of both of our minds. How to get more time! Ha! But also the rewards of doing a good efficient job. The long commute for you. Geez. But yes, I can see how Pikes is a nice setting in terms of options. I'd make that choice as well probably.

The internet? Yes, I have opinions on why it works. 90% is attitude.(?) To me a web store is like any other store. You put in your time at the register or not much happens. I made up my mind it is my store. I am going to be there. Hardly a day goes by I am not editing pictures, tweaking something, and for sure dealing with customers. All a server does is give you an address, a space to keep your site. A domain, of course is a must. After that, who hosts it is not so important.

I have slow speed dial up and that hampers me, no real chance for high speed without twice the cost and less reliable (more server down time). If the server gives plenty of Megs of space, that is important. I finally maxed out and had to pay for more space. My goal is to make it a Gigabyte. As for 'several sites linked together.' My server has nothing to do with that. The server gives us so much space, a user name and password. How we use that space is up to us. The program I use is not a common one, called 'Web Studio'; there is a free trial version if you want to download it, look at it and try it. It's maybe a $150 program. Not spendy. Dreamweaver I'm told is best, but I did not understand it, so gave up.

What I do, is create new web sites, rather than more pages. So the home page is www.milesofalaska.net. There is www.milesofalaska.net/custom knives. Also wood, /bio, /under$50, /for women, and so on so now have over 50 addresses. The viewer does not know they are being forwarded to another site rather than another page. The advantage is, each site gets a new set of search words for the search engines to pick up. So my site exposure is multiplied fifty times compared to one large site. Also, it is called 'web' and search engines like to see lots of links reaching out to many sites. The more links created, the higher the search engines rate your site. The price is all the same with the server who only charges for space, not how the space is used.

Then I treat my web like a real store. I invite people to go. I talk about it, and it is on my business cards, and it is the place I ask people to go look at pictures, to get my address or phone number, to email me from. I could actually do double the business if I had help. I'm limited by how many emails I choose to reply to. Some I dump and turn away. I stall people, do no follow ups, do no real soliciting. Do not get back to people. I lose a lot of business, a whole lot. I could expand if I wanted, if I had time. I could sell other people's things beside mine.

I have this idea too (smile). To sell stuff I do not have but can get. (?) So I take pictures, talk about local Native art and offer it on the net. I get a buyer. I get a deposit, and then I go buy it from the Native. That is like 'back ordering.' I do that now with raw materials. I have a photo of a pile of antlers at a friend's place. When I get an order, I go see my friend and buy it. My buddy Crafty is upset that I can wholesale his product, and make money after paying his asking price. He is the one who told me the internet is nothing, just a fancy new fangled gadget destined to fail. His market then, is whoever walks in his shop in Alaska. My market is the world. He shrugged his shoulders and told me as long as he gets his asking price, he has no reason to complain.

There are a whole lot of ways to make money on the net. 'I' think anyhow. Smile. It is totally untapped. Getting people to my site in the first place? Oh—tons and tons of pictures. Stories. The right search words. Choosing words few others would use as key words on their site. It took me a short time to understand using 'art' as a keyword is less than useless.

For you? I mean for sure I would not use 'cards' or 'art'. Describe what you do, and, offer, that makes it yours and no one else's, then search that description for the key words. Maybe even play on 'model' and 'James bond,' create an image, a story to go with it that is real. Lines like "My life as a James Bond girl inspired me to..." Or "After all that excitement in my life, I just want to make cards of my cat and flowers, but as you see, my thrill for life is not really gone, it has just taken another form..." Bla

bla. Find an angle. Combine things in the search words no one else would or could do. That to me is about everything—the key to getting hits.

Further into your letter. Romantic. I decided one part of the definition of 'Romantic' is 'lack of knowledge'. So ya', I tend to agree with you—I guess. I mean I do, and wish I did not. Sigh. Reality of married life? Hmm. And ramble on **Sunshine, Miles**

There are women like this I have as friends, write, get to know. They arrive in my life, most leave. I forget who they are, or we get to know each other and write sometimes for years and they are, well, 'friends.' We never know how the relationship will be, or change. Any could be potential life partners. Much has to do with time and place. 'Only if,' like if we lived near each other. If we needed to move and wanted a change. If the others were willing to relocate. There must be a dozen women at any given time who are like Susan.

There is Bev from Oregon who wrote a book about Sasquatch and built a huge sculpture. There is Moon, the beautiful Indian who does sand painting and leather. What's her name in Canada who makes slippers, who is small like me, loves my lifestyle, but will never leave Canada. There is Heidi who I have known forever here in Alaska. If she ever said, "I am tired of being alone and we know each other. I want to share life with you, here I am," I'd be glad—honored to share a life with her. I think it could turn into love and trust. But another 'only if' situation.

She has a friend I know almost as well, and lived with a short time. Really pretty, with waist long hair and maybe South American look. These are a few I have known for years. Others come and go. None are 'girlfriends.' I'm as likely to give advice about another guy, or ask them advice about another woman.

Lye Lye might even show back up again, and we work things out. It is hard to know the future. I have no idea where Lye Lye went and with whom. She kept it a secret.

Someone I know in Manley Hot Springs calls me, "Miles, the Postmaster told me Lye Lye has picked up mail here. She has been living remote, not coming in, but looks like with Jessie, you know, near Moonshine, on the river." So yes. That makes sense. She and I had stopped at Moonshine's camp for a rest. Charlie was not there, but had hired Jessie to feed dogs and watch the place. We had stopped, visited with Jessie. Jessie sort of knows the outdoors. Lives in the wilderness, but barely squeaks by. Always broke. Often cannot afford to come in for mail, as he can't afford gas and his transportation is usually broken down.

Anyhow, Jessie was bragging about all his knowledge, and dispensing advice to Lye Lye. *I recall now.* I had been irritated as she was ignoring me, all ears as he talked. Not quite flirting, but showing almost worshipful interest. Ideas on how to build fires that I felt were nonsense. How to make lanterns using bear fat and such.

Very fine and wonderful, but having 'been there and done that' I know it's not that easy. Sooty, and one bear might give enough fat for a month's worth of light, at best. The fat needs rendering first. The real issue is that Lye Lye cannot even build a fire in the stove in a house.

Why get all excited about 'complicated' stuff that is fun, but not necessary. At any rate. Yes. Now I remember them, secretly talking while I fooled with the boat and wondered what was keeping her so long. Did a conversation go something like, "I'm stuck with Miles for now, trying to get away. Can you help me? I want to live like you do, can you show me?" So. It sounds like now she is with him in a remote one room cabin living the life she dreamed of. Whatever. Sigh. I suppose I hope she is happy.

Miles,

My head is exploding!

You are a reality show all with yourself.

Read some of the book before I went to bed, I had wild, wild dreams. I am learning so much. Couldn't put it down! Will write more later or maybe I will call tonight. I sent the boxes yesterday. Hope you get them before you leave. We are so different but similar in some ways. You are helping me grow.

Thank you. I keep seeing the guy from Kentucky in the tent, he looked at me and said you are a great guy and that he knows you for years and he was so true and sincere about it. You are loved by many. You make a difference. What more could you want in life. You are the deepest person I have ever met. Anyway, I'm sure you have heard all of this before that is why you attract people to you. You are right out there not afraid to show who you are, you are bold and beautiful. Raw and real, tense and tender. Amazing Wild Miles!

Walmart needs your books!

I sent you a shirt I wear at night. Hope you like it!

Have a great day,

Wren

Wren has been helping me at the Tucson show each year. We have an attraction for each other, but still an 'only if' situation. She hates the cold. I live in Alaska. She has a variety of health issues. Wren showed up at the Tucson show with a meter that measures radiation coming off power lines. My tent happened to be under a major power line.

"Miles, I can't work here and neither should you. Your booth needs to be moved. Look at the reading on this meter." She shows me a meter with a needle over a red line and beeping, very concerned and agitated. "Magnetic pulses, rays from electrical objects are bad for us. Mess with our brain." I politely listen. My help, Andrea, begins to look nervous and wonders if he should quit. I need 'good positive energy' around me. I do not want anyone being fearful or talking 'bad stuff' attitude in my booth. "We are all going to die if we stay here," is not going to work. I try to be polite. *What a waste of such a gorgeous body.* Sigh. But no. I am not going to say anything like that out loud.

We need to be vegetarians today for some reason. But only today. It would not surprise me if it is because aliens ordered it. Wren cannot go through this street light because the sequence of the past three lights spells out help. We have to go around the block instead. Wren happily tells me she just spent $5,000 for a weekend retreat with a medicine man and twenty other believers. She has been given an assignment, that if she completes, she gets to graduate. *Do tell me. The prize is, you get the honor of sleeping with the guru?* It has to do with cosmic energy in relation to the energy of our inner soul. "It all has to be balanced you know."

Yes, I know. I sell crystals all day long to just such people, who smile, hold the crystal and hum. *Where do these people come from?* Can they dress themselves in the morning? I'm curious. I could see one person getting their wires crossed, but a whole army of them? Pretty spacey all right. I vaguely suspect, these people come from parents who were taking acid in the '60's. However, how do I myself explain certain events in my life? One time only, I handed a lady a crystal, she holds it, opens her hand and the crystal has changed color.

"Because it absorbed the energy out of my body Miles" Crystals in fact vibrate to things we cannot see, and this is called 'radio.' Voices come out of the crystal. Is that spacey or what!?

Wren arrives at the show with her rich, spacey friends one day, who all wanted animal energy that day. They all bought teeth and claws, spending over $500. In my role of Oz, I sent them all out on a variety of missions, blessed the claws, and with a straight face listened to how the new claw made them smarter. One friend looks and dresses like Cher, from Sonny and Cher. All of these friends of Wren, talk, look, and dress like movie stars. Wren dresses more like their spiritual guide.

Her relation to me in front of them is. "Here is the guy I told you about, Wild Miles. Can't you just feel the animal energy?"

With replies of, "Ooo!" "Ahhh" and "Can I have some enlightenment?"

If I open door number one and say, "Get out of here, you kook!" I do not get $500. If I open door number two and it is Pandora's Box, or door number three— $500 and a free spin of the wheel of fortune... let me see, *what door will I choose?* Such a hard decision! $500 dollars later..... Huh? Oh yeah. I had to send them all on missions.

"This lion claw really needs something from Africa. I know this bead guy in the African village..." I get out the secret card and contact. "And tell this guy that Wild Man from Alaska sent you. He'll connect you to the right beads that came from the area the lion lived—possibly the same village. Be sure to have both red and blue, that represents the sky and passion. When mixed with energy within you it should all come out pretty catty!" *"And so on and so forth," says Oz. Rats, we forgot to mention what moon sign it needs to be! Hey, do not laugh! There are people who need direction, are lost, unless someone guides them.* The good news is, I do not rip them off. The odd good news is, they all report feeling better, stronger, more alive, and how worth it is to know someone like me.

"We are so honored to meet you, Sir!"

Wren returns with a variety of gifts, ideas and help. She brings me lunch, watches the booth, and takes me out to dinner. Takes me home 'and such.' *No, we did not have sex! But we lay together and talked and fell asleep together.* She just said, "I do not like to be touched, sorry—forgive me please?"

She is, in fact, giving and kind. Capable of freaking out, but somehow, I seem able to—how do I put it— calm her down by…well. Like I did with the freaked out dog, and Lye Lye, and Karen, and on and on. It's a stupid gift I have. God, with a sense of humor. The ability to keep a straight face, but more than that. I suppose I forgive where people's heads are at. Or, somehow, be there where she is, speak her language, without agreeing. Just accepting. I guess. I really have no answer. Wren is simply not a bad person. Is that enough of an answer?

Wren suddenly stops in the middle of her prattle babble energy. In mid breath, "Miles!" Like something stupendous just struck her. "Miles! How did you do that? I mean I can see Connie and the lion claw, she asked for something from a cat! But the whale tooth for Judy…" I have to keep my smile. That was not actually a whale tooth. *That would be illegal.* It was a fossil sea lion acquired before 1972. But who could tell it from a whale? Few experts would know for absolute certainty. Anyhow. It served its purpose. "And Miles! Miles! How could you have known Zera needed a unicorn tooth? How could you have possibly known? And yet you told her what she needed, and it was true, so true! You are so gifted Miles!"

I can only smile, nod, and reply, "I'm the man! Seek and ye shall find!"[1]

"So true Miles, you are so wise!" But in truth? Well, this Zera lady was the wonkiest of the bunch. So I just have to ask, if I were in La La Land hanging with a bunch of animal freaks, what would I need? Something mythical of course. I might have said 'dragon.' But no, she is so Celtic and… the blood line says unicorn—and so fearful, so very against anything to do with fire. She'd be much too scared of dragons! Dragons would never do! She holds back, shy, and does not talk a lot. Something cute and cuddly. It's pretty obvious that would be a unicorn. Just as it is obvious to anyone who is a pack animal needs the wolf, anyone who likes to sneak up from behind, thinks of cats. Crystals are for people who look like they take acid. Jasper is for hippies who wear sandals and are down to earth who do not have much money. Basics like that steer me in the general direction. *Profiling!* By hinting, and the art of suggestion, it's easy to get more information.

"And Miles! The way you proved it was an authentic unicorn tooth was so filled with absolute irrefutable proof! Where did you get your wealth of knowledge! Nobody but you could have ever given her a real unicorn tooth! I am so lucky, so grateful!"

I tell her, "Well, I spent a lot of years among animals, and in nature alone, meditating...." I review how I can authenticate unicorn teeth. "There is only one issue. If it is unicorn or horse. We can eliminate camel and sheep by the size and shape. I stumbled on the difference between unicorn and horse." *I know their habits!* We all know unicorns eat flowers. We all know they are environmentally conscious! God gave the unicorn the correct teeth for the job. "The unicorn tooth is very sharp. This is so they can snip the flower off the plant. The plant lives, and grows more flowers! "Whereas a horse eats the entire plant whole, and has dull teeth to grab and pull." We are talking ancient teeth—about 40,000 years old. "I find unicorn teeth at the edges of ancient frozen ponds that were at the base of 100 foot tall glaciers. The sun hits the ice face and makes it melt, giving water in a vast dry grassland. This is where the spring flowers emerge first. This is where unicorns hang out. *One only needs to read 'Clan of the Cave Bear' to know this'* The teeth fossilize a robin egg blue. No, I have never found a horn yet, or a hoof. "I'm not sure mankind in this age deserves them. So they remain hidden until we are more deserving." She understands and agrees with me completely. It is easy to see why she does not want to have sex, as it is a trust issue. She needs someone who is honest. She thanks God she has met someone who understands. I believe every word I say at the time I say it, as one in a hypnotic trance.

Wren would say, "Yes, that makes sense, you do not have to believe all this, having to live in civilization and trying to survive! You must enter another state to connect for a short time, then come back! Of course*!" Even as a non-believer one can have a gift.*

I am curious where such people get their money, how they take care of themselves, what they do for a living, how they pay the bills. Wren, Moon, and some others have wealthy parents. Wren's parents run a diamond business in a high end Jewish section of New York. They bought her a house, and give her an allowance. Pay her to stay as far away as she can get. If she moves because the heat in Tucson is too much for her in the summer, I might never see or hear from her again. Yet I enjoy seeing her year after year at the show, a familiar happy face. She often talks fast, then looks at me to see if I accept what she said, or—seems fearful of something. Never very confident. She often has great insight and intelligence.

She knows how to appear normal when it is necessary in public. Very high class, with breeding. She can speak French when she orders wine. I have seen odd things in my life

—the impossible, stranger than life. I once sold a 'magic ancient wolf fang' to a customer, who bought it for a newborn son. Word got back to me the baby in a crib grabbed the fang and would not let go. Ever since the baby has worn it, and stopped having colds, learned to talk early…and what not. As often as nine out of ten times, customers coming to me for 'magic' are very satisfied. I have never once been asked for a refund from such a customer. I do not recall seeking out this position, claiming any special abilities. Customers tell me I have a gift, and ask for help. I joke about it, put it down, make light of it, however, there is much that cannot be explained. *If by chance I have any power, I am afraid of it. I do not like the responsibility. Yet am attracted to it anyway. I do not like making promises. It could all be a placebo, or a form of brain washing hypnosis stuff. The power of suggestion. I feel it sometimes, and yes, it scares me. Because I believe in freedom and not control.*

From my diary:

Nome trip

Back from a ten day trip to Nome, looking for fossil ivory, and selling at an Iditarod bazaar. I met Dodger in Tucson. He's from Nome. I shared my selling space with him to help him out. He appreciated it, and informed me his wife runs the show in Nome. I could stay with him if I come do this show. I took him up on his offer. Cost me $400 to fly, spend a total of $800, made about $1,000 in five days of selling. I got to see the dog racers come in. I got to go crabbing with Dodger. We had a meal of a King Crab, all we could eat. I made some contacts in Nome, and got to see for myself what is going on with the ivory prices. I came home with a lot of materials I can sell. Probably not worth going again financially, but was a worthwhile trip.

Dodger is someone I met in 2007 or maybe even the year before. It turns out his mother lives in Tucson, as mine does! He is from Alaska as I am, but from the far north, in Nome. I take him on as a second vendor in my booth for $100 so he has a place to sell his Eskimo artifacts. He had good sales, and we get along well. I ask him questions about getting fossil walrus ivory for me.

I'm still trying to figure out where to do shows, how to get the materials I need myself, or sell. Dodger has a snow machine for me to use. It's an amazing way of life to see. Dodger subsistence hunts musk ox and wants me to go out hunting with him. I did not go because it was after midnight cold and windy. Dodger comes home in the morning with a huge muskox in his sled pulled by the snow machine, a site to see. There are, in fact, some rich customers to sell to, but most want to buy from an Eskimo, which is understandable. I email from Nome to a customer eager to hear the word on materials, even eager to front buying money if needed.

The diary reminds me of how it was. I got only a little fossil walrus ivory while in Nome. I learned a lot about what is going on with the market. Big buyers show up four times a year to do major purchases, acquiring 75% of what is available for sale. This makes it not worthwhile for smaller buyers to fly into the villages for what is left. Big buyers appear to be buy raw fossil ivory cheap, then have it carved in Bali, making way more profit than buying the finished carvings off the locals in Alaska. I know about this, because I met Jay, one of Eaa's friends in Tucson who is the go to guy for having the Bali carvings done.

The Eskimo for many years was exploited, keeping ivory prices artificially low by these big buyers who have a monopoly on the major markets. Much was acquired in trade for drugs or alcohol. This created problems and distrust between the races. The Eskimo had three major recent changes. One is the oil pipeline going through their land, meaning revenue for them. Second was a land settlement, where all Natives got land rights, formed corporations to manage the land and its resources. Third is the internet became available.

The money enabled the Eskimo to form corporations, and one result of this has been to offer an outlet for the Eskimo to sell ivory in an organized way. One example is that one corporation in Savoonga just acquired a $30,000 grant to buy ivory to sell, to help the village economy. If this is tax dollars, then the government is interfering with free enterprise that private investors cannot compete with. Free government money, fronted to buy with. The government guaranteed $200 a pound, a slightly high retail, effectively putting the wholesalers out of the market. This may have been a good thing and I even am in favor of this, even if it hurts my income. *But who else gets economic free help from the government because of exploitation? More than Eskimos get explo*ited…

The land title allowed the Eskimo to protect the beach and ancient dig sites where the fossil ivory comes from, legally restricting digging to local Natives only. In the past, tourists dug on public beaches unrestricted. The internet allows the Eskimo to offer much the ivory retail on their web sites. Ebay later banned the sale of all ivory, including fossil walrus and mammoth, believing any ivory sales effects the illegal elephant ivory trade. Still, the Eskimo has set up individual selling sites run by the corporations. It looks to me like there is also just less fossil ivory to be found, after 100 years of easy pickings. Much of what is found now is found by divers, not beachcombers. Diving takes equipment, skill, more effort. As everywhere, a majority of the young are not industrious, prefer to play video games, and accept handouts, rather than take pride in being hard working, responsible and self-sufficient.

The smart, sober, industrious Eskimo understands he has a limited resource. It is not a good decision to sell it raw wholesale, cheap. He wishes to sell his limited resource as an end product for more profits, with add on value as his carvings. It is possible to find an Eskimo who is not smart, or is drunk, and make buys in the bar and on the street. I'm unwilling to do this. Those in charge who see what is going on are not happy and make problems, and it is unethical.

There are still a few stashes of ivory people collected who have no use for it. Some want to sell it off for a profit. Some want it to be used in a good way. These sources are available, but not dependable, are hard to locate, requiring trust and friendships, and in limited supply.

I tend to agree the resource should belong to the Eskimo. So if the high end old time buyers who ripped the Eskimo off are out of business now, this is fine with me. But if I can find a local source at a fair price that I can pass on, this would be nice.

I explain what I learn at the Nome show to one of my customers and friends. Like the Tucson show, I can go and see for myself, and form my own opinions when I am at the source. This alone is worth a lot to me. I was disappointed I could not find a good, reliable source for fossil ivory. It seems to me, I am better off trusting Dodger, and just dealing with him as the middle man. I think it would take me a few years to be accepted as an honest dealer in fossil ivory in this Eskimo country. Fossil walrus ivory is just not a big priority for me. I also think the laws about fossil walrus ivory make dealing with this material risky. A person could get stuck with a lot of material, and be unable to sell it.[2] However, the knife makers ask for this material. There are not a lot of sources, so those who can get it can make some good money in the selling of it. I think I will not get back to Nome. The trip does prove my theory, that I could go about anyplace I want in the world, and at least break even selling my art.

One place I'd love to go is Siberia Russia. One guy, through Highways Companions, books vacations in unique places, and has literature on trips to Siberia. The information is looked over. I dream I might make such a trip.

As a child, 'things happened' in my world. I do not know what, when, where or how. No one's version of events matched. Is it me who knows the truth and everyone else is a liar? Or, am I twisted, mistaken, hallucinating? Who can I trust to supply me with the facts and the truth? How do I have confidence in what I know, and how do I confidently act upon it with any hope of doing the right thing, if I cannot grasp the facts and the truth? *Much like Wren!* How many people have told me it is impossible to drink creek water and live, eat food a month old in the refrigerator, sleep when it is light out, wire your own house and have it work, live without a credit card, etc., etc? It is impossible. Can't be done. Not a fact, not a truth, not reality.

I am crazy. Solutions to problems are not solutions until we recognize them. If we cannot dream something, it can never happen. An entire culture can live in denial, ignore obvious facts. Families find ways to cover up family secrets. Relevant to me if I try to explain in a kind way, truths, facts, and reality, to those in a world the listener is not familiar with, and denies is valid. "You can't do that" or "That doesn't count." I can hold my hand out to them and say, "Behold what is before you," and they shake their head no. It is in fact not before them if they have their eyes closed. I have to sigh, and leave them behind.

Speaking of reality, Dodger gets my attention when he stops by my selling table which his wife lined up for me in Nome,

"Miles, did you check out what shipping to Nome, Alaska costs? See some of the prices for food?" I did notice prices being about three times higher than Fairbanks. I point that out, that if you live in Nome, it may not matter if wages are three times higher. "Somewhat true, Miles, wages are higher. Not sure if wages are twice as high as Fairbanks, but it's true, we manage to get by." I had noticed this about Alaska in general. How folks on vacation, or contacting me are 'shocked' at Alaska prices. I chuckle and explain $10 an hour is normal slave labor here, where in some places in the lower states it is under $5 an hour. So those of us who live here can afford a higher standard of living cost.

Some prices seem to be going up at a fast rate though. Dodger points to a package he got, and the shipping cost. "Miles, $30 for a package that two years ago cost under $20. And five years ago cost $10 to ship."

"Yes, I notice the increased shipping costs too, Dodger. It affects my business, since I sell on the internet all over the world. The shipping cost is a big deal to me! I see the price of stamps goes up every year or so. I recall when years and decades went by with no change in stamp price. I think it is the internet and emails that hurts the post office."

"Maybe private mail carriers hurt too, Miles."

"Could be Dodger, but here in Alaska anyhow, we tend not to deal with FedEx or UPS. They can't find us! Ha!" But yes, I suppose in the big picture Alaska plays no part. We are a drop in the bucket. Like when we vote, like for President. The winner is announced, while Alaskans are still voting. That's how little our vote and opinion counts. No use grumbling about things we have no control over. "Oh Well!" I laugh. I can't complain. Sales are decent and I'm having a good time.

It is exciting to see the dog racers come in at the end of a 1,000 mile race, after ten days sleeping in the snow, and traveling through the wilderness with no roads to follow. Exciting, because I know most of the racers, and know many of the sled dogs. I can look at sleds and know who built them. I look at dogs, and know whose blood line, and what village. It all gives something to talk about that we have in common. I watch my friend Josh come across the finish line. Not one of the front runners anymore. My long time explorer friend Norman Vaughn shows up. Bill Cotter comes in, who is from Nenana. Joe Runyan used to live in Nenana. We all know each other. I am invited to the banquet for the racers. A lot of speeches are given. Good food is had by all.

Nome life is different than what I have seen in the interior villages, yet similar.

Dogs drag whale bones and polar bear fur down the roads. Not much wood is stacked in the yards, because Nome is above the tree line in the Arctic. Everyone depends on oil. Nome is the source of oil. Yet the crude is shipped far away to be processed, then transported back at a high cost. Many of the villagers off the surrounding remote islands are here for the big event, and to get in on some of the business, or just the chance to hang out. For many it is the bar, but not the hang out for everyone. I'm still figuring out how to run a good business.

I brought some grizzly bear claws to tentatively see if any of the natives wanted to trade for fossil ivory. I have a pile of claws acquired over the years through trades, gifts, naturally dead bears, and what not. Not legal to sell, at least under most conditions. Though I am told by a reliable source, black bear claws are legal to sell. The public has not been notified.

As a judge friend tells me, "You are obligated to know what the law is, the government is not obligated to make the law available, or honestly tell you what the law is." This was confirmed by a friend on the Game Board who is the one who actually got the black bear claws law changed. I'm beginning to suspect however, that it is not the law that matters. The government does not always follow the law. What matters is what do those who carry the stick feel.

I see a local vendor selling grizzly and polar bear and other claws openly, with price tags. We discuss what we think the law is. "Huh," I sum it up. "The customer owns the claw and pays me to do art on it. We set out on the table samples to show people the kind of work we can do on their claws if they bring them to us." The Nome vendor does not agree. "I've been selling bear claws here for years, no problems!" I'm not trusting enough to agree.

A lady comes up to me inquiring, "I like your grizzly claws, this one in particular. Is it for sale?"

I hesitate to reply, and decide to say, "If you have a claw you already own, like one of these, I can do this metal work on it for you. I am not sure of the legality of my selling it outright to you like this."

This may have been a good call, as she says, "Oh! Well, my husband is the wildlife officer here in Nome. I can ask him and see you tomorrow to buy this if I can!"

I am not sure I want a law officer looking closely at my life. The same as, who wants to invite the IRS in for tea? So the next day I am careful about my signs saying, 'Samples! Not for sale'. The other vendor is still outright selling his claws. So I might be losing business. *Dang.* Towards noon, Eskimo time, a fish cop shows up. I see him head to the table with the grizzly claws for sale. I see the vendor getting a ticket! *Hmmm.* The cop wanders over to my table and gets out his ticket book and begins filling it out.

"What's wrong, officer?"

"You're selling bear claws, I'm giving you a ticket! It's not legal to sell bear claws."

In a shocked tone I reply, "No sir. I'm not selling bear claws! I'm a law abiding citizen!" I point, "See the sign, 'Not for sale—samples only'?" A pause while he notices the sign for the first time. " I am showing people what I can do with their claw." The officer frowns. I interrupted the pleasure he was having, writing me up, and yanking my chain. What I am doing is legal.

The officer frowns."OK. Well, I'll be back at the end of the show and you better have the same number of claws out on the table as you have now!"

With a humble and straight face I say, "Of course, officer!" I have other claws under the table put away. So it will not be hard to have the same number of claws at the end of the show. I am sure the officer's wife said something to him. I am pretty sure he came here to get his wife a free grizzly claw necklace, by confiscating mine, writing me up, and keeping the claw. So even in remote Nome, things are changing. Even in remote small communities there is government corruption. Selling bear claws is something I might win in court. *It is in fact legal, but most officers do not even know that. So It's better to just play along.*

I wander around looking in local shops and see an opportunity. There are a lot of finished Eskimo ivory art pieces that look like they would make great handles for knives. I buy a few carvings of dancing natives. Even though I have to pay $150 each, the going price. I think these carvings can go on knives that sell for close to $1,000. I can see if I can get high end knives to move. It is legal for Eskimos to sell any kind of ivory they want. For sure. Not a problem to resell it for me, as long as I have not altered it or removed the Eskimo artist's name.

There was a time not so long ago, it was legal to buy Eskimo art, cut it up and rework it as my own. I only 'think' that law has been changed, but no way to find out, since Fish and Wildlife is not obligated to tell the truth when asked. Or more, most officers do not know the law. They are not lawyers. They themselves are not sure. So rather than taking a chance, be wrong, and get in trouble, it is just easier to reply, 'No!' Few lawyers specialize in Fish and Wildlife laws. Experience shows lawyers do not know how to easily get the latest cutting edge this month's answer. My friend on the Game Board, who is at the source, who studies only game laws does not know.

WHEN I GET HOME from Nome, I see an email concerning something I ordered, asking about shipping and how I want it shipped.

Subject: RE: Order from the Web

Mr. Martin,

I received a quote to ship your order through Fed Ex at $173.56 approximate time is 5 business days to get to you. We have secured a large discount through Fed Ex which has consistently beat UPS prices. I will get a quote from UPS and email the number to you as well.

I apologize for the delay.

Kindest Regards,Lori Tucker

PACE Technologies

My reply

Hello Lorie

My order can be shipped by US mail Flat Rate Priority for $15. Why do I want to pay $173.56, or twice the value of the product being shipped? Or let me put it this way... Alaska sells you gas. How would you like to pay $173.56 a gallon for shipping?

What goes around comes around. Do to others as you would have them do to you. I guess my answer is "no thank you". Please cancel my order. I have learned my lesson, to never order anything unless I know what the total cost is before I click 'yes!" Thanks for the educational lesson. **Miles**

This is becoming an increasing problem, totally outrageous shipping costs being asked. I've been taken only one time so far. I paid $73 shipping on a $5 item, by giving my credit card number and being in a hurry, just saying, "Send it, thanks." I of course expected $3 shipping. I should reply with more kindness. I sigh, because as I get civilized, the kindness and forgiveness of the savage disappears. I am getting caught up in the shark frenzy and road rage mentality. We choose our rewards, and accept the price. Not much time goes by before the subject of 'the rules' comes up again, in a different way than the mail.

"I understand saving money by reloading your own shotgun shells, Miles. But you are saying how you are experimenting with different components. Why would you think you can improve on what the factory has done, the ballistics published, the loads already offered for sale? These people are experts with a lot of money, and a lot of motivation to figure out the best loads, it's a very competitive market! I'm not sure what you are doing is even legal. Shouldn't you be following the rules?" A neighbor is asking why I want to mess with the directions? Am I that arrogant, I think I can improve on what the experts come up with?

I reply, "The loading data we are given is a result of a lot of tests that are motivated by several factors, that may not have to do with 'best performance.' Such as safety, comfort (stopping sharp recoil), cost, politics, laws and environmental impact. 'Being most lethal at the furthest distance,' is only one factor they consider.

Also, all guns do not perform the same with the same loads. One big factor is what will work most reliable, in the most number of guns. Compromise. Companies prefer to deal with their own products and contacted sources. Mixing companies products could give better results. I'm saying it is not that difficult to come up with something specifically for my gun, for a specific need, that is better than anything commercially offered. It may not be as safe. It may cost more. It may not work in other guns."

I pause to see if what I am saying is having any effect on my neighbor. I remember another point. "It is suggested, even mandatory, that we use steel shot instead of lead in shotguns. In fact, it is very difficult to buy loaded lead shot shells in the store. But I can reload myself with lead. Lead is heavier, and denser, so carries energy better and much further than steel. My lead is as lethal at 100 yards as your steel is at 50 yards. The assumption is, we hunt for sport, because 99% of the population does. Being environmentally conscious is the number one priority, not the ability to eat."

"OK, but what about reload data for lead shot? Why not follow what is suggested?"

"I'm thinking my shotgun has a longer barrel than most. So I am wondering if a slower burning powder that builds up the pellet speed over a longer time span because of the longer barrel, might result in less pellet deformation, and less kick and pressure." If so, I could increase the weight being pushed, more pellets moving faster, more uniformly round, will perform better at longer distances. Only maybe. I'm testing it. It's fun. Why not? If it doesn't work, 'oh well.' You may be correct, chances are, everything I try has been tried already.

I have an expert friend with a chronograph, to test speed. He tells me that, in fact, I am better off with less weight moving faster if long range is my goal. It is true, only one in 100 exciting ideas I have panned out. The economics are there. I can make a shell for five cents, when it cost one dollar to buy one. If we factor in my time, who knows how it works out. I am not the one trying to push what I think and do on anyone else. I am here defending myself. I'm not trying to be arrogant or stupid. You asked, and I replied. If we do not agree, I am not bothered. Is there some reason why what I do bothers you?" [3]

Our conversation will go no place. He ends with, "But the law says…" Yes. A last resort when not getting your point across, is to get out a big stick.

The truth is, I am hearing some rumors of changes in laws along the lines of what this guy is saying.'No more lead shot allowed—period.' Then I hear, 'Only banned over water.' The concern being the lead lands in the water, ducks and water birds ingest it and get lead poisoning. Lead is still legal for grouse, turkey, fox, wolves, bears, and other kinds of hunting, 'for now.' —as of a month ago. Also here in Alaska, the enforcement people are not concerned, because we do not have a high population and not much lead is in the environment from shooting, like in the lower states.

I find myself saying, "Yea, I take steel with me when I go out waterfowl hunting, to make sure I am legal." *So I can wound more birds like you do.* This neighbor is getting to the point I fear he wishes to make a report to ensure I become a 'person of interest.' I try to be honest, give my opinion as I see it, and find this is not working.

DON SHOWS up at my doorstep, the older Don out on the trapline, out behind my homestead on the Kantishna. I do not recognize him out of context until I know his voice when he speaks. He's a bit fidgety. Clears his throat.

"Vern and Kevin are becoming more of a problem for both of us Miles."

My recollection of the situation is, this Don character tried to ace me out of the area taking sides with the young industrious kids. I suspected he had chosen the wrong side, and would come to regret it. Now here he is, problems with these kids and is looking for my help. *Changing sides.* I pause a while. "Well come on is I guess, have some tea." He looks relieved.

Long ago he wanted to park his truck in my Nenana yard, so I could watch it for him. He wanted to keep it plugged in to my electric. In the far north all vehicles are outfitted with various electric heaters so they start in the extreme cold. These heaters draw a lot of electric power. It was only for a few days at a time, but think it cost me $10 in electric every weekend. He never offered to pay, and from the looks, I appear to be money poor so any descent person who wanted this service should be happy to offer to pay.

However he and his wife sometimes buy my artwork. It is possible they figure buying my art, as a favor to help me out, is a way to pay me to watch their truck. Or maybe because they bought my art they assumed we are friends now, and friends do not charge each other for favors. *Sometimes relationships can go like this.* However in the middle of winter I got concerned about my increased electric bill. I am not even able to run my power equipment to create art! I had said,"Don, sorry to ask, but I cannot afford the electric your truck heater consumes. I can not run electric in the shop to do my art. Can you pay for the electric you use, like maybe $10 a week-end?" He did not reply, changed the subject. But never saw him again at the house. He never brought the truck around again. So here he is again, in my view, with a need, not here to help me in any way.

"Don, I think there is nothing I can do to help with these kids at this point. There was a time when Vern first showed up, I was working out a deal, and your concerns could have been included, if you and I came to an agreement." I let this sink in, then continue. "So it looks like you felt you could get along with them and did not need a good relationship with me. That deal went wrong, now you want my help, after I got aced out."

"Miles, it is not like that!" He acts shocked. " I always respected you as a trapper and lived up to my agreements concerning your trails, you know that!"

"Don, you set traps on my trail."

"Later on, after you gave it up, not while you were out there and it was yours!" Possibly he is correct in living up to his own sense of ethics and bush laws. This is an issue with nothing in writing anyone agrees to. Lots of misunderstandings. *There were other issues. Are they minor and my own misunderstanding?* "He could have come and asked, talked to us!" *Yea, but admit it, we ourselves believe it is better to beg for forgiveness then ask for permission.* "I do not like confronting people." *Me neither.* Don adds,"Anyhow Miles, I am not really here to ask for anything. Just visit. As an older wiser Man."

I decide I have no use for creating an enemy. He is not asking for anything, so I have nothing to lose by simply accepting that. This is as close to an apology as I'll get. There was a time all this could have escalated into something serious. But I am not trapping anymore, it's all in the past.

"You still trapping hard, Don?"

"I wish! To hard, getting old. I get out now and then on the trail with the wife. We bought two new machines, sometimes the kids come with us." I recall a new machine a few years ago. I had passed him on the trail way out close to the Kantishna near Chicago.

I remind him. "At the time, I had my old Tundra machine, a 300. You had a new big 800."

Don had trouble keeping up and was getting stuck when I was not, so the new machine did not look so hot to either of us. "Yea, Miles, forgot to tell you. On the way home from that trip I got on the sidehill at Chicago and the machine stopped and rolled over on my leg." He pauses as I take this in.

"Wow"

"Yea, and I could not get it off. I was there two hours until my son came along and helped me. Now I have newer smaller lighter machines, but as you must know, the really nice ones like your Tundra are not made anymore." So we get off on a discussion of snow machines and the merits of each size and brand.

"The Bravo that Arctic Cat makes was another old small standby no longer made." We agree the new generation wants the hot fast powerful toys "These customers have the money. The manufactures have figured out the smaller machines trappers and those who work machines need, do not earn them a lot of money, we do not bring them in for service. We hang on to them, so are not good profit makers."

"Profit is off the weekend warriors."

"You figured that out too, huh!" We laugh. "Same with boats!" We review the marketing strategy of boat sellers. It is nice to talk to one who has knowledge of such things. There are not many people who can discuss the subject with any kind of knowledge among those I associate with.

Time for Don to go and—who knows what our relationship is. I think of something."Do you know Sandy, out on the lake below Wien Lake?"

He thinks,"I might know him by Sinclair, his last name, Yea, he flies like I do, but hardly know him, he did not want me over there trapping, he's not around much."

"I trapped with dogs up his way long ago, had his permission, but kept traps off the lake, so know what you mean." I pause. "I asked, and wondered, because he is an elder like us, from another generation, with things in common."

Don waves good bye and I wonder if I will ever see him again. I think of Sandy now. We keep in touch. He has a magazine he writes and I have articles in it. The magazine is about and for explorers, odd thinkers. I saw an article about a guy who travels the world by hot air balloon. Another teaches sky diving. Sandy lives on a big square rigger ship that reminds me of a pirate ship, and he teaches sailing. I am the mountain man. We write about views on life, stories of inspiration.

One article I liked a lot, was about a pilot who crash landed in Mongolia who had to walk out and it took months, He met a nomadic stone age tribe that helped him get out. Written in his own words for Sandy to print. More like a small town xerox printed low budget not a big circulation. Written for a small exclusive market. Through this, I can see what Sandy is about, why he does this. We all share things in common. We have views and a way of thinking ordinary people do not understand. I feel close to Sandy. On my mind, because when we first met, our relationship could have gone another way. He was protective and defensive of 'his lake' and wanted me to give up my trail, stay away!

My gut feeling was the Clint Eastwood approach. 'Do you feel lucky today?' Have it out in a war. I decided to hear Sandy out, try to see his view, find out if we could work things out. Now Sandy is someone I admire and respect a lot. So could it happen with this Don guy? Could things have gone different with Joe at Hanen lake? *Maybe not, he tossed out all my supplies, told me I have no rights. I have no view worth considering. How do you work things out with someone like that?* "Still, he is a respected person in civilization with a lot of influence and clout who would make a much better friend then enemy!" *We make our choices and live with them.*

THE CALL I have been waiting for arrives. Seymour calls with some survey work coming up this spring, jobs are starting to shake lose. As soon as the phone rings I answer, "Hey Seymour!"

"How did you know it was me Miles? How often does this happen? I notice, Miles!" I change the subject. I do not know. I just think of Seymour, and he calls. I do not want to make a big deal about it. Others as well notice, how they have the phone in their hand to call, and I call them at exactly the same time.

"The state is offering remote land at the mouth of the Cosna River Miles. Our job is to pick out the parcels that look nice, and survey them after approval on another trip. The state is no longer allowing the homesteader to pick out the land and stake it." We have discussed this over the years, after noticing the issues as a result of homesteaders having no clue where they are. Staking land they cannot find again and we cannot either, or staked five miles from where they think, and it turns out, they are out of the staking area. Some have already cleared land and started building. A few times we have even rescued stakers who got lost on their property, trying to walk their lines in a square. They get turned around, go over the hill, into the next valley, and could walk 1,000 miles in the wrong direction and never find a road or village. One had been lost for six days. We guessed the state would change how it offers it's remote land.

"Sounds like a nice boat job, Seymour. I know people who homesteaded years ago at the headwaters of the Cosna, back in the '70's.

"Yes, I already contacted Wiseman, who says he knows you, to see if he can help us find some good parcels. He himself is interested in another piece of land closer to town and might move on down to the mouth." So once again I will get paid for work, plus boat rental. "This job involves mostly selecting good spots. Nothing difficult to survey." Seymour is careful to pick the kinds of jobs we can handle as we get older, me with my back injury.

Not much happens worth mentioning. Life is often just a routine now.

THE COSNA RIVER

We camp out in tents, cook over a campfire, and get paid for having fun—sort of. There is time to fish for our dinner in the early morning and evening. The Cosna River is interesting. Very deep for its narrow, twisty width. The water is dark brown —caused by acid in the leaves falling in. There is not much current except during break up in spring, there is a great rush of water that does a lot of damage. The banks are steep and hard to climb. This is a factor in choosing good pieces of ground for home sites. Wiseman meets us on the second day. The Cosna is about a long day's boat travel from Nenana, but not so far from Manley—just forty miles. But forty miles on the river is not like forty road miles.

"Interesting boat, Wiseman! Hard to get them like that anymore!" He has a very old style, maybe from the 1940's. Extremely long, twenty-eight feet, narrow like a canoe. Not especially fast or maneuverable, but good on gas and ability to haul lots of weight.

"And runs shallow, Miles!" he adds. I wish I had such a boat in my earlier days on the Kantishna River with all the heavy loads I had to haul."

We talk boats around the camp fire. There is a set of large grizzly bear tracks on the beach, but we hardly mention this. Bears are common enough. We do briefly talk firearms. Wiseman prefers his sawed off shotgun in the tent with him. Seymour swears by his light magnesium 44 Magnum pistol made by Taurus. They make fun of my Ruger 357 Blackhawk, as not enough firepower against a grizzly.

"Top of the line back in the 80's!" We all agree on that at least. "Beats fighting off bears with sticks, bows, or even black powder!" We agree on this as well. "Black powder is powerful all right, but just the one shot!" We all nod. It is all the usual talk around campfires in the wilds.

Wiseman is someone who is going to use lead in his shotgun. Though he laments it is hard to find in the store anymore. He thinks steel would not even penetrate a bear. Not enough energy. He says, "Well, I am glad the rest of the U.S. is so far away. Civilization with all its hare-brained ideas! Telling us how to do things, when they do not have a clue how we live. If they tried being in our shoes, they would perish. With the gall to tell us how it is done!"

This is a pretty universal sentiment among remote people. We are glad civilization is so far away, and has such little effect on us. We agree civilization would feel differently sleeping in tents next to grizzly tracks in the sand like us.

"Where is anyone who is going to tell us what to do and how to do it?" He looks around for such a person, and of course, such a person would be 100 miles away, and not know we are here. Thus civilization can go off the cliff like the lemming, but is not going to drag us along. I note the 'them' and 'us' mentality. On that note, we all retire to our tents for the night.

We all have small compact dome tents with no headroom inside. All we use them for is sleeping. We are in a flat grassy field about an acre big, surrounded by wild mint and low willows. This is a bend in the river that gets both morning sun and evening sun. Wiseman might want to select this piece of ground as his new parcel. Five acre parcels might cost a thousand dollars.

"Getting to my home now requires switching boat engines to get into the shallower water, it's hard." He realizes he does not have to go that far for the isolation and freedom he wants. The cost of traveling such a long way hurts more with the economy going to heck so fast. "Another fifty miles upriver is more then I want to deal with." We all nod.

"Wiseman, you found any ancient fossils up your way, heard Ken used to bring them in to Tusk off and on, so was just wondering, heard the upper Cosna is a source." I know Wiseman knows both Ken and Tusk. I know these remote people need a way to pay bills, make money—fossil hunting works. I know Wiseman is not a big fossil hunter, so will not be protective of the area, might divulge information if he has any.

"I'm more into gold then fossils, Miles!"

A lot of people are. Upper Cosna was part of the gold rush ages ago. I assume there is still some gold to be found. I heard from the fur dealer that Wiseman traps a little.

"I found a leg bone once, so know the area produces the tusks you look for, Miles." It sounds like Wiseman does not know where or how to look and does not have the knowledge, so I am not going to get the information I want, but suspected it might be like this. No harm in trying. However he knows Ken well. "I saw Ken with a whole boatload of fossils once. He told me he sold them to Crafty." Tusk is known for not always having the cash to pay, so the next option is to go see Crafty. Crafty could have told me, I'd expect him to. Thinking on it, Crafty may not want me to know Ken has fossils, I might be a competitive buyer, paying more than he. This is true. Seymour is just listening in, not so much part of this conversation. He is not a true wilderness person like Wiseman and I are. Seymour changes the conversation so he can be part of it.

"You see the size of those bear tracks at the edge of camp?" We all nod in agreement, they are big and for sure grizzly. Seymour hints we should be concerned. Proving again he is not one of us—comfortable in the wilds.

Wiseman comments, "Just a week ago I was camped out in a tent overnight and a bear, just a black bear, tried to tear into the tent at night while I was in it." We all say how this is not usual and wonder why the bear did that. "Curious I think." We all nod as we stare into the fire.

"You shoot it?" I ask. I'm wondering how that shotgun of his works from inside a tent. I think a sawed off shotgun is a dumb idea. It is not good for anything else but up close shots on bears or people.

"Hit it with the butt of the shotgun through the tent to get it off me." We agree the odds are slim a grizzly would show up and try to get in our tents. Though it is still a good idea to keep the firearm handy, just in case. We are tired, fire is going out, misquotes are getting worse as the smoke from the fire goes away. We have all been burning pic in our tents so they are bug free when we go to bed. Pic is not good to breath, so we let this stuff burn while we are away.

Before I fall asleep I hear a beaver come up the riverbank and get into some mint. Rustling sounds. I know what the sound is. Most sounds I recognize now, not so many unknowns. Talk of bears and seeing those huge fresh tracks has me more aware. *I'll stay awake and let you know if a bear jumps on the tent, ok?* "You do that." No reply. Nothing wakes me in the night. I wake up in the morning with a smile, and my 357 resting on my chest.

A FEW DAYS LATER, after we have a few nice parcels picked out for the state land disposal, we smell smoke from a forest fire. Wiseman has picked out the parcel he wants, and will file on it. It's one of the perks of the job, I guess, to get first pick! Neither Seymour or I see any land we are especially attracted to. We both have quite a bit of land already. Or more, we have our future planned out, how we want it to be, and where we expect to be going when we need to get away. This part of the job is about done.

Seymour says, "Well, these tentative spots need approval. We took pictures and descriptions. We get back together later in the summer once these spots are approved with any added instructions or adjustments." A few other jobs in the past went the same as this, so I understand the sequence of events.

The forest fire smoke gets thick along the river. We see the flames. It is time to get out of here. More and more we notice summer jobs involve being around or in forest fires. We do not recall this from the past. We think it has to do with climate change.

Seymour and I both notice Wiseman is hard to work with. He means well, but I think his lack of communication with others has him off in his own world, marginally able to function around others. I see a little of myself in him. Wiseman made the choice to stay out in the wild longer than I did. He has now been isolated for over thirty years. Seymour and I feel he may be permanently tweaked at this point. He does not understand why we do not do everything his way—the right way. He wonders why we haven't figured out that his way is the most efficient, and only way to do it. From how to make coffee, to how to set up the tent, to how to put gas in a gas tank.

Seymour sent him off on his own to pick out parcels of land, since Wiseman lives here and knows the good spots. He gave him a set of instructions, explaining the rules the state is going to live by and uphold. Out of ten parcels Wiseman picks, only one ends up approved by the state. There are rules about how much water frontage a parcel can have. The angle of the side lines, leaving the river—which need to be close to ninety degrees. There are setback restrictions for a cabin site. Parcels need to either share a common boundary or be at least 300 feet apart. I have heard these rules for so many years I do not think much about what the state wants, it's memorized. Wiseman does it his way. He feels because he lives on the river and knows the most, he should be the boss. "The state doesn't know what it is doing!" Well, maybe not, but guess what? The state is our boss, handing out the money. We are in no position to tell them how it should be doing things.

Seymour and I understand he lives alone with his wife. He is always the boss, and has never had to listen to anyone else, or have his opinion questioned. But the truth is, Seymour and I could have done a better job without him. Seymour pays him for quite a few days. There is only one parcel to come of it and we will have to totally redo all his work, take down all his ribbons, and ignore all his drawings. Seymour is kind enough to understand it is not his fault, he has gone bushy. However I understand, being kind is coming out of Seymour's pocket, to the tune of thousands of dollars.

Wiseman goes upriver to pick up his wife, and meets us at camp as we are about to leave. His wife ignores us, staying in the boat while Wiseman talks. I notice the wife giggling, talking to herself, peeling the bark off a little willow stick. After half an hour she tosses the peeled stick in the water. *Looney tunes.* Wiseman seems not to notice. *So this is normal.* "Suggesting this has gone on a long time." It gives new meaning to the wonderful life alone in the wilds. It's not free.

This reminds me of another reason I came out of the wilds as I once knew it. I forgot! I noticed my reality was getting to the level of unacceptable. I'd relate a series of events and people who had been with me would frown and inform me it did not happen like that at all! So it dawned on me, shared stories are required to be on the same sheet of music as the rest of the world.

Seymour asks, "Miles, are you going to head on downriver to look for mammoth?"

I feel bad to have to be evasive and vague about my plans. Much of the fun of fossil hunting is gone, when I can't even share the experience with my best friend. I'd rather no one have any details of when and where. The price of ivory goes up fast. There is a scarcity worldwide. Word is, the Chinese are making more money. It is a mark of prestige to have an ivory carving in China. Mostly they want elephant. So there is a black market in elephants and killing them. Mammoth ivory is a number two choice. I'm not sure how the number two choice affects the killing of elephants, but somehow there is a connection being made. Enough of a connection that there are frowns concerning any ivory whatever. Everything is connected if we think about it.

However, I have an opinion. It is best to weigh and balance, between a gain and a cost. By the same argument, if people are selling poached wild deer meat and other wild game meat, should we stop the sale of legal beef, as a good solution? Who would accept this? Any time we extract something from nature, there will be a price! Of course! Something is lost! Be it wood, oil, water, rocks, topsoil, or mammoth tusks. I am not trying to give Seymour a song and dance. We have discussed such things over twenty years of working together sitting around many campfires.

The Federal government seems to be taking over what used to be state jurisdiction. With a different interpretation of the law. The state is closer, and understands the local reality better, so seems more sane and reasonable to many locals. The Feds are far away, and seem more inclined to use a baseball bat to get our attention. There is no forgiveness, or looking the other way, at the same time expecting its citizens to do exactly that, look the other way and forgive Federal indiscretions.

The bottom line being, it is unclear exactly what might happen if caught with a mammoth tusk off the river by the Feds. So far, no one has been arrested. Yet people I know are more cautions, more afraid, less certain everything will be fine. So whatever wonderful adventure I may or may not have shared with Seymour in the past, times have changed. I do have permission to look for ivory on the Burke family Native claims, and there are four to five claims that have the mineral rights. Dim Burke told me he would be upset to have to go to court and verify mammoth fossils were found on his land! "Legal or not Miles, you know the University can take your find, confiscate my land. You know if there is money involved, the Feds will figure out how to screw it up!"

I have a conversation with one of the big mammoth ivory dealers I know when in the village. Tusk sees changes as I do. "Miles, there is a new definition of mammoth ivory now. It used to be called a fossil." I nod and understand mammoth ivory is not strictly a fossil. This is just a legal definition, not a scientific one. A fossil, strictly speaking, means all the animal part has been replaced with mineral, and it is now a rock. The true term for 40,000 year old material might be 'mineralized,' meaning a material on the way to being a fossil. The process has started, but is only a few thousand years to sixty, maybe seventy thousand years old. A true fossil might be millions of years, for total mineralization to take place. The law has applied the term 'fossil' to mammoth material. Meaning anything older then 1972, when the CITES treaty was signed. Tusk is now saying this is being corrected, "So now, mammoth ivory might be called an artifact!"

I see how this changes the legality. I have heard such rumors. Those of us in business have discussed it amongst ourselves. None of us knows anyone in the government we trust to give us a correct answer. Or even let us help be part of a workable solution. All I hear are horror stories of those who went to ask questions, and ended up on the dreaded 'person of interest' list. Like a Jew trying to discuss discrimination with Hitler.

"Miles, I have been working with legislators for years trying to get a workable definition we can all live with." Mammoth ivory is not a true fossil, but neither is it an artifact. An artifact involves something altered by man. Taking mammoth ivory off the land would be classified as 'grave robbing' if called an artifact. I also understand that as a fossil, or being mineralized, means mammoth ivory falls under the mining laws as minerals do. As such, mammoth ivory in the past could come from any land that has mineral rights, such as early homesteads, native claims, and some mines. Of course, it only matters to a handful of people like Tusk and I. *Who cares!* Nothing on the subject is clearly in writing. There is no quotable official answer. The unofficial position of the state has been for many years, "If you stumble upon a mammoth tusk while out camping, you can keep it."

For those few of us who are more serious, the policy is more vague. But goes like this, "If, if, and if." Meaning, if you are not excavating with equipment, if you are not altering the course of the river, if you do not interfere with other users out of the area. If no one complains. Mostly, be reasonable, be kind, consider others, take care of the land. We are trusted to understand what that means without a contract, or a spelled out set of rules as thick as a phone book. I assume fossil hunters are appreciative, trust, and work with, our local government. At least to a much higher degree than the relationship with the Federal government. This 'understanding' with the state has a lot to do with why I am not greedy, not out there all summer long making a fortune. I dabble. A week out of the whole year as a camping trip. I believe the state finds this acceptable. This should help keep me out of legal trouble. This is the difference between being in business and being in jail. What are the Feds up to? What is the objective? Tusk and I both know the story of how the University buried and lost all the mammoth tusks. There is no shortage.

"Tusk, I was at the Tucson show and read an article in the local paper. The article was a put down on the entire Fossil Show! I could not believe it, Tusk! Such an article during the show certainly hurts the show. I wondered if Tucson wants the show or not! We bring in millions of dollars, then get this kind of reception?" Tusk asked about the details. I said if I found the article I saved, I'd copy it. "Basically saying most fossil dealers are crooks, and be careful. That most of us bring illegally smuggled goods to the show. That most of these fossils belong in a museum for all of us to enjoy, and should not be sold to the general public."

Tusk frowns and points out that there is the same smuggle issue with all products—food, clothing, gem stones etc. No one enjoys paying duty. There is often corruption in the system when collecting fees, or imposing restrictions.

The article quoted gem show promoters, who said there is no affiliation with the Fossil Show. Meaning, "Do not associate those hooligans with us!" I take the attitude to be a nose in the air. The high end Gem Show looks down on those of us who like to play in the dirt. Even though some fossils are worth as much as high end gem stones. It's about perception, and my guess is the Gem Show has the ear of the press, and are among the protected. The Gem Show sees the Fossil Show as a rival, and would as soon see the 'fossil' part of the show disappear. The city is buying into that.

"But Tusk, the entire show makes it the biggest event of its kind in the world. It takes the fossils, minerals, and gems to make it happen. Many customers look at and buy both. Neither detracts from the other." But that is only an opinion. I see the same outlook in the Nenana Chamber of Commerce. Many business people want to cut off the competition at the knees, be nasty in order to get ahead. They will not share advertising for a big community add. Each business pays for a one inch spot tucked away where few see it, separated throughout a magazine. When I believe a single half page Nenana add would help us all!

There is a point to be made, and a partial truth. Some fossil finds should be in a museum. But why not say some gems belong in a museum, using the same argument?

Tusk expresses a similar view "Well, where do universities get money, and what is the purpose of a university? Money comes from people who pay for and take classes on subjects of interest that they heard of, like, and see a job in down the road, right?"

The state is still saying it has jurisdiction over the waterways. The Feds are beginning to argue the state, in fact, does not have jurisdiction. So Tusk and I ponder what exactly does all this mean? Tusk says, "Are we supposed to say 'Sure no problem, we'll stop making $50,000 a year while you sort this out.'" We both ponder this. It's exciting, it's fun, it's sort of easy, once you know how. This is what we know, and it seems not to be hurting anyone or the environment. And no one has come right out and said, 'No!' Yet we both feel the tension and issues coming to a head.

"It's like wanting to arrest Indiana Jones or Crocodile Dundee, Tusk!" I am reminded. "Hey Tusk! You remember that time long ago I had a tusk and brought it in my boat all the way to Fairbanks? You met me at the boat landing to buy it." There were folks launching their boats. It was a nice hot summer day. Families were having picnics at the outdoor tables. Several were curious what I had in the boat. Tusk and I struggled to load a big tusk in his truck that was longer than the bed of his truck. I bet over 200 pounds, and twelve feet long. It happened so fast and right under the noses of these people who could not believe what they were seeing. Tusk laughs too. The days when tourists might have a chance to see such a sight, get pictures, hear the story and repeat it to the grandkids when they got home, "And this boat pulls up and there is a 40,000 year old tusk sticking up! A guy pulls up in a beat up old truck and this huge tusk is loaded up. We got to touch it! Met the guy who dug it up!" No. Such times and stories are over. If it happens anymore, it is a big secret.

Tusk and I are both glad we are getting older and got to see, 'the good old days' before our country fell apart.

"Or is this just a sign of old age Miles?" We both laugh. We recall our own parents saying the world is coming to an end because of the Beatles wearing long hair. "And other changes," we laugh, "And how they used to walk to school five miles every day," and such that no one does any more. It could be just change, and we can't keep up.

Someone I do not know, but who knows me says, "Miles, you seem like a workaholic! Every time I see you, you are working, selling, making. No weekends off, no vacations! Maybe you need to back off and take a break now and then!"

I give the usual reply to this, since I hear it often, "It is common for my work day to begin at 4:00 am and end at 10:00 pm. As I get older, I seem to need less sleep. I do not think this is being a workaholic, however, because I am doing what I like to do. I can also say my play time begins early and goes till late... and I am a 'playa-holic'—depending on the perspective." I do not elaborate any further, as this is not a friend, and this guy is more making a comment, or observation, then asking me a question. To him, what I do is work, and nothing I say will change that.

Tusk understands. He adds, "Sometimes I need a break from carving, though! My hands cramp up, I run out of ideas and need to walk away." I do understand that.

"Tusk, when that happens I work on my book, fool in the garden, go on a boat trip to find materials. I just change what I do. I think of it all as part of a subsistence life. Sometimes I am food gathering, other times working on my shelter or source of heat. We either do it ourselves, or we pay someone else with money we made working the same job over and over. It's a choice we all make." We all note though, that the laws are changing. We do not have the right as much as we once did, to do it all ourselves. We cannot necessarily build our own home, or even work on it ourselves. Nor can all of us burn wood, or go cut trees without buying the wood. And other aspects of taking care of living. But anyhow. I do not want to go on about the subject today. Things to do, places to go. I hope I chose a lifestyle and a place to live where I do have the freedoms that mean so much to me.

I HAVE an email waiting for me at home:

Wednesday, July 02, 2008 Gmn [gmn77@bigpond.com]
Hi,
I would like to purchase an authentic complete Mammoth Tusk (finished & polished & mainly blue in color) so if you have one or you can get one please let me know the cost and a picture of the tusk. Just out of curiosity, I would like to know if you carbon date or if you can carbon date the tusk to see how old it is.
Thank you **Gene**

The first person I show the matched set of tusks to knows someone interested in buying them. They tell this friend and the friend drives up all the way from Anchorage to look, 300 miles. We talk ivory, the world market, people we know in common, and past deals we made. Once we establish 'walk-the-walk-talk-the-talk,' we get down to business. I want eight grand. He says he does not like to pay over $100 a pound. I have sixty pounds, so six grand. "But these are matched, I'd agree if we talked only poundage. If dry and ready to display they'd be worth ten grand." We agree that's retail value, after they have been polished and a year from now after curing. He asks me what I'd take in cash money now on the spot. I said I might go seven grand. He asked me to split the difference for $6,500. I go for it. My guess is this is about what he had in mind when he left Anchorage.

We are counting out piles of $500. He is sitting on a gas can. I am squatting on my haunches in the shop. An overhead bare bulb swings in a cave like atmosphere. I feel like Indiana Jones. The Dungeon of Doom or selling the Holy Grail. Money piles up on an old box of rotting potatoes. Not just 'money.' It occurs to me *I used to live on $2,000 a year*. This transaction represents over three year's wages. *Try to imagine that*. It is all relative. I mean six grand is a lot to anyone, but imagine it is three years wages. The equal to 150 grand to most. Imagine counting out 150 grand on a potato box in a dark room. Money for three days of work. Almost beyond imagination, unless you are a drug dealer. Whoever gets three years cash in their hands at once? A good feeling does not describe it. Nor is it like winning the lottery. I earned it. I took a gamble, I risked my life. It paid off.

Oh, I had hoped for eight grand, or even the ten grand it might be worth in a year, maybe. But chances are I'd have to wait, and then ship it, and it would probably be hard to find any customer with ten grand cash. Talk is cheap. I'd almost for sure be accepting payments.

I have $700 invested, and three days of time. I was gone a week, but five days was survey work. Even the gas for the whole trip was paid for by the survey boss as part of boat rental. *I can do a lot with $6,500*. I also know how this buyer works. Same as me. Cash talks. Show anyone a pile of hundreds and make piles of thousands and the price comes down. That's life. No mess, no waiting on checks, and hope they are good. No paper trail, no records, just hard cash in my grubby hands. It's like being a pirate. Divvy up the booty. Pieces of Eight. The buyer is a pro. He's serious. He drove four hours to be here and brought cash. He's not playing games. He wants, expects, and deserves, 'a deal.' It's only a few days out of the ground, still wet. I have little invested in it. Not even advertising or putting the word out. Not time, not money. Move it in and move it out. He'll be back for more if this works out.

Yes, I was hooked on that, 'wads of cash life,' the first deal I ever made, selling my first pile of furs, and getting a year's wages in one fat wad. I knew I'd never work for anyone else, or enjoy wages and like it. I knew this was how I wanted life. Big wads of cash, mixed with months of poverty if need be. It beats working for a living. Life is good. I have to email this Gene guy.

Sorting and cleaning fossil bones and ivory after a river trip.

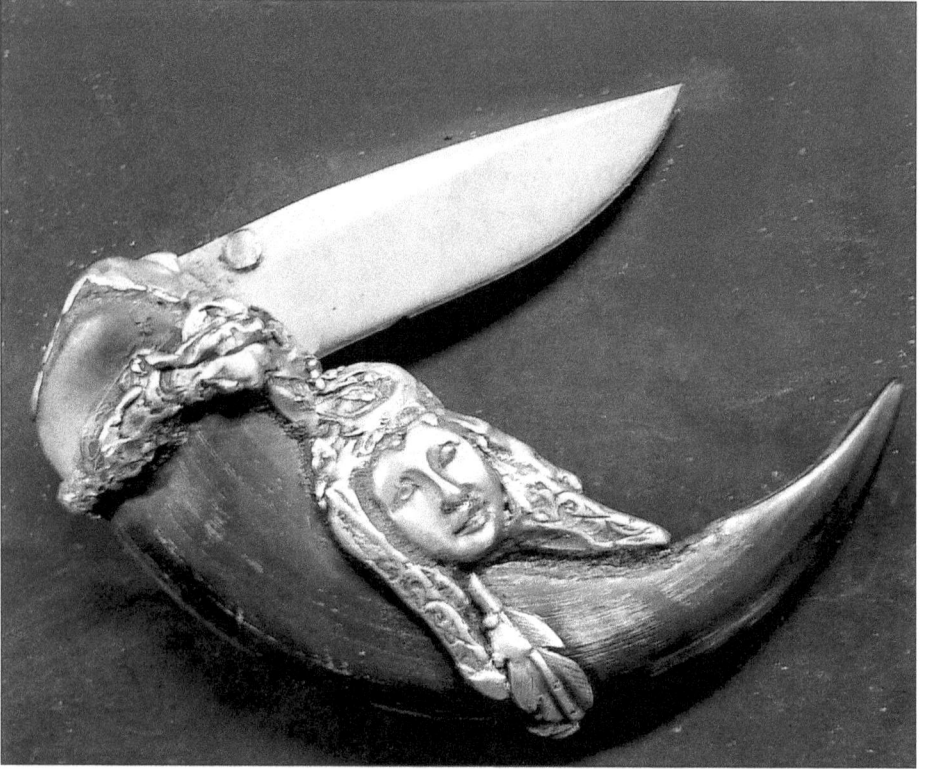

Grizzly claw folder custom cast work.

CHAPTER TEN

MEET IRIS, BECOMING A SENIOR

Tuesday, July 08, 2008
  Iris Atlantic City NJ 08401
  Hello Iris!
Nice to get a second letter from you. Yes I know, I never did answer the first.(?) I intended to. 'But.' Often, if I set something aside and plan to do it later, then later never arrives. My world has changed. It has rewards, but one price is less time. I have an internet business, and often get thirty emails a day. I got about 19,000 emails in six months. It's a lot of people to be nice to, care about, who want me to remember them. I am used to a life outdoors, being active. Now I spend more time sitting at the computer than I'd prefer. But it's my main way to communicate. One thing I like is it's an easy way to store and organize correspondence! I can make a file with your name, and it will not get lost. From you I get a letter. I set it 'someplace,' it is not long it is buried in the pile of other savable valuable stuff.

I think it is interesting—finding me again. I spin back in time. So much has happened since 'then'—where to begin? More than I can write. A lifetime of events. Four to five homesteads, 200 miles of trapline cut, sled dogs came and went, the snow machine days came and went. A forest fire wipes out all I have. Several women, a marriage, a child, a divorce, all sorts of work of all kinds. Doing well as an artist, trips to shows, a book, the New York Times, being a murder suspect, finding mammoth tusks and being an ivory dealer, moving to the village, more social now, head of the Chamber of Commerce, asked to run for Mayor. On the Library Board, the Historical Society, a web page designer, a land surveyor. Some things are the same. How can I fill you in on all this? I'm overwhelmed.

A certain sadness. Something lost, a fork in the road, hard to get back to. Us not being the same people now probably. A life time ago. It's difficult to pick up where it ended. It's meeting all over again as strangers. Not as young, hopeful, sure happiness and getting along is just around the corner. I accept that I am alone, probably always will be. Make the best of it. Try not to think a lot about it. Focus on the good things, the success I have seen. I make an effort to smile and wave your direction. At the end of a ten hour day, what does it mean?

One week of my life seems to be as much as some see in a lifetime. But sometimes I am tired and need space to reflect, be alone, have a life that is mine. Far from those who want to know me. I am a character on the other side of the wormhole, through the Stargate. A time traveler. Who will be at my side? Who would dare to? Who will keep the home fire burning? I am a comet burning bright across the sky. Not good material for getting close to. I have learned a lot since the early days.

So hot where you are? I can hardly imagine it. The low 80's out in the direct sun is as much as I can manage. Ha! I'll take fifty below any day! Your Mom and the time with her. Sounds like fun all right. Tend to mix work and fun. I see what I like to do and find a money angle. Then I sort of get paid for having fun. It means I never work or I never play, depending on the view…

That's my life these days. You have an email? I could send pictures then (?). You never married? Had kids? What is the purpose of your life? Ya', I suppose I see life as having a purpose. A reason we are here. Fitting in to a big picture somehow. Welcome to my planet. Have a good day! **Sunshine Miles**.

I am a senior. My health slowly winds down as is to be expected. Not complaining, but it does cut down on the level of excitement in my life! Ha! I now take four to five pills a day for high blood pressure and diabetes, slightly over-weight these days. Sigh. The internet business grows. I suppose almost doubles each year. Began with a yearly income of $2,000. Next year four, next year eight, next year sixteen, next year holding my cards closer and not saying or knowing for sure, but in the ballpark of thirty two. Then perhaps sixty four. May be headed for $128,000, but not saying.

I clear my throat and add,"Gross of course, not cleared money!" *Of course! We obviously do not take home as an employee of the company that much!* "I put most right back in the business." But it gets to be difficult to stuff it all back into the business as it bursts at the seams. Lots of work! *Yes, lots of work!* Not sure I have been any happier than when I made two grand a year. Doing well, maybe became a game? Something to do for fun? See how far I can go. Just to do it. Prove I could. My blood pressure increased along with the stress. I am not as free.

"Miles, as your accountant, I notice something you might consider." And my accountant offers advice. I notice we have not paid a lot into my retirement plan or social security or health insurance. I have, in short, not looked out well for my old age.

I explain my viewpoint to Bean, my accountant.

"Well, I sort of have. I acquired homestead land I knew would increase in value faster than money in the bank, which I could sell off in my old age as needed! Also, as part of my business I invest in a lot of raw materials I use in my art and offer for sale. It is difficult to put a value on it as 'value to whom'? In the right place at the right time I might have half a million dollars in materials." It is in fact difficult to estimate. I have nine buildings full of materials from forty years of collecting and stockpiling, measured in hundreds of pounds. I have a good 500 pounds of mammoth ivory alone, worth as much as $100 a pound. But also worth as little as 'nothing' if I die and no one knows what it is, or what to do with it, or who to sell it to. It's a specialty market.

One view is that this is just so much 'junk.' Twenty five pounds of high end opal, a hundred pounds of musk ox horn, if cut and polished as knife scales as high as $30 an ounce. But again, it all hinges on knowing who the buyers are. The bottom line is, in theory, I could 'retire,' and live off selling this inventory. But yes, it is a job, and yes, the most money is in retailing and running a store. If I wholesale this amount for ready cash, I would get less than ten cents on the dollar. The amount declared on taxes as stockpiled inventory is not the same as the optimistic, 'what I'm worth' I might tell a fan.

"Miles, if you put in a couple, maybe few, good years, and show some nice income, pay into your retirement, you could easily double what you can collect every month for the rest of your life." This thought is inspiring, and acts as a motivator. If I understand right, social security bases it's payment on the past three years average income. Earlier income not relevant. I can head in to the home stretch sprinting, rather than just fading away. I had always felt there would be no retirement money when I reached retirement age. I'm a baby Boomer. I believe all the funds my generation paid into social security got spent by the government and are gone—basically 'stolen.' I am among the lucky, and did not pay in a lot to lose a lot.

There are many stories among friends my age. How they lost their retirement. In many cases, companies went bankrupt, out of business, taking the retirement fund down with them. In other cases, someone in the company embezzled the funds. In such cases, I get told how the thief is punished with minimum time, while those who paid in all their life suffer for it. In my mind 'big government' and 'big company' is synonymous. Even if not, the government borrowed from Social Security. Calls it 'government money.' Perhaps I am confused as to who and what the government is. *I thought it was 'us'?*

I tell my accountant Bean, "If we are the government, I do not recall saving my money and spending it. Do you recall that? Nor do I recall being asked how I'd like it spent, or if I want it spent. I do not recall gambling with it, investing it in the Stock Market. I recall not having a choice! If I had a choice, I would have deposited the money in coffee cans in the back yard and still have it, even if inflation ate up its value, at least there would be something." I understand the money is not only 'gone,' but we are in debt, and worse, can't afford to pay the interest on the debt to China.

"In my opinion, that makes us the poorest country in the world. If our country was a private company, they'd be in prison for fraud and theft. " My accountant agrees, but tends not to be vocal about it. Though now and then he tells a humorous accounting story, proving my point. I do like his attitude. Bean tends to find it all humorous! I never thought I'd be good friends with a number crunching, bean counter. Normally, such a person does not believe in magic, passion, nor has an exciting life.

Bean has stories of partying with Mick Jagger of the Rolling Stones. High level scams he has observed, and again, finds funny. He is the accountant for a large school. He is not afraid of the IRS. Even gets along. Thus knows what they want. When we met, and I asked about 'taxes,' I laid it all out before him. I asked, "What do the numbers say, what does this tell you?" His reply was,

"What would you like them to say?" Followed by working together to make it happen. I liked this approach very much. Most accountants tell me there is only one answer, you are screwed, but maybe I can minimize the damage. And it's too complicated for me to understand. Bean tells me it is easy enough to understand, or at least I can do my part and give him the numbers.

He might say, "Are you sure this cost is for this reason? It would fit better over here."

I say, "Yes, sure, that works." Nothing illegal. It's just my life is complicated, and can be defined in a lot of ways, shifted from here to there financially. I have a single business, 'Miles of Alaska'. I sell art and raw materials. I'm a trapper. I sell a few vegetables, flowers and starter plants from the greenhouse. I have a dog culling business. I haul freight, sell firewood. I'm an author. I record and sell tapes. I rent homesteads and traplines. I have aspects of my business I never even thought of, that I legitimately make money on.

"Miles, did you use your boat for business purposes? Like haul any art, use the boat to get art supplies out of the woods?" Well guess what! We get to deduct that use. Just about everything I do is 'business,' and as such, everything I have is a business deduction.

"Getting paid for what I like to do," is my motto. "Find a money angle to everything." And one of the rewards—everything is a business deduction. The government practically owes me by the time we are done. Bean is wise as to when to show a profit, when I might show a loss. Many business expenses could go either way. I make a dinner appointment with friends and pick up the tab.

"Yes, we talked about my book and art among other things." Maybe a lot of that we need not call a business deduction. I can accidentally forget I had dinner or what we talked about in a year I need to show more profit.

"This would be a good year to do that." *I can make that happen!* Some things are better off depreciated over time, other items it is better to outright declare. I think all this is what he means by being flexible, adaptable, and making the numbers come out the way we want. Because I work for myself, if I have a heads up, I can adjust my business to suit my needs ahead of time. When it is a good year to show a loss, I can spend more time creating than selling, or more time writing, with the profit showing up down the road at some future date. If it's a good time to show a profit due to some deduction I need or qualify for, I can liquidate, sell off inventory, pay more for advertising to get more business sales, or do another show. In this way, I control both my income and my taxes. No. I am not 'screwed.' I can either cut my income in half or double it without a huge effort. I live subsistence and it is not the money so much that defines my standard of living. I grow the same garden, kill the same moose, cut my own firewood, just the same regardless of my income. So really, what is income for? Whatever I want it to be, right? I mean, once the basics are covered. So here we are again with 'retirement,'

Bean shows me how I can pay into my taxes, contribute or invest a few thousand dollars. Then what I can collect will go from $400 a month to $800 a month for the rest of my life. So, 'cool.' I set aside a few thousand to basically invest in high yield returns called my retirement, that we will call, 'taxes.' It's not complicated, or hard to understand. I have to show matching income to justify paying thousands in taxes? It's partly about receipts. It's partly about—well, I invest so much back into inventory. Since I am a pack rat I might have at any given time $200,000 in inventory. That I could sell any time. I just do not, since it is like money in the bank at a much higher interest rate. It's like investing in the commodities market. Only I physically have the commodity. Some items I sell are so off the wall and absurd, the value is whatever I say it is. What would you pay for a musk ox hoof? I sold a moose knee cap bone to a guy who threaded it for a gear shift knob. Is it garbage, or a $50 item? I have a hundred of them.

"What about inventory tax, Bean?" Well. It is difficult to put a value on a pile of moose antler. Boxes of musk ox horn scraps. Some mammoth ivory chunks.

"Would the IRS in an investigation, coming out to Nenana, Alaska to look into this, be able to place a value on all this, Miles?" Ah yes. I see the point. When I sell, it is worth whatever I say it is, whatever someone pays. Value is quite flexible with the current market, the quality and condition. Till I sell it, it's a junk pile. *I paid how much?* "I find most of it." I trade for a great deal. I get gifted a great deal.

I keep repeating till it sinks in, "It's worth, whatever I say it is."

I never trusted the government to look out for me. However, I am amazed to see I am getting close to retirement, and there is actually money I could collect. My game plan changes after talking to my accountant. I can work the hardest I ever have in my life now. I think of it as having lived my vacation and retirement when young, when I could enjoy it, but having to make up for it now in later life by working, at a time most are winding down.

I am not the happiest I have ever been, but there is the light at the end of this tunnel. In just a few years, I can reap the rewards in collecting twice as much social security every month. I do not dress, act, look, the part of someone who is successful. I'm the same old story teller we have all known for forty-five years. It's not to my advantage to look like I make money. I enjoy the privileges of being poor. Old habits die hard. I do not have the habits of the rich.

If I had a million dollars I'd still be a dumpster diver, and my socks wouldn't match.

Behind the scenes other things are going on. At least a few people are jealous? I got all this cool stuff, and do not appear to be working hard like they are, and it's not fair. In my defense, few know I get up and start my day as early as 4:00 am every single day. By the time 9 :00 am rolls around, and I stroll in to spend an hour having coffee, most folks are just getting up and assume so am I, and do not realize I have already put in five hours of work. 95% of my socializing is done on my terms, away from home and shop. I doubt even one person knows my habits.

Once the guy who delivers papers says, "I go by your shop at 4:00 am and it is common to see the lights on and you working inside, Miles." I have never followed anyone else around for an entire normal day in their life to see what their life looks like. I have no idea. What do people do when they get home from work? What hour would that be even? What do they do with their weekend? I very rarely visit people at their home, and if I do, it is for a few minutes to an hour. I do not see what their routine is like.

"Jealous, are you kidding? Dream on!" Their view may have more to do with my lack of social skills. I recognize I tend to focus on the positive, do not dwell on the negative. Defined by others as, 'Has selective memory.'

I say, "If you do not see it, it is not there. If you forget, it never happened." Poof. Like that.[1] Life in my own world, on my own planet.

I am watching old rerun Westerns my son got me. The Jim Bowie series is on. Looks like it started in 1956. I remember some of the episodes. My hero. Each episode begins with the theme song. Something about, "His knife is tempered steel, and so is he," and words about him being a defender of the country. Most episodes begin with him carrying a rifle and knife, then using one or the other. Often shooting game for dinner. In one episode, he meets the famous painter, Audubon. In this episode they hunt together and kill game.

I repeat a quote of Audubon, "If I do not kill at least 100 birds a day it is a bad day." Audubon spent time in prison for not paying his bills, and if I recall correctly, died almost penniless and unhappy. The Audubon Society today is an environment group. They would lynch Audubon if he were alive today. I am very puzzled. This appears to me to be an entire society having a selective memory. Forgetting the truth and reality, making it suit what we want it to be. Like believing Columbus discovered America. Or the United States is a democracy. Or there is no discrimination. Just what is reality anyhow?

My planet has no names, times, dates, or proof. I have a huge database in the computer of customers filed by date and name. I match the name to a file, and the file can be a key in, and suddenly I recall the data in the file, once I open it and read the first line or two of saved emails. Till then you are a stranger to me. I cannot accurately depend on giving my own date of birth, phone number, or spell my mother's name or know her birthday or any member of my family, or myself even.

"When I need to know that, I can look it up." I fill my brain instead with 'useful stuff.' Or, stuff not the average bear could know or even look up. That makes me 'special,' 'unique' (as we all should be), 'an individual' and 'valuable.' My brain is filled with every trap I ever set, and what it caught. Every bend of every river I ever ran. I can visualize a scene and run it forward in time or back in time, then freeze it and draw it like a photograph. I know the story behind most of my raw materials inventory. Hundreds and thousands of items. I have no room for data I find boring. That I can look up, or ask someone else about or... I do not mind being eccentric. Or, that's my version of the story. Or, if my role is that of 'story teller,' who wants to hear the same memorized story about Columbus?

"Miles! What a nice piece of jewelry on the website, but why are your hands so filthy in the picture! It distracts from the fine art!" *Hands. Nothing but scars and the ravages of time. Broken nails, deep wrinkles. The things these hands have done! Beyond imagination.* "So Miles, I have a friend who knows how to take pictures if you are interested." *These unworthy hands of mankind. The instruments of such beauty. How is it possible? Look at the picture and behold! Be amazed! Out of compost comes the flower. Out of the storm comes the rainbow.* "Anyhow Miles, think about it, he's a good photographer and his pictures might increase your sales." *In the madness of the world, the loud noise and angry voices, behold the beauty and be silent, still—and be moved. Ponder the mysteries of life!* "Or at least wash your hands before showing them in the pictures!"

"I'm not ashamed of my hands." Is all I say throughout the conversation. *Why would God put such an amazing artistic gift into such hands? I want you to ask that question, and think about it. Am I unworthy of the beauty I create?*

"I didn't say you should be ashamed! Oh, never mind!"

From the very beginning in Book One, back in 1972, I had a purpose. To answer questions. Questions concerning why anyone would leave civilization to go live alone in the wilds facing bears, and all the hardships. I almost died more than once, but kept going back. What makes such a person tick? How might such a person be different from others in society who do not make such a choice? That is what I have tried to be true to—answering that question. As honestly as I can. With no regard for where the answer might lead. Having survived and finally adjusted to such a life, why return to the world I struggled so hard to leave? I meticulously record my experiences, thoughts, opinions. The answers are here to be deciphered.

"I suppose, Miles, just geeze, tell it about someone else, please? My personal life is no one else's business!" So, yea, women came and went. I'm not trying to embarrass anyone. So here comes another letter. One letter out of many hundred of such letters.

Friday, April 10, 2009
Hello Miles,
It's about 2:30 in the morning and I couldn't sleep so I thought I would make an attempt to send you an e-mail. Earlier today I went into Atlantic City to pick-up my last check. After taxes were taken out I have $1500.00 left. $600.00 of that is for the plane ticket you got for me. Hopefully, with the remainder I will be able to get some winter clothes when I get there. I also sent a flat rate box there this morning. It should be there on Monday. Some of my friends from my job took me out for dinner at Caesars Casino Buffet. I did not pig out! I only had a salad, cup of coffee, and a small slice of sugar free shortcake. I came back to Pat's house on the train. It took me about forty minutes to walk from the train station. The night air was a refreshing forty degrees and the moon was full. Seems I was the only one on the street. This neighborhood is very quiet all the time. Quite a difference from the city.

I don't have any plans to go anywhere until Monday morning, when I get back on the train and start my journey to your planet!!I am only two trains and two planes away!! The only thing I will need when we get back to Nenana is a shower and some sleep. Travel time and layovers will be about eighteen hours. I will try to sleep some on the plane.

I will call you tonight about 7:00pm your time. I enjoyed your last email you sent me two days ago. The pictures were a nice touch too!! Please send me an email sometime today and let me know that this went through. For now I will try again to go back to sleep. **Iris**

Reality has not set in for me. I have in the past paid plane fair for women to come be with me and try us out, see if we can work out a relationship. I stopped getting my hopes up very high. I got an email earlier from Iris, all excited. I do not even think I saved it. Basically saying she finally found me again! Wondered what happened to me! Apparently we had written off and on for a while, a long time ago! Do I remember? *Um, yea, sure, I guess* "Nice to hear from you again! Wow, what have you been up to!" I begin to key in better as she writes a couple of times about how her father used to record music and she'd send it to me on a cassette. I guess I remember. *The question is more if I want to. Why am I supposed to remember?* I do recall the picture she sends. Yes, I knew her a long time ago. I knew a lot of people a long time ago. *What's your point?* Well, her situation is different than it was 'then.' She had been taking care of a sick father who needed her. He has now passed away. Her job is sort of ending or at a turning point to where it would be a good time to start over. She is simply ready for a change, available now.

I am not sure why we lost touch. My guess is I went out into the wilds and lost her address, or sent a letter she never got, or she wrote and I never got it. Life simply raced on by. She, at the time, did not seem available. I wrote because I like to write. But had a lot of such relationships by mail. *Over 100.* I pause. *That does seem like a lot. Hmmm* Well , OK. Maybe that many I have written once or twice. Half that many at least a few times, and a good twenty I have written and got to know for several years and more. *That sounds more believable.* Not that it matters, only in that, this was not as unique an experience for me as for her. I did not want to feel guilty about that. Her being all excited to finally find me again, she fell off the chair when she did a web search and found me and what not.

Iris recalls I wrote, "Shit or get off the pot."

She called my bluff and said, "I'll be there."

I said, "OK, here's your ticket, we'll see," and "Veni, Vidi, Vici" (however that Latin goes).

She saw, she came, she conquered. That pretty much sums it up. She gave up everything she had come to be with me and start a new life over from scratch.

This seems a good enough place to finish my book five! Friends joke the next book needs to be called "Now Tame" Or 'Domesticated' or some such. *Very funny, everyone!*

THE END OF BOOK 5

A personal note—

Reviews help! If you enjoyed this book, please leave a review where you purchased it—it would be greatly appreciated!

Sign up for my newsletter, "Keeping Up With Miles," @ www.milesofalaska.com

Deals, new books, comments, links to YouTube. Stay updated!

The Alaska Off Grid Survival Series Summary

Book 1 - Going Wild

In 1973, I am 22 years old, and a city kid. I enlisted in the Navy and got out after the Vietnam War.

I travel to interior Alaska, a 'Cheechako' (Greenhorn) by Alaskan standards. But I have been raised on Walt Disney and feel qualified to be a mountain man!

I arranged with a pilot to drop me off in the wilds of Alaska. I do not have everything I need and have things I do not need. I learn about guns, trapping, and the loneliness of living in the vast wilderness with no other humans around.

I do not see anyone for many months, then walk out of the wilds to civilization in the spring. After working odd jobs to make supply money, I return to the wilds in the fall and have a hard time my second winter. I almost die, and need to be rescued.

I decide to build a houseboat so I can travel around without having to build another cabin. I have to accept summer work in Fairbanks to pay for the boat materials and work under a builder. The boat takes much longer to build than expected.

I live as a street person much of the time to keep expenses down.

Book 2 - Gone Wild

I have many adventures on the houseboat and acquire a dog team. There are issues with the police, a bear on my boat, and a trip to see my family who live a civilized life.

My houseboat sinks. I get lost and learn other hard lessons. I start doing artwork and end up on TV. I win a land lottery and start my first homestead.

There are mail order women, and I live with a woman and her kids. Ten people are murdered in a village we visit, and myself and the family are almost among them. Family life is more difficult than I imagined.

Fish and Game becomes a concern.

I head back into the wilderness, which leads into book 3.

Book 3 - Still Wild

I acquire a couple more homesteads and cut more trapline.

I give up sled dogs and enter the world of snow machine adventures.

I winter in Galena and visit many native villages. There are bear encounters, and many survival situations to learn about.

I become a serious mammoth hunter and find fossils as part of my living. I work with a land surveyor specializing in homesteads and wilderness surveys, getting paid to use my boat.

My art sells well, so I do some big shows. I become more social and understand civilization better. I see the wisdom of being accepted by others. I learn. I grow. I try to change, as the world does.

The economy changes. It is less acceptable to be a trapper. I never become totally civilized as a city person defines it, but maybe I do, relative to the life I had in book one.

Book 4 - Beyond Wild

I am getting past just survival and doing well, even prospering. I own more than the houseboat can easily haul. Gas gets expensive. I need a new houseboat engine.

There is a homestead and trapline that keeps me in one place now. There are more bear stories and adventures into the wilds, including a 300-mile boat trip looking for mammoth tusks, which has disastrous consequences.

I find where I want to live on the Kantishna River. A river 300 miles long with about five people on it. I hang out in the native village of Nenana, spending a lot of time here.

I get my first computer and learn to build a website. People are looking at the pictures and buying my raw materials and art. This is a chance to make a difference.

Life is beautiful. Life is precious. I Dare to live it.

Book 5 - Back To Wild (This Book)

I acquire a home in Nenana and start a web store. I am forced out of my subsistence lifestyle, partly because of changes in the laws. I do some serious mammoth hunting.

Unstable power causes a lot of computer data loss. I learn by punching keys to see what happens. It takes a long time to get good enough to create a book.

I continue the Mammoth hunts. The Tucson fossil gem show and State fair do well for me.

This period of 'being civilized' that I am trying out, has advantages, but also a price to pay—a big change from the wilderness life and being alone!

I am a suspect in a murder investigation. Another trapper tries to move in on my territory. There are neighbors and infringements on my property.

I fear I cannot change who I am. There is difficulty blending the two lives and ways of thinking. There are mail-order women coming and going, as well as the usual adventures and situations I manage to get myself into.

Book 6 - Surviving Wild

Iris is my partner. Business grows, with money coming in, but causes 'complications.' I understand why I left for the wilds in the first place.

I get better at fossil hunting and have some exciting trips getting mammoth tusks and other ancient treasures. I am viewed as an expert on a few subjects and Discovery TV and reality shows contact me several times.

The new life in town causes legal issues that have been nipping at my heels off and on throughout my time in Alaska. Fish and Wildlife ask, "Why are you alone out here where we cannot keep an eye on you? We know you are up to something. What is it you have to hide? We will find out!" This mentality is that different is bad and of concern. I end up being investigated. A SWAT team shows up at my property with a dozen cars and 20 cops.

My arrest makes headlines. I'm sentenced to Federal Prison for six months as a felon. This is a stark contrast to 'Book 1-Going Wild,' where I have as much freedom as it is possible to have.

How did I get from there to here?

Book 7 - Secretly Wild

I am a convicted felon, describing life in prison from the viewpoint of someone used to freedom and the wilderness life. The same feather in the hat I wore on the cover of Ruralite magazine in 1979, is now worth five years in prison.

What do I need to do to survive here? There are classes to take, books to read, farm work to do, and people to help. There are interesting felon stories.

I observe more crime within the prison system by the system than I am accused of committing. "The prison could not survive if we operated legally," I am told by officials. I do my time. Now what? Am I a better person? I see the error of my ways. I am saved. Society is safer now.

Book 8 - Retiring Wild

I talk about news relevant to living off the grid as an individual in the wilderness that few citizens are aware of. I adapt my business, and still have adventures, depending as much as I can on the subsistence life I love and understand that is now becoming illegal as a white man.

I ponder whether the end of my life is in agreement with the views I held dear from the beginning. I have hope that even in times of control and suppression, I can still focus on the plus side, and continue to find ways to enjoy personal freedoms and individuality.

I continue to explore choices, how to have better control of my destiny, happiness, and success. I refer to this as 'Survival.' I have few regrets, and hope my life's path as written can provide entertainment and insight.

As someone who is interested in being different, not one of the sheep, I look realistically at the rewards that choice offers, but also the price that has to be paid.

Please visit www.alaskadp.com for links to the books.

Visit www.milesofalaska.com to find a bio of Miles, additional photos, stories, how-to videos, handmade artwork, and raw materials for sale.

Magazine and News Stories

Alaska Magazine

Alaska Magazine July 77—Survive by Miles Martin two pages, Photos. By Miles about my rescue, walk out on the Yukon River, five days at 50 below zero.

Nomadic House Boater Have Cabin Will Travel January 81—by Miles. Three pages, four color photos, a map. About life living on a houseboat, trapping and selling art (photo of my art), and all the adventures I have had on the river.

Would You Make A Good Bush Homesteader? June 86—by Miles four pages, six color pictures (One shows my custom knives.) A story I wrote about what it takes to be a homesteader.

Surviving The Big Lonesome— March 98—by Jim Rearden five pages, two color photos, one double page photo of Miles. Photos by world-famous photographer Jean Erick Pasquier. Describes life in the wilderness.

GEO Magazine

GEO in Germany is like "National Geographic" in the US.

Life in The Wilderness Alaska Special—87 by Miles Martin ten pages, sixteen color photos, a map

Photos by Jean Erick, one of the best photographers in the world, I Wrote it myself, winter life in the wilderness.

Alaska Special - 95 Einer gegen den Rest der Welt

Eight pages, seven color photos, three are double page. A follow up story to the first, written by New York Times reporter Ted Morgan, with Brigitte Helbing, photos by New York Times photographer Rex Rystedt. My fight for a lifestyle.

The New York Times

New York Times Magazine an insert to the paper, April 17, 1994, section six, The Vexing Adventures of the Last Alaskan Bushrat.

Six pages, four color photos, one is a double page Written by New York Times writer and bestselling author Ted Morgan. Photos by Rex Rystedt (World-renowned photographer). Facing twenty years in jail and a $10,000 fine for putting artwork on a bear claw and selling it.

Book-- A Shovel Full of Stars 95—Published by Simon and Schuster — New York

By Ted Morgan about ten pages with Miles. About one of the last homesteaders, and the lifestyle I live, of a Subsistence person.

Ruralite Magazine

Put out by Golden Valley 180,000 circulation
Wild Miles August 79, two pages, four black and white photos, Full cover page photo of Miles doing artwork. Story and photos by Margaret Van Cleve — Mostly about my artwork, some about my lifestyle on a houseboat

Newspaper, Daily Newsminer, Fairbanks Alaska

Associated Press, date unreadable, think a Thursday, and think spring of circa 74 **'Trapper rescued by Chopper;** Vows to Return to the Bush' headline, one column, National news, about my rescue after five days walking at 50 below.

Alaska Trapper Magazine

Put out by Alaska Trappers Association, a cover photo of me with Wolf. Five-page story by Miles comparing snowmachine and snowshoe trapping Nov. 99—four pages. Over the years, another six-seven articles on various trapping and related issues. Contact organization for exact issues.

Me in 1975.

OTHER TITLES AVAILABLE FROM ALASKA DREAMS PUBLISHING

Visit www.alaskadp.com to see these titles.

Books by Miles Martin:

- Going Wild
- Gone Wild
- Still Wild
- Beyond Wild
- Back To Wild
- Surviving Wild
- Secretly Wild
- Retiring Wild

Titles by other ADP authors:

- Rookie
- Alaska Freedom Brigade
- Apache Snow
- In Search of Honor
- A Coming Storm
- Arizona Rangers Series – Blake's War
- Legend of Silene
- Inspiring Special Needs Stories
- My Life In The Wilderness
- All Over The Road
- Ghost Cave Mountain
- Inside the Circle
- The Silver Horn of Robin Hood
- Alaskan Troll Eggs
- Through My Eyes
- The Professional Ghost Investigator
- The Adventures of Jason and Bo
- Seeds Of The Pirate Rebels

NOTES

CHAPTER 1

1. A cop shoots a twelve-year-old who has a plastic squirt gun, justified because the cop felt threatened. A commercial pilot deliberately flies a jet into a mountain with 160 passengers on board. This is becoming almost daily news. It is easy to think there is a fly in the soup.
2. Several children went on to take art classes in college based on this experience. One became an outstanding professional. Thus another 'win' As I said, if even one child was very positively affected and it changed their life forever, it was worth all the work.
3. Later I add bag phone or ham radio after I get my ham license. Cell phones are not in use yet, no cell towers this far out. The old analog phones work better then cell out remote.

CHAPTER 2

1. I get a run around from new people I do not know. My items may have gotten lost. All I know for sure is, I never get paid, never get my art back, and never get contacted on the subject. So much for $700. But cannot dwell on the negative. I press on with good happenings!
2. I end up with as many as 1,000 molds to choose from.
3. I've been using past flashes throughout my books. I make up a term taken from old songs 'knock out nifties of the past;' that we hear, and the song spins us back in time. We are there, like it was yesterday.
4. Free gifts over time ends up being a legal issue. I never kept proof, receipts, because at this point in time there was no need, it was not a legal requirement, and no one cared. I've always done deals on a handshake. A piece of paper means nothing without lawyers, courts and civilization. Many primitives, mostly suppliers I deal with do not know how to read or write. The problem has not arrived yet, but is developing.
5. Many who know me feel I get scammed often, even most of the time. "Oh yea, I forgot that time" is my usual reply. *Why did you remind me?*
6. Thirty years later I still have the slippers

CHAPTER 3

1. This murder was well covered in my previous book.
2. Not true. But the truth is involved and complicated, raises too many other questions, and I felt in this case the easiest reply is no. If I can sell the guy a less legally controversial lynx claw, I'd much rather.
3. About ten years from now what I hoped for, does come true. A brilliant hard working honest native runs the gift shop implementing ideas I believed would work—focus on local, no imports, hardly any Eskimo. Hundreds of tourists a day come through.
4. I later come to believe Crafty does have honest respect. He does in fact have a great deal of knowledge. And his selling methods are just 'life' and 'Oh well.' I'm the one who ends up in prison a felon, not Crafty. The law may care little about ethics and morals.

CHAPTER 4

1. A few years later the librarians are sent to take classes on internet, web site work. They end up knowing more than I do, but in the beginning none of us knew much!

NOTES

2. And as I predicted, about two years after, I am forced to buy a snow machine because I am not allowed to fish for sled dogs. The Indians got shut off and stopped from Subsistence fishing as well.
3. Well covered in my previous book I think
4. Various power outages across the country seem to be more frequent. Hurricane Katrina and 'Frankinstorm' hitting New York cause outages, supply issues lasting weeks. How dependable is public power and water?

CHAPTER 5

1. Someone I used to have adventures with reminds me in 2014, that I once tied my boat up to a tusk, ran my boat up on it at his fish camp and did not know it. I do not recall, but he has this memory.
2. Over a long time, I lose the drive to change the way things are.

CHAPTER 6

1. Over the years computers have gotten a lot more user friendly in terms of not needing to know much to run them, or transfer settings to a new computer. Now an expert can actually access your computer on line and fix it. I still had slow speed dial up internet.
2. I forget how it happens. Moon ends up with quite a pile of my art on consignment. She is going to sell it for me. I hear from her about once a year. No money, no art. Beyond "Oh yea, I'll get it to you." Ten years go by.

CHAPTER 7

1. An extremely hot topic in 2014 when residents outside the city limits feel deliberately excluded from discussions, and rumors of being annexed due to oil gas discoveries cause an emergency investigation and funding for a study. Many say a now divided, distrustful community will never be united again.
2. In 2013, a lot of citizens outside city limits accuse the city of holding secret meetings, making secret deals, making decisions outside what is legal, with some extremely hot feelings. This divides the community in ways that some say will cause lasting distrust and anger.

CHAPTER 8

1. Just read book one 'Going Wild' like the four page poem I wrote about seeing the ice go out for the first time.

CHAPTER 9

1. I read a popular best seller book, 'Blink' that scientifically explores the ability to make unconscious quick and amazingly accurate decisions based on 'we do not know what for sure ' but it works.
2. In later years this becomes true, for me anyway. Lots of restrictions and papers needed
3. In later years I hear this 'no lead' law is based on a study where lead was found in bird gizzards. But further study showed lead poisoning was not the cause of deaths. The lead might be 'in and out' of the system before doing damage. I therefore assume the restrictions remain for other reasons then environmental.